HOW TO SAVE
A FORTUNE ON
YOUR LIFE INSURANCE

HOW TO SAVE
A FORTUNE ON
YOUR LIFE INSURANCE

BARRY KAYE, C.L.U.

cp
CAROL PRESS

Carol Press
Suite 200
2029 Century Park East
Los Angeles, California 90067

Library of Congress Catalog Number: 80-71051

ISBN 0-936614-01-3

Printed in the United States of America

10 9 8 7 6 5 4 3 2

This book is dedicated to the public and to the life insurance industry. Only through a better understanding by the public of the true workings of life insurance can the industry serve the public better. It is with this purpose in mind that I write and dedicate this book.

Life insurance is a very complex subject and generalizations are not applicable to everyone. It is important that your own specific situation be analyzed by a qualified life insurance agent. If legal advice or other expert opinion is required, the services of a competent professional should be sought.

In this book the author describes situations where all facts were available to him. Without that knowledge of your specific requirements, the author and the publisher disclaim any liability or loss incurred by the use of any direct or indirect application of the material contained herein.

ACKNOWLEDGMENTS

My acknowledgment to my wife Carol and children Fern, Alan, and Howard whose love, consideration, and understanding made the time available for the completion of this work.

A special acknowledgment to all of the personnel at Barry Kaye Associates, who contributed in many ways, with special thanks to my executive assistant, Dianna Simmons, for her valued contributions.

I particularly acknowledge the time, energy and creativity that my friend and editorial advisor, Steven Jay Rubin, contributed to this project. His patience, advice and enthusiastic support in helping to edit and organize this book made possible its publication.

CONTENTS

Part Two: The Basics

Part Three: Practical Applications

LIST OF TABLES

Introduction:
———— Why I Wrote This Book ————

My NAME IS Barry Kaye. I am a Chartered Life Underwriter—a C.L.U.

I have studied and passed all the tests necessary to earn my degree in the field of life insurance. I have practiced my profession for eighteen years. I have been a general agent for a major New England insurance company. There are forty salesmen who work through my office. I am also an agent who works every day in the field with various clients, including individuals and organizations throughout the United States.

Why have I written this book?

In the world of business and finance—topics that have become very close to all of us in these times of economic uncertainty—books are usually written to aid consumers by filling an information gap. In the past, we've had few such books about the life insurance industry. Those that were done were often written by outsiders, attacking the industry in sensationalized exposés, or, if done by an insider, turned out to be technical handbooks, often dry and uninteresting, designed to appeal to no one outside the insurance industry.

I have great respect for the fine consumer journals that have taken the time to examine the fundamentals of life insurance, offering their succinct and painstakingly produced cost comparisons. But these publications suffer from a major flaw. Writing from the outside, they are in no position to delve beneath the complex surface of the insurance industry. There is a series of simple, logical facts immediately apparent. If these facts are right or wrong, what makes them so? No magazine or periodical has so far taken on this perspective. And today, with so many dynamic and revolutionary crosscurrents in the industry, that is a serious lack.

Wouldn't it be more interesting and truly revealing if an experienced professional agent, who really knows his business, could present for the first time a behind-the-scenes analysis of the real life insurance industry? I think that it is vital for a member of the profession to do just that.

I realize that I'm leaving myself exposed. When an insurance agent like myself makes a public observation, he's immediately attacked as being biased or seeking publicity for his own purposes. The fact that many of the points are controversial will only add fuel to the fire. The attacks may come from unknowledgeable people from within my own industry, as well as those from other industries affected and the consumer who may not understand my true purpose. But one professional had to do this, explaining, clarifying, and correcting the many existent misconceptions. I am willing to risk the criticism in the hope of creating a better understanding of life insurance for the public's benefit.

One of the most vital issues in the life insurance industry today concerns the continuing controversy between the proponents of permanent and term insurance. Yet I maintain that term insurance is the greatest myth ever perpetrated on the American public.

Everywhere I go, term insurance is lauded as the only form of insurance the consumer will ever need. It is presented as not only more economical, but more practical as well. Out of this wealth of opinion has sprung the "buy term and invest the difference" concept in which the consumer takes the excess cash he would have used to purchase a permanent insurance policy and invests it in the traditional marketplace (stocks, mutual funds, real estate, municipal bonds, oil, etc.). And in chart after chart, it appears that such a concept actually works, that you do make more money over the course of a lifetime.

But there are other questions to consider. Term insurance usually runs out at age 70, but if it does continue, the rates are totally, exorbitantly prohibitive. Defending this, many people comment, "Fine. Who needs insurance at that age anyway?" But life insurance needs in later life cannot be dismissed so readily, especially when one's investment portfolio has not panned out exactly as planned, when emergencies arise and drain cash reserves, or when one's estate needs protection from tax encroachment. You may not need insurance to support your children who have grown up, but you might desperately need the money to protect the estate that has taken you a lifetime to create. Term insurance proponents fall silent when it comes to protection of this type.

In fairness to those in favor of term insurance, which does have its appropriate uses, I would like to make another interesting observation.

Could it be that the very concept of term insurance has been actively promoted and encouraged through the years, as part of a massive, well-calculated sales campaign engineered outside the life insurance industry by the investment industry of America, which viewed the billions of dollars going into permanent insurance policies as a potential source of funds for their investment products?

And, over the years, could these same unknowing investment brokers, be they in real estate, oil, mutual funds, stocks, tax shelters, etc., have not only promoted term insurance to their clients as a wonderful opportunity, but simultaneously damned permanent insurance as bad?

Could such a campaign then have been taken up by many

of the consumer journals of the period, which have continued
to castigate permanent insurance?

Now a segment of the public has been massively swayed
away from the concept of permanent insurance and directed
toward the misconception that term is the "only way to go."

In most cases, term insurance is not the only way to go.
While it does sometimes serve the purposes of the very young,
the low-income family, and the individual with short-term
insurance needs, no one has taken time to explain that term
insurance does not hold up. The fact is that in later years,
when the person insured passes age 70 (and people are living
longer these days) insurance protection stops, and new policy
acquisition costs are astronomical.

The low starting price of term appealed to consumers who
hadn't wanted to bother with life insurance in the first
place, and it was easier to sell. After a while, people began to
ignore the agent who was selling permanent insurance. Thus,
for some, the correct form of insurance (permanent), which
protects a person during an entire lifetime, has been replaced
by a form of insurance (term) suitable only for the few.

How could such a misconception be perpetrated? It takes
a great campaign to sway the population, and it is becoming
clear now that the campaign was indeed fueled from outside
the insurance industry.

While the solid corporations, the substantial individuals,
and the educated insurance agents in this country have attempted to explain why permanent insurance is the only
practical approach for the long run, others are leading seg-
ments of the population on their way to a security that seems
low cost, but that is going to break down somewhere in the
future when it is most desperately needed.

It is time someone exposed this dangerous myth, presenting for the consumer's benefit the true facts about term and
permanent insurance. With the lowering of permanent insurance premiums, that form of insurance is now, more than
at any time in its history, the proper route for the majority.

I hope that if this book accomplishes one thing, it will put term insurance—an excellent product for the right purpose—in its proper perspective. Thus the "term insurance myth" will be put to rest and the public will understand the true value of permanent insurance.

Along with the basic consumer information in this book will be some observations on the realities of the life insurance industry today, information which you will not find in the basic texts of consumer journals or publications of the federal government, since only someone totally involved in the industry can truly provide that perspective.

Life insurance is going through a transformation. In fact, I've decided to go one step further and refer to it as a full-blown revolution. Prices today are coming down to record levels, and new plans, such as the Extralife-Economatic, are being created that are already changing the very course of traditional insurance buying patterns. But the word *revolution* covers not only the pricing substance of life insurance, but the theory and form as well.

In the following pages, I examine every aspect of the life insurance business and, for the consumer's sake, reveal the many myths and misconceptions that have pervaded the industry throughout its history. I strongly feel that the consumer must understand life insurance beyond simple cost comparisons. Once you get the right price, the buying process is just beginning. In these inflationary times, every consumer who owns a life insurance policy, or who is considering the purchase of one, will benefit from reading this book.

In Part I, I reveal this revolution in insurance. In Part II, I discuss the basics of insurance, insurance planning, and insurance buying. And in Part III, I explain the practical applications of lower premiums, the miracle of compound interest, and the resulting astronomical savings in all different situations, in all different amounts, at all different ages.

With the help of this book you too can learn "how to save a fortune on your life insurance."

PART ONE

THE
REVOLUTION

In this section, I survey what many agents, consumers, companies, and journalists are beginning to call the insurance revolution. This is a revolution not only of new products but also of extraordinarily lower prices, making life insurance coverage much more easily attainable.

It is also a revolution in ways of thinking. Both consumers and agents are beginning to reevaluate their whole concept of the life insurance industry. Only when dangerous misconceptions are eradicated will the public be able to take advantage of new products and prices. As in most revolutions, it is ways of thinking that change first; action comes later.

I have brought together these facts and observations about the insurance revolution in the hope that consumers will begin to ask questions about their current insurance situations, whether they are about to buy for the first time or have owned policies for many years. Asking such important questions could result in saving thousands or hundreds of thousands of dollars over the course of a lifetime.

1

The Revolution in Life Insurance

A REVOLUTION IS occurring in the life insurance industry today. Like many revolutions, this one is starting slowly, with a great deal of caution and diplomacy. Since the life insurance industry is a creature of habit, it is not prone to springing surprises on the public.

Last year, over 14 million *new* individual life insurance policies were sold in the United States alone. This year, insurance prices have plummeted, interest rates have soared, and new insurance plans are being created almost daily. The insurance industry in most cases has nurtured the growth carefully, promoting the stability and professionalism of the service more than any wonderful savings elicited by the new products. However, as in any business, certain companies prove to be more innovative than others, and a few years ago, products began to appear on the insurance market that were substantially lower in price, featuring not only lower premiums, but astonishingly lower net costs. This was especially true with permanent insurance. A few leaders in the insurance industry suddenly realized that the new lower prices were more than just the result of slow progress over the years. These prices, as well as other developments, would have revolutionary effects on the entire insurance industry.

Why Lower-Priced Policies?

What caused these insurance companies to come up with this new low-cost product? The rise of interest rates meant that insurance companies were achieving higher yields on their investments, establishing larger cash reserves, and creating greater dividends. Larger profits and dividends received on their investments allowed the companies to lower the cost of their premiums.

At the same time, actuaries were studying mortality tables that revealed that people were living longer. When people live longer, they pay premiums for a longer period of time. And, resultingly, the insurance company is given a greater period over which to honor the policies, allowing it to invest over longer periods of time, building up larger cash reserves, which in turn can lower premium costs.

While the inflationary spiral has indeed raised certain operating expenses, the computer revolution has actually reduced overhead in many cases, turning insurance companies into computer banks filled with information that formerly took thousands of person hours to compile and disperse. With operating overhead reduced, insurance companies are able to concentrate their work load on developing new products that can offer further reductions to the consumer.

At first glance, insurance agents thought that the new lower pricing would mean lower commissions, and that more would have to be sold to make the same money. This impression tended to pervade the company level, too, where lower premiums were immediately assumed to mean lower profits. However, this didn't keep a number of companies from developing the new lower costs, not only because they had the money to back them up, but because they shrewdly realized that once these plans were made available to the public, greater volume would replace any loss in revenue. In any event, companies would have to be competitive to remain in the business.

In addition, due to inflation and increasing salaries, the public needed more life insurance than ever. And if the companies featured lower premiums, consumers wouldn't hesitate to buy the larger amount of insurance they needed.

A Change Is Coming

But before all these changes could really have an impact for the consumer, certain real transformations had to occur in the industry itself. At the time, I was of course most aware of what was occurring within my own area of influence.

I first heard about the lower rates in October 1979. Up to that time I had no idea they were finally coming, even though I had been pushing for them for years. Since different competitive price structures were being developed by other companies as well, I soon realized that comparison advertising, something the insurance industry had scrupulously avoided for most of its history, would have to be used.

I also realized that for the first time we were going to have to talk about "replacement," a word the very mention of which was considered outright heresy in the insurance industry. People who possessed older policies could be saving a great deal of money—perhaps into thousands, tens of thousands, hundreds of thousands, and even millions, depending on how much life insurance they currently owned. Discussing the replacement of their policies was taboo, and it was out of the question to mention the topic in advertising. These were ironclad unwritten rules because if an agent writes a replacement policy, another agent's commissions are lost. This was the type of competition that had always remained below the surface in the industry and was never openly discussed, but had been going on for years.

As the new rates began to appear, I was astonished at how

the resulting savings could be compounded. I couldn't believe the dramatic amount of savings generated. With interest rates skyrocketing, consumers were going to be able to save fortunes in life insurance premiums.

The new rates apply principally to permanent insurance sold in various forms, including a type called Extralife-Economatic, which allows the consumer to purchase, say, a $100,000 face value by paying premiums for only $70,000, the balance of the face value being made up by dividends that purchase additional insurance. This in turn results in lower commissions on the policy, and a much lower premium. I soon realized that this new low-cost format permanent insurance would become the dominant product for virtually every future situation.

Such insurance was the most effective answer ever developed to refute those who claim that the best method of buying insurance is to buy term insurance and invest the difference. At last, the permanent insurance premium had been lowered to a point where, compared with the term insurance, the differential would not be great; within a much shorter period of time, the term insurance premiums would become more expensive than the permanent insurance premiums, and would have no surrender or loan values.

Since it appeared that permanent insurance premiums always offered higher commissions to agents, many consumers naturally assumed they were going to be sold that product regardless of their need. This is simply not true. While I will discuss this in more detail in later chapters, I will say here that term insurance will eventually run out, especially when the consumer is unable to maintain the larger premiums in later years, when he is most likely to die. And in many ways it is now advisable from a strictly financial standpoint to purchase permanent insurance and invest that difference. But let us discuss that controversy later.

Getting the Word Out

It is one thing to see something as important to the consumer and quite another to be able to convince the consumer of its importance. We had to develop a strategy to provide this useful information through the most likely means, that of advertising. Several companies did just this, and created a consumer response.

One key slogan even asked the question: "Should you replace your current life insurance policy if it is clearly in your best interest?"

Strong consumer response then created a need to develop a system for comparing old policies with new ones. We had to make it clear to consumers that the original policies they had purchased were not bad ones, but rather that new pricing structures made it necessary to review all the insurance they currently had.

At the outset, this wasn't as easy as it sounded. Agents had to be prepared for the initial negative reaction from many of their clients or their advisers. The consumer had to understand that what might have been sold prior to the revolution was not incorrect, but simply that insurance had changed.

One of the most difficult tasks was to explain how the agents were going to adopt a lower premium and thus earn a lower commission but at the same time do much more business. Of course, the lower premiums would result in happier clients. In years past it was standard procedure for us to go to clients for leads, asking them if they knew of any friends who needed life insurance, and if they would recommend us to someone else. Now, however, the revolution was changing all that. Clients were now saying, "I've got some friends you could really help, why don't you go see George or Jane or Robert and show them what you did for me."

While we were in the process of retraining agents, we also had to devise a system for comparing proposals. To make a comparison, the old policy's cash values and dividends had to be analyzed with those from the new policy, along with compound interest factors based on the difference of premium savings and the difference if the cash values were surrendered and compounded. In many cases, these numbers were available in industry manuals. However, many of the policies were from old series and the dividends might have changed or not been published. Thus agents had to secure exact information about the previous policies in order to do the best job for the client.

In certain cases, the old companies were uncooperative and the proper information could not be secured. Besides this, many clients did not really realize the full impact of the savings that could be effected and thought this was a selling ploy, so they weren't very cooperative in making sure that this information was provided.

I had to impress upon the agents that we were truly providing a service for the clients in looking at their policies and making these comparisons. It took some effort to impress clients with the absolute need for accurate information, which only they could secure from their previous companies. Those clients that did not wish to cooperate for their own benefit were informed that we could not proceed further with any comparison until accurate information was made available.

At first, agents were frustrated because they really didn't understand how the new rates worked. But then we showed them how we did these comparisons. We gave each agent the basic ten or twelve different forms to use to make the comparisons, and finally they saw how the system worked. As they learned how the numbers applied, they saw how effective it was.

Some agents are still not selling correctly but change will come with time. When agents aren't doing well selling $30 per thousand premiums, they certainly are not about to switch to a $16 per thousand premium, where they will make much less money. However, if they are well trained, the agents realize that they could possibly sell four $16 per thousand premiums for every $30 per thousand premium they now sell.

A Widespread Revolution

The idea that consumers are actually bringing other consumers to insurance agents would have been totally farfetched five years ago. It just didn't work that way. But because of the "telling it like it is" type of advertising, and the extraordinary lower prices, consumers are buying these policies in record numbers. Insurance today is passing from a phase of skillful selling to one of intelligent buying. We are talking to consumers now, and consumers are reading advertisements carefully. They want to understand what effect the new pricing will have on their policies, old and new.

But the revolution isn't only producing lower prices and happier consumers; it's creating a large number of new agents who are more intelligent, who understand the business, who have adapted to the new pricing, and who possess the knowledge and ability to service clients with a product that is going to save them more money than they ever thought possible.

With better agents who are more knowledgeable about their product, more logical and succinct in their approach, there will be a much better future for the entire life insurance industry. At last, the industry will no longer be presenting in mysterious tones a totally misunderstood product. These new products will provide individuals and businesses all over America with the security that they so badly desire and need.

When this is fully understood and the myths and misconceptions have been swept aside, the life insurance industry will regain the full respect of the American public and take its rightful position as one of the basic industries of America.

2

Myths, Misconceptions, and Sacred Cows

FOR ANY REVOLUTION to succeed, old preconceived notions must be dropped, to let in an entirely new, fresh, objective attitude. In the life insurance revolution, this means eradicating the crippling effect of the myths and misconceptions that have plagued the industry for years.

As long as these misconceptions remain, there can be no true understanding of the potential value of the revolution. The need for education applies not only to consumers but also to many agents who, through no fault of their own, have nurtured and advanced these misconceptions. No one has simply ever explained the alternatives to them.

This chapter will equip consumers — and their agents — with the tools to develop an entirely new perspective, to see through to the reality of the insurance revolution.

Myth One: Never Drop an Old Policy

One of the most dangerous, ironclad .nyths has been, "Never drop an old policy even if substantial savings are available!"

It was cut and dried; you just didn't do that. And as we were brainwashed to think in this way, we advanced the myth to lawyers and accountants until they too began to suspect any insurance agent who dared encroach on an old policy.

How did this myth develop in the first place? First, it was felt that you bought that policy when you were young, so you were never going to be offered those same rates again, simply because you were never going to be young again.

That was fine. But what happens when the insurance rates drop and new price structures emerge? The new product may still cost less and save you substantial money. Are you still going to hold on to your old policy because you're older? *Of course not!*

There are three other arguments occasionally used by those who defend the "never drop an old policy" myth.

One is the incontestability period, which is usually the first two years of the policy. Some agents point out that a new policy forces you to go through this two-year period all over again.

But what the incontestability clause really means is that if you lied about your health, etc., on your insurance application, after two years the life insurance company is liable for all claims and cannot contest whatever you said.

This is great information, but what if, like most people, you haven't lied? If you have given the true facts on your new application, who cares if you have to wait out a new two-year incontestability period? There is simply no reason to hold onto a policy because its incontestability period has passed, particularly if you're about to save a large amount of money on a new policy.

Another argument for holding onto your policy is the suicide clause. What the consumer doesn't realize is that most insurance companies will pay your death benefit even if you commit suicide—as long as your policy has been in force for two years. This theory is based on psychologists' reports that if you really wanted to commit suicide to get insurance money, you wouldn't wait two years to do it.

Those in favor of retaining old policies claim that if you drop the policy, you have to start the suicide clause all over again. That's fine if you're thinking about committing suicide, but does this apply to the average consumer?

Finally, if you're considering dropping an old policy, it's pointed out to you that the agent's going to make a new commission, and that you will thus have a new acquisition cost.

Well, what's wrong with that? You don't keep one stock for a lifetime, you change the stock and you not only have to pay commission to drop it, but a new commission when you buy another stock as well. Yet did anyone ever say there is a "new acquisition cost" on that stock and maybe you shouldn't sell it, or buy a new stock, because of that?

Insurance agents have to maintain a business. This includes the expense of office space, the time to arrange appointments and visit clients, and the effort of carefully analyzing policies and maintaining quality work. They are also very likely going to have to spend more time on replacement analysis than on a normal analysis. They will certainly have to expose themselves to what can potentially be more problems, since they will, in all probability, have to face the current agent and the company whose policy they are replacing. Their credibility is on the line, and they may be assuming an even greater responsibility as a result of this entire process.

But, from the consumer's point of view, if the bottom line shows that your premium is lower over a period of years or that your net interest adjusted cost savings is substantial, then the new acquisition cost will certainly be worth it.

All of these are ridiculous myths, but put together they sound terribly impressive, enough so that you might think twice about dropping your old policy, even if you could save a lot of money.

Myth Two: Life Insurance Is an Investment.

One myth that has taken root over the years (and is often used as a sales incentive) is that "insurance is a good investment." That is what I call an accurate inaccuracy. If you were to die tomorrow after having made the first premium payment, life insurance could turn out to be the best investment you ever made.

But when you get right down to it, life insurance isn't a good investment *or* a bad investment. It's simply not an investment at all.

Over the years, people who failed to develop savings found that the cash values of their permanent insurance policies became sizable amounts of money. Should they need it, this money could be made available to them like a savings account. Life insurance looked like a way of accumulating a nest egg. If the consumer felt like calling it that, the insurance companies certainly had no objection. In fact, the cash value in a permanent insurance policy was nothing more than a reserve to sustain a level premium over a lifetime. It did indeed produce a sizable amount of money that was available on surrender or as collateral for a low-guaranteed-interest loan.

But investment counselors who sold stock, mutual funds, or real estate took a very dim view of those who looked upon insurance as savings. They saw a wonderful source of available cash for their own products. Thus, it wasn't long before life insurance was assaulted as a bad investment.

Only one product, life insurance, provided your beneficiaries with instant money upon your death. If you had a little cash value, it was considered a bonus for having paid higher premiums in the beginning to keep your premium level. Some insurance salespeople stated that you would have cash available as in a bank while at the same time having a death benefit that no bank could provide. That may have been too simplistic, but it was often left at that.

Myth Three: You Don't Need Insurance When You're Older.

Another huge myth is, "You don't need insurance when you're older." This one really bothers me. The word was falsely spread that insurance money would be needed only during the time when children were being raised. But no provision was made for the wife.

That she might have been supported in a certain style and might lose her husband at an age when she could not re-enter the job market was not considered. The children may have left the house and completed their education, which may have left the bankbook depleted, all at the time of her husband's death. If we were to believe the myth that you needed no more insurance after the children had grown, where would this woman be?

Isn't it criminal that a woman who has stood by her husband the greater part of her life, and for whatever reason cannot work, suddenly finds that her spouse is dead and hasn't left her enough money to replace the income she has just lost. She now has to go through the final years of her life with not only the emotional trauma of having lost her husband, but also with the economic trauma of not having enough money to make ends meet, or of losing all of her self-respect and pride by turning to her children or to public assistance for support.

Finally, those who have substantial money, paradoxically, may need life insurance the most, because they're subject to estate taxes, which for the wealthy are astronomical. With life insurance, though, you can let the insurance company pay the taxes. This is a typical, though dramatic, case of how the "the older you get the less life insurance you need" myth really falls apart.

Myth Four: All Insurance Companies Are the Same

Another major misconception is that "all insurance companies are the same." This is probably the biggest myth in the insurance industry. People believe that all insurance policies cost the same and that all insurance agents talk the same. This is patently *not* true. Did you know that for the same type of policy, some insurance policies are as much as 400% more expensive than others?

Along with this goes the myth that you're doing the agent a favor by buying from him or her. This myth shows a real lack of understanding of the actual need for life insurance. Life insurance is a business proposition; shopping around and making comparisons is only good sense. Consumers find that the knowledgeable and creative agent may make a major difference to their family's future.

Does the consumer really think he's doing the agent a favor by purchasing a policy? I have never accepted an apology from someone who didn't want to buy life insurance from me. All I lost was the commission, which might have been $1,000 on a $2,000 premium. On the other hand, if the client died, his family might have lost $100,000 in income-tax-free money. Why apologize to *me*?

In my opinion, one of the worst things that can happen to anyone is a bad salesperson. If the salesperson is not good, he or she will eventually lose a commission. But the real losers are the clients who never completely understand the benefits of insurance; they become the biggest losers, because they do not have the advantages that would come from a proper purchase. Good salespersons can show the advantages of the product to consumers, so that consumers *truly understand* what is in their best interest to buy.

Myth Five: When You Borrow on Your Policy, You're Borrowing Your Own Money.

One misconception that must be eradicated once and for all is, "When I borrow on my life insurance, I'm really borrowing my own money."

You pay a premium. The insurance company provides a policy on your life. The policy builds cash values, which are reserves that enable the premium to stay level over your lifetime. Those cash values are an asset. If you check your financial statement, you will see that the cash values appear as an asset. And right next to your cash values, you'll find your stocks, your real estate equity, and your savings. All of these are assets, and any one can be used as collateral to borrow whatever the bank will lend you. There is no difference in the character of cash value assets, savings account assets, or any other liquid asset on your financial statement.

Yet have you ever gone to the bank or to your stockbroker and said, "I'm going to borrow my own money"? But with life insurance, there is this ridiculous misconception that if you use that cash value as collateral, as you would have used any of your other assets for collateral in a similar transaction, you're borrowing your own money.

We have discussed some of the major myths and misconceptions that have confused consumers and their agents over the years. As you read on, you will discover how these, and other misconceptions, apply to specific situations that affect you.

3

The Industry and Its Image: ──── Cleaning Up the Act

THE LIFE INSURANCE industry has received its share of attacks in recent times. Many of these have been patently unfair. In the introduction to his book, *The Tired Tirade*, insurance expert Halsey D. Josephson pointed out that despite a consistently good record, reflecting over the years a tremendous dedication, honor, and commitment to its clients, the life insurance industry was still being attacked by critics who castigated life insurance as a "racket, immersed in shocking, unscrupulous, and even contemptible practices."[*]

Such critiques continue to appear sporadically on the scene, each serving the author's own purpose. A sensationalized attack can probably sell more books than the true story of life insurance can. More importantly, though, it may help sell the author's own product if he discusses life insurance in such a negative manner that more money is suddenly channeled to his own investment medium.

Halsey Josephson supported the insurance industry in his book by explaining many of its practices and motives, and, especially, its image. He pointed out that these periodic

───────────────

*Halsey D. Josephson, *The Tired Tirade*, rev. ed. (New York: Farnsworth Publishing Co., 1976).

attacks on the industry were written by people who did not understand life insurance, and that their simplistic approach was usually incorrect by omission. Twelve years after his book was first published, the insurance industry is *still* waging a constant battle to improve its image.

Does Life Insurance Mean Death?

Defending the image of the life insurance business from muckraking journalistic outsiders is only one side of the image problem. There are other more vital problems, some dating back to the beginnings of life insurance history.

Certainly the most detrimental image factor is life insurance's obvious association with death, and the incumbent need to make decisions for the future. There was a time when the life insurance agent was symbolized as a man driving a hearse up to the door of a prospective client, or carrying a coffin into the client's living room. Many people thought of the agents as people dealing in death—and that what they were selling had no benefit for them in life.

The simple truth is that they were selling *death* insurance, a term that would hardly have encouraged sales. While there is no question that this type of insurance is meant for the eventuality of death, it serves a vital and uplifting purpose in life for people who have purchased it, since with this purchase comes peace of mind.

Most people do not like to be reminded of mortality, and certainly don't want to take time out to actually contemplate their own death and its effect on those left behind. And talking about life insurance forces people to do that.

Do I want to leave this to my wife? Do I want to leave this to my husband? How should the children be protected? Who's going to get what? Who wants to talk about this in the first place?

So people procrastinate, telling the agent to "Call back, call back." In defense of the consumers, perhaps this uniform "Call back" and "Not now" is a result of believing that they must eventually face the facts of life insurance.

Such a situation tends to reduce the insurance agent to a pest. A pest has a terrible image, and over the years, the insurance pest has become a part of our vocabulary, even though most people end up buying insurance eventually.

People view insurance agents who force immediate unwanted decisions about the future on them as men and women who are hungry, unprofessional salespersons interested only in their own commissions.

This biased attitude dates back to the great Depression of the thirties when many of the unemployed entered the life insurance industry. It was felt that however bad times were, a person could always get a job as a commission salesman who collected ten cents door to door, in order to make a few pennies of commission. Since then, the door-to-door image has been hard to get rid of.

Due to the high turnover rate, many agents who failed to make the grade were not above knocking the very industry that they had failed in. It gave them a rational justification for their own failure. Many of them told untruths which further tarnished the insurance industry's image.

Life insurance has also often been hurt by being lumped in with health and casualty insurance. Many people who have been denied casualty claims, or were not reimbursed properly for an accident or another claim, or were denied insurance altogether, are inclined to distrust all insurance agents, regardless of what they are selling. Life insurance agents, who have nothing to do with automobile, fire, home, or casualty insurance, often find themselves being put off by someone who doesn't give them a chance to explain their product. It is a frustration common to many agents and to the industry as a whole.

In addition, there are agents who are not competent and who simply don't know what they are talking about. And there are part-time agents or others who are out of the business before they are even in it. The knowledge of these people is sadly inadequate, and they spread information that is frequently inaccurate. They don't understand the clients' needs or the product, and indeed try to sell them the proverbial "bag of goods." There are so many agents like this that the public is in many cases exposed to grave misconceptions about the whole basic premise of life insurance. Damaging as such agents can be for the consumer, they also make life miserable for the competent agent, who must now confront the dual problems of misinformation and poor image in addition to explaining a very complex product.

Cleaning Up the Life Insurance Image

The three most difficult things to sell in our society are education, religion, and insurance. Each appeals to a basic intellectual aspect or character of an individual. Insurance forces people to think about the future—something to which they may never have given much thought.

Cleaning up the insurance industry's image is an enormous task. On one level, people like Halsey Josephson have launched a successful counterattack against the castigators who labeled the life insurance business a ripoff. But he was writing a book primarily for the benefit of his fellow agents, to teach them how to survive these false attacks. Few consumers knew of Josephson's book.

In this book we are more concerned with the consumer's problem. How can we clean up the image so the consumer can benefit directly? This is a vital problem for the public and the life insurance industry today.

As in all business, the resurgence of truth is a basic factor.

Truth will rebuild the image. Unfortunately, truth is very difficult to cultivate because of its subjectivity.

However, a well-trained agent can present the facts in a clear, precise way. The life insurance industry today includes a growing number of detailed training programs that produce responsible, well-informed agents. They are trained in helping clients to establish priorities and needs. Along with truth and understanding, communication, and credibility, agents learn to satisfy the client's needs without generalizing, without creating needs where there are none, and without looking at their own commission before they look at the client's policy.

Agents have to be able to define the true needs of a client so that consumers are never left to the mercy of Sunday paper supplements that advertise wonderful mail-order insurance plans for $7 a month, which actually computes to an astronomical $60 per thousand dollars of insurance at age fifty-two, versus the normal $24 per thousand for a better policy at the proper price.

The buyer must beware of the new mail-order, instant insurance syndrome, sold through department stores, credit cards, gas companies, and practically any business with a mailing list. With simplistic approaches and total generalizations, they offer what usually turns out to be a very high-priced solution to problems that they don't even know about. No consumer should have to pay so much for so little. Complete personalized service is available—and for far less money—through a reputable agent.

Another example is the tremendous use of computer software for various types of insurance programs. While the program itself may be excellent for an individual or for a business, it often is so complex and so creatively exciting that little heed is paid to the actual insurance product that is used within the computer program. In many instances, substantial savings could have been effected using a different life insurance product. New available insurance products on the market can greatly enhance the value of these computerized approaches to clients' problems. The program may be the right one, but was the lowest price policy used and should that program be reviewed to assure its cost efficiency?

Education Is the Answer

I believe we must continue to educate the public on how to buy insurance and why to buy. As more agents are educated to know what *they* are selling and why they are selling it, the insurance industry will change. Insurance companies will swing around, conforming to the new intelligence levels of clients and agents.

As consumers themselves realize that the industry is changing, they will force agents to comply with higher standards— or they will take their business elsewhere. Agents will have to become more knowledgeable, and the companies will become better-run. Better informed consumers will respect representatives who take the time to understand and communicate the need life insurance fulfills, a need that detractors can never entirely disguise.

All of this will improve the image of the insurance industry, making it more competitive with other forms of business. And as education and communication grow, insurance companies will be better able to serve client needs, substituting for distrust and confusion a new intelligence and understanding.

New Waves:
The Coming of Extralife-Economatic

YOU MAY BE glad to hear that the insurance revolution will produce better communication, more intelligent agents, and increased respect for the life insurance industry. But what you're probably most interested in is price. The revolution we are speaking of here is a price revolution.

The consumer will soon notice this effect when the insurance companies of America begin gearing up their new advertising campaigns, demonstrating a degree of competitiveness unheard of in life insurance history. Comparison advertising is on its way. Certain companies now realize that they have the lowest prices, and rather than keep quiet about it, as they have done in the past, they are beginning to shout. In these inflationary times, savings are vital to every consumer's pocketbook.

Extralife-Economatic

That price revolution is already here with the creation of new insurance products, that are ushering in a new era of life insurance. Leading the way is the new low-premium plan known as Extralife-Economatic.

Extralife-Economatic, simply put, lowers the price of permanent insurance policies by allowing the consumer to purchase an insurance policy of, for example, $100,000 while paying for approximately $70,000—70% of the policy. The balance is then made up by a combination of additional paid-up insurance and one-year term insurance purchased from the dividends, which provides the total face value purchased—$100,000 in this case.

As the paid-up additions grow to $30,000 (bringing the full face value to $100,000), less term insurance is purchased until finally there is no term insurance at all. This is usually within twelve to twenty years. Eventually, when the policy reaches its crossover point, the dividends can either be taken in cash or used to purchase even more insurance.

The full impact of such a plan is still being studied. But already some insurance companies in America are doing a substantial amount of business with the new permanent insurance format featured in the Extralife-Economatic policies.

Critics point out that the Extralife-Economatic generates lower cash values because of lower premiums, that dividends are not really guaranteed, and that the consumers give up flexibility in the use of their dividends. Some agents claim that this type of insurance is only for someone who is really cost-conscious. (Because of this very conservative attitude, a number of companies are not sure they want to advertise this plan as being anything more than another low-premium plan, when in fact it is one of the lowest permanent insurance premium policies ever created by a mutual life insurance company.)

Each of these points of criticism can be refuted, however, to show that the Extralife-Economatic is the revolutionary plan it claims to be.

First, everyone has to be cost-conscious these days. Those people who really want high cash values can buy a lower-cost premium policy and simply have more of their own cash available.

A second objection is that dividends in mutual companies are not guaranteed. Theoretically, should the company suffer a reverse in profits or a change in mortality tables, dividends could be cut and thus would not be able to support the policy. In fact, dividends are not as unstable as people may think. Some companies have paid dividends regularly for over a hundred years. While these may not be guaranteed, there is little possibility of their dropping out of sight. Moreover, some companies state that even if the dividends should decrease, the face value will be supported—even if the dividends are only 50% of their original amount. So the chances of losing the face value because of dividend deflation are very slight.

Finally, it is meaningless to state that the flexibility on your dividends will be lost, because the cost of the premiums is so much lower with the new price structures. The lowest cost permanent insurance is now available through the Extralife-Economatic plan. Consumers can join those who advocate the new concept of "buy permanent insurance and invest the difference."

Extralife-Economatic is the most workable form of permanent life insurance ever created, and many consumers are realizing this fact.

Other Forms of Permanent Insurance

Previous forms of a modified permanent insurance were less substantial and were usually prone to agent merchandising.

Modified premiums bought policies at lower rates, possibly for the first three to ten years. Clients paid the first, second, and third years at the lower rate and then the premium was automatically raised to the existing rate for the appropriate age group at that time. I've never been in favor of that kind of policy. Because of the lower premium, the client gets no real cash values the first three years, and then the premium is increased substantially. The client is better off buying term insurance and then converting it to permanent at the end of the third year, or whenever the client wishes.

Modified life was a form of selling permanent insurance in a painless manner. Consumers felt they received a discount in the beginning, when in fact this was nothing more than a form of merchandising. Either consumers buy a term policy because they need it and can't afford the permanent policy, or they buy the permanent policy because they can afford it. But I have seen many instances where a person who *could* afford it was actually talked out of it through merchandising and ended up buying the modified plan. Agents will have to abandon this type of merchandising and appeal more specifically to the consumer's needs.

Buyers must also beware of modified combinations of permanent and term insurance that actually cut the face value in half in later years, leaving them with a smaller death benefit at a time when they are actuarially closer to death and really need full coverage.

Certainly there will still be consumers who wish to purchase high cash value or term insurance. But for many, Extralife-Economatic plans are providing unusually good benefits. In cases like "minimum deposit," for instance, they can buy insurance with the lowest possible outlay by later borrowing against the cash values to pay back the cost of the premiums each year. With the Extralife-Economatic plan, consumers can borrow a lower premium, which creates a smaller interest factor. While there are other ramifications (which will be discussed later), Extralife-Economatic does offer a substantially lower cost over a lifetime using this minimum deposit approach.

New Alternatives

As Extralife-Economatic becomes more accepted, the arguments for term insurance are going to be affected.

As the premiums go down, even the most ardent critics will find it actually possible to compare the costs of permanent insurance favorably with those of term insurance. The new rates demand such a comparison. Many people who have been buying term are now at least considering permanent policies under the Extralife-Economatic plan. This is one of the most dramatic developments in the insurance industry in recent years.

For many years, mutual or participating companies (owned by the policyholders) were at a disadvantage when compared with stock or non-participating companies (owned by the stockholders). Despite the fact that in the long run mutual companies offered a lower net premium and net cost because of their dividends, stock company premiums were always lower in the beginning—a reality that was constantly noted by the consumer. Now that some mutual companies have introduced Extralife-Economatic plans, their premiums are more competitive with the non-par premium, and in many cases lower right from the outset. When coupled with the lower net costs the mutual company has usually had, the Extralife-Economatic is truly a revolutionary plan.

As competition increases for the consumer's dollar, the non-par companies are eventually going to launch a counter-attack of their own. In fact, right now many non-par companies are going back to the drawing board and projecting higher interest rates to build larger cash values, which could possibly lower premiums on non-par policies.

But in the long run, if a non-par policy again develops a lower premium, consumers will be paying that premium for the better part of their lives. The mutual companies, through Extralife-Economatic plans, will eventually lower the premiums by using the dividend to reduce payments. And when the dividend exceeds the premium, consumers will have no cash outlay and will have cash in hand to the extent that the dividend is in excess of the premium.

Both mutual and non-par companies are researching and

creating new products during this revolution. Many combination annuity and term products combining the cash value and death benefit, such as the new Universal Life policies, are now surfacing. There will be variations on this type of product, including the new Adjustable Life. Each will have its advantages and disadvantages but as a trend it will mean more consumer-oriented, lower-priced approaches, based on new higher interest assumptions, introduced to the marketplace. This is all to the advantage of the consumer.

$$5$$

The Numbers Speak for Themselves: Pricing and Savings in the Revolution

To HELP UNDERSTAND this revolution, let me give you a basic, simple explanation of life insurance—how it came to be and how it works.

Constructing the Policy

Let's suppose that, many years ago, a thousand men of the same age got together and decided that they wanted to provide some kind of financial protection for their families. They would all contribute equally in order to make sure that the family of any man who died prematurely would receive $1,000.

It was figured out actuarially that during the coming year three of them would die. They then knew that they needed a fund of $3,000 available by the end of the year. All premiums would be paid at the beginning of the year and all death benefits would be paid at the end of the year. One thousand men contributing $3 would provide the total needed fund of $3,000. Therefore, each man would have to contribute $3 for the year.

Since the money would earn interest from when the premiums were paid at the beginning of the year, the premium was discounted by whatever interest factor was used—in this case, 5%. Thus because of this interest factor each man's premium only had to be $2.85. Someone would have to keep the records, so they added a cost of administration factor—five cents, bringing the total up to $2.90. Therefore, if each man contributed $2.90, by virtue of the interest that would be earned on the principal fund from all the premiums paid, then subtracting the cost for administration, the proper amount of money would be accumulated in order to accommodate the three men's families.

If a profit is to be added to the figures, a percentage would have to be allowed in order to accommodate that desired profit.

This simplified process is utilized for each and every age group, and continued each and every year.

In simple terms, insurance benefits an entire group by the pooling of the money of many to protect the families of the few that will die in any given year.

The introduction of the Extralife-Economatic plan that lowers premiums to new levels has launched a pricing revolution. It is already saving the consumer a great deal of money. In order to obtain the best savings, the consumer must understand how the pricing and savings work.

Premiums

Let's start with premiums. Obviously, there is a difference between a $350 premium and a $250 premium: one is cheaper than the other. However, a cheaper premium doesn't necessarily mean the *insurance* is going to be cheaper.

This brings us back to the question of non-par versus par. A premium on a non-par policy, in most cases, is never going to change for the rest of your life. In most cases the premium on a non-participating policy is guaranteed not to go up. But it is also guaranteed not to go down, regardless of how much the company is benefiting from its investments, the new mortality rates, and more efficient operating expenses. New policyholders may benefit from new rates resulting from higher interest assumptions and new mortality tables, but old policyholders of the same age continue to pay the old premium.

A premium from a participating company may be high now, but because of the dividends you will be receiving over the years, the premium will eventually dwindle.

The new Extralife-Economatic plan makes the participating companies even more attractive, because it features a lower premium, sometimes even lower than the premium of non-participating companies.

New competitive products are constantly being developed. One type, from the non-par companies, could produce a lower premium policy based upon a non-guaranteed, higher interest rate of return on the cash value. Instead of using the conventional dividend approach, this policy could adjust the premiums yearly, based on the rate of return the insurance company achieved. However, this would eliminate the guaranteed premium and might cause the consumer to pay more on a prearranged higher guaranteed premium if the projected results are not accomplished. Policies of this type might either eventually cost more money or their death benefit would decrease. While they offer excellent merchandising potential, they eliminate the peace-of-mind guarantee that most insurance buyers are looking for.

Interest-Adjusted Indexes

The premium isn't the only factor used in determining how expensive your policy is and how much you might save.

If premiums alone were used to figure the net cost of your policy, you would simply subtract your cash value from the total amount of your premiums paid over, say, twenty years.

Figuring this way, if Jeff R. paid $500 a year in premiums for twenty years, he would have paid a total of $10,000. Let's say his cash value at the end of twenty years was $8,500. Ordinarily, you would say the net cost of his policy was $1,500. However, net cost is no longer figured in this way.

Recent government regulations now require that an insurance policy be "interest-adjusted" to determine its net cost. This simply means that a 5% net figure must be tacked on to the calculations to allow for the cost of money over the years. Supposedly this will reflect the *true* cost of the insurance policy.

In other words, the government says, "You didn't have to buy this insurance; you could have made an investment. Therefore, there's a cost of money to this policy. So, if you spent $500 on the yearly premium, you lost the use of $500 on which you could have made interest. Thus, on a net 5% after-tax basis, we will interest-adjust your life insurance rates. We will say the insurance didn't cost you $500, it cost you $500 *plus* 5% compound interest."

Interest-adjusted net-cost indexes—something you will become very familiar with when your insurance agent produces his rate cards—allow consumers to determine how much they are actually going to be paying for their life insurance.

Cost Comparison

More importantly, the cost index provides a basis for comparison. While other variables should be taken into consideration, the basic true cost index gives consumers a way to compare all policies and companies.

For example, with this cost index, consumers can truly determine the actual cost of so-called "discount insurance" plans that are often advertised in supermarket fashion. Often, they will offer permanent insurance for only $7 a month. But the cost index shows you are paying $60 per thousand, compared to an average permanent insurance policy offered by another company giving you a similar plan for only $24 per thousand. In this case, interest-adjusted cost-index tables can save consumers a great deal of money and protect them from a costly insurance plan.

When you compare non-par and par companies, the par companies are usually cheaper in the long run because of their dividends, which reflect the return of their profits to the policyholder. Of course, if there is a complete reversal in our economy and we enter a period of depression, then the guaranteed premium could be lower.

For example, let's choose a $100,000 policy for a 35-year-old male in an average non-par company. For this policy, his premium would be $1,334 per year. His net cost, interest adjusted, comes out to $4.94 per thousand dollars' worth of insurance, over a twenty-year period.

Now let's consider the same policy in a participating company. The premium for this policy is $2,062 a year. That's over $700 more than the non-par premium. Many consumers will immediately stop right there and say, "That's obviously more expensive; I'll take the other one."

However, when you use the interest-adjusted figure, you find that the net cost of the par policy is only $2.29 per thousand dollars of insurance. So, over a period of twenty years, the participating policy clearly costs less.

People have to stop thinking about how much their policy costs at the beginning. At 35, the cost over the next five years is not as important as the cost over the next 35 years, and how much you're really going to spend and, in turn, save with the right policy.

Cash Values

Let's consider another factor in determining cost structure and resultant savings: cash values. Some consumers prefer high cash values because they see them as an emergency or retirement fund for the future. So they ask, "Which policy produces a larger cash value?"

I believe that it is important to have enough cash value to keep the premium level, which is the true and only reason for permanent life insurance. There is no need to have excessive cash values, provided you can still keep the premium level and pocket the extra savings by purchasing a lower cash value, lower premium policy. Why not pay lower premiums, keep the policy level, and invest the savings difference somewhere else, perhaps in tax-free municipal bonds, or real estate? Diversify whenever possible, but never build up excess cash values when they're not necessary to keep a premium level.

True Value

In the insurance revolution, consumers are becoming less concerned with cash values and more concerned with lower premiums. And because of the lower premiums available, and the resultant lower net costs, consumers are definitely buying policies that are much better values for their money.

Saving a Fortune!
The Miracle of Compound Interest

IN LIFE INSURANCE, savings are seldom what they seem—especially in the area of interest. Therefore, it is important to understand how your potential savings are affected by interest.

Interest benefits the consumer in two ways. First, high interest rates produce better investment results for insurance companies, allowing them, in effect, to reduce premiums. Second, with substantially reduced premiums, consumers receive better value for their money and can take advantage of other investment opportunities with those savings.

How Compound Interest Works

When banks were offering 4% interest for their patrons, compound interest was hardly exciting. With those rates, it took eighteen years to double your money, and that certainly does not create a miraculous return. But when you can get as much as 12% on your money, compound interest takes on a new light. Not only can you get tripl: the old rate of interest, but you can also *double your money* in a third of the time. And if the tax-free interest rates should rise to 15% in the future, the possibilities are nothing short of miraculous.

If you would like a quick financial overview, use the "rule of 72," a basic formula that demonstrates how long it takes for money to double.

Here is how it works: Just divide the rate of interest return into the number 72; the result is the number of years it takes for money to double. For instance, if you're making 8% on your money, then 8 is divided into 72, and the result is 9. It will thus take you 9 years to double your money at 8%. If you make 12%, it takes 6 years. And if you made 20% on your money, it would take only 3.6 years to double.

Conversely, to find out what percentage of interest you *need* in order to double your money in a certain number of years, you simply divide the desired number of years back into 72. If you want to double your money in 8 years, you divide that number into 72 and get 9. Thus, it takes 9% to double your money in 8 years. And if you want to double your money in 4 years, you divide 4 into 72 and get 18%.

How Much Can You Save?

Since permanent life insurance is a product for your lifetime (or, in the case of term insurance, for a period of years), it is important to note the value of any savings you can accumulate over the same period, as long as you purchase the insurance product that meets your objectives. It is imperative that you make all comparisons on an apples-to-apples basis only.

If your life expectancy table shows you probably will live thirty five more years, and you can save $3,000 per year on the cost of your policies now, you're saving $105,000 ($3,000 x 35 years). And that savings will be compounded by the available interest rates. At 12%, this could amount to as much as $1,450,389 in thirty-five years. Even at 6%, you would accumulate $354,362. Astonishing, isn't it?

The figures are so unbelievable that they strain credibility. However, the figures speak for themselves. (See Table 1.)

Compound interest is a fact. Even if rates were to go down, the savings over a lifetime could still be substantial.

I can now show clients a lower cost insurance plan and say, "You're going to save $3,000 a year on this policy. And those savings can amount to between $354,362 and $1,450,389 over the course of your lifetime." You'd be surprised how many people never think of money in this way.

Surrender Value Counts, Too

We also have to take into account the surrender value of an existing policy, and its resultant compounded interest value.

For example, if I replace a client's current $3,100 policy with a $2,600 yearly premium, on the surface it would seem that we were saving the client only $500 per year. But in addition to compounding that $500 at 8% for the next thirty years, we also take into account the $2,200 of cash surrender value the client had accumulated on the old policy. By compounding the yearly savings, along with the cash made available upon the surrender of the old policy, we then obtain a total saving of $140,000 over the next thirty years. I'm sure you'll agree that's quite an impressive figure.

It's Real!

Remember, compound interest has nothing to do with insurance. It's merely a principle of finance. I'm simply showing you how important your savings become when you buy insurance properly.

If more agents used compound interest tables, the consumer would be able to understand the meaning of savings and see why the new lower-priced premiums are causing such unprecedented interest and excitement. When such spectacular savings are possible, the consumers of America will want to take the time to listen to the insurance agent explain compound interest tables and the impact interest has on savings. For we are not talking about sales merchandising here, but facts.

If you have a $10,000 surrender value on a policy, a thirty-five-year life expectancy, and can achieve 12% compound interest, in thirty-five years that $10,000 will amount to $527,996. Even at 6% you would accumulate $76,860. Perhaps now you understand why we call this the "miracle of compound interest."

On the next two pages, you will find two charts that fully detail the effect of different rates of compound interest on a specific sum and yearly savings. With these numbers you will be able to see how they work as well as how they make an impact on your money.

TABLE 1. INTEREST:

$3,000 YEARLY SAVING

YEAR	CASH FLOW	COMPOUND VALUE AT 6.0%	COMPOUND VALUE AT 8.0%	COMPOUND VALUE AT 10.0%	COMPOUND VALUE AT 12.0%
1	−3,000	−3,180	−3,240	−3,300	−3,360
2	−3,000	−6,550	−6,739	−6,930	−7,123
3	−3,000	−10,123	−10,518	−10,923	−11,337
4	−3,000	−13,911	−14,599	−15,315	−16,058
5	−3,000	−17,925	−19,007	−20,146	−21,345
6	−3,000	−22,181	−23,768	−25,461	−27,267
7	−3,000	−26,692	−28,909	−31,307	−33,899
8	−3,000	−31,473	−34,462	−37,738	−41,326
9	−3,000	−36,542	−40,459	−44,812	−49,646
10	−3,000	−41,914	−46,936	−52,593	−58,963
11	−3,000	−47,609	−53,931	−61,152	−69,399
12	−3,000	−53,646	−61,485	−70,568	−81,087
13	−3,000	−60,045	−69,644	−80,924	−94,177
14	−3,000	−66,827	−78,456	−92,317	−108,839
15	−3,000	−74,017	−87,972	−104,849	−125,259
16	−3,000	−81,638	−98,250	−118,634	−143,651
17	−3,000	−89,716	−109,350	−133,797	−164,249
18	−3,000	−98,279	−121,338	−150,477	−187,319
19	−3,000	−107,356	−134,285	−168,824	−213,157
20	−3,000	−116,978	−148,268	−189,007	−242,096
21	−3,000	−127,176	−163,370	−211,208	−274,507
22	−3,000	−137,987	−179,679	−235,629	−310,808
23	−3,000	−149,446	−197,294	−262,491	−351,465
24	−3,000	−161,593	−216,317	−292,041	−397,001
25	−3,000	−174,469	−236,863	−324,545	−448,001
26	−3,000	−188,117	−259,052	−360,299	−505,122
27	−3,000	−202,584	−283,016	−399,629	−569,096
28	−3,000	−217,919	−308,897	−442,892	−640,748
29	−3,000	−234,174	−336,849	−490,482	−720,998
30	−3,000	−251,405	−367,037	−542,830	−810,877
31	−3,000	−269,669	−399,640	−600,413	−911,543
32	−3,000	−289,029	−434,851	−663,754	−1,024,288
33	−3,000	−309,551	−472,880	−733,430	−1,150,562
34	−3,000	−331,304	−513,950	−810,073	−1,291,990
35	−3,000	−354,362	−558,306	−894,380	−1,450,389
36	−3,000	−378,804	−606,210	−987,118	−1,627,796
37	−3,000	−404,712	−657,947	−1,089,130	−1,826,491
38	−3,000	−432,175	−713,823	−1,201,343	−2,049,030
39	−3,000	−461,285	−774,169	−1,324,777	−2,298,274
40	−3,000	−492,143	−839,343	−1,460,555	−2,577,427

TABLE 2. INTEREST:
$10,000 SURRENDER VALUE

YEAR	CASH FLOW	COMPOUND VALUE AT 6.0%	COMPOUND VALUE AT 8.0%	COMPOUND VALUE AT 10.0%	COMPOUND VALUE AT 12.0%
1	10,000	10,600	10,800	11,000	11,200
2	0	11,236	11,664	12,100	12,544
3	0	11,910	12,597	13,310	14,049
4	0	12,624	13,604	14,641	15,735
5	0	13,382	14,693	16,105	17,623
6	0	14,185	15,868	17,715	19,738
7	0	15,036	17,138	19,487	22,106
8	0	15,938	18,509	21,435	24,759
9	0	16,894	19,990	23,579	27,730
10	0	17,908	21,589	25,937	31,058
11	0	18,982	23,316	28,531	34,785
12	0	20,121	25,181	31,384	38,959
13	0	21,329	27,196	34,522	43,634
14	0	22,609	29,371	37,974	48,871
15	0	23,965	31,721	41,772	54,735
16	0	25,403	34,259	45,949	61,303
17	0	26,927	37,000	50,544	68,660
18	0	28,543	39,960	55,599	76,899
19	0	30,255	43,157	61,159	86,127
20	0	32,071	46,609	67,274	96,462
21	0	33,995	50,338	74,002	108,038
22	0	36,035	54,365	81,402	121,003
23	0	38,197	58,714	89,543	135,523
24	0	40,489	63,411	98,497	151,786
25	0	42,918	68,484	108,347	170,000
26	0	45,493	73,963	119,181	190,400
27	0	48,223	79,880	131,099	213,248
28	0	51,116	86,271	144,209	238,838
29	0	54,183	93,172	158,630	267,499
30	0	57,434	100,626	174,494	299,599
31	0	60,881	108,676	191,943	335,551
32	0	64,533	117,370	211,137	375,817
33	0	68,405	126,760	232,251	420,915
34	0	72,510	136,901	255,476	471,425
35	0	76,860	147,853	281,024	527,996
36	0	81,472	159,681	309,126	591,355
37	0	86,360	172,456	340,039	662,318
38	0	91,542	186,252	374,043	741,796
39	0	97,035	201,152	411,447	830,812
40	0	102,857	217,245	452,592	930,509

The Danger of Inflation:
How It Will Affect Your Insurance Values

IN OUR INFLATION-RIDDEN WORLD, life insurance is one of the few products that has actually gone *down* in price. This is something that the entire life insurance industry can be proud of, and is only now beginning to promote. In fact, "Buy life insurance as an inflation fighter" is fast becoming a battle cry in some sectors.

But inflation is a double-edged sword.

Inflation Affects the Insurance Industry

The insurance revolution, combined with the effects of inflation, is going to be expensive for the insurance companies in the competitive 1980s. There will be higher salaries to pay. Computers will bring new efficiency to the industry, but those computers and the technicians to operate them are going to be expensive. Climbing postage rates, expensive new cost guidelines and brochures, higher rents, skyrocketing gasoline prices that affect traveling agents and commuters, all contribute to the cost and effect of inflation on the insurance industry. As competition increases, these expenses will rise, forcing the insurance companies to keep up the pace, or lose business.

Inflation and the resulting new price structures have forced the abandonment of traditional methods of business in favor of more direct sales approaches. Such new-wave marketing and promotional campaigns are very expensive, yet they are necessary in a fiercely competitive market.

Inflation Affects the Consumer

While inflation increases operating expenses, it also creates a need for more life insurance. Consumers discover that they need more coverage than they had originally thought. However, because of those new low prices, they can increase their coverage at the same cost, or for only a few dollars more.

Salaries are also increasing in order to keep up with the rampant rise in inflation. People are definitely making more, but money buys less. Obviously, since the insurance death benefit is meant to replace the income that a person's family will no longer receive upon the wage earner's death, additional amounts of life insurance must be purchased to accommodate as well as maintain a certain standard of living.

Consumers worry about what money will be worth in twenty or thirty years, and how much insurance they should purchase. Undoubtedly, consumers are purchasing as much as they can afford. This is particularly true among people with large businesses and estates, where, without insurance, inflation could cause confusion and panic. Whether an estate is worth its inflated value or not, the consumers are forced to protect their property at its *current* worth, or risk losing a major portion of their estate to taxes.

As inflation continues to inflate home and business values, consumers will continue to buy more and more insurance to protect their heirs from perhaps insurmountable mortgage and other debt obligations. Prices may stabilize, but values seldom go down. Some protective measure must be taken to keep as much as possible in the family and to prevent large losses to taxes.

Many people feel that the insurance they are buying today will not be worth as much in future years because of the reduced buying power of the dollar. This argument should not be a deterrent to purchasing the present needed amount of insurance. In fact, quite to the contrary, it is the very reason for purchasing more insurance than ever. The combination of a cheaper dollar and a lower premium only serve to make the purchase of insurance more attractive.

Inflation's Positive Effects

As we enter the 1980s, I think the insurance industry is at the most creative period in its history. Not only are the benefits to the public increasing, but the survival of many insurance companies in their present form is at stake, causing many company executives to begin to change their conservative approach for a more aggressive and competitive one. This is good for the consumer.

Certainly, inflation is responsible in part for this new aggressiveness. Needs are changing and agents are no longer able to make do with old methods. People need more insurance and yet they don't necessarily have the money to buy it. Property and investments produce a greater need for unprecedented amounts of life insurance. It is the responsibility of insurance agents to stay on top of the latest developments and tax ramifications of insurance, and understand how they can affect a client's needs during this period of super inflation.

There was a time when agents sold policies and then retired to their offices to wait for renewals, sending out an occasional Christmas or birthday card and thank-you note. Inflation has taken the waiting out of the life insurance industry.

"You Are *You!*"
Stopping the Trend Toward Generalizations in Life Insurance

YOUR NEEDS, objectives, and desires are different from those of anybody else. You are an individual. You have your own opinions, and you also have your own budget. In most cases the generalizations that you hear or read are totally inapplicable to you.

Clients can learn how to prevent generalizations and protect their interests by understanding how to communicate with an insurance agent, and spotting the problems that may hamper that relationship. Then they will be able to purchase what they need—and not what someone tells them they need.

It is my goal to educate the consumer so that he or she is aware of current life insurance trends and practices, and also understands the value of a strong relationship with the agent. With such a relationship, consideration of individual needs becomes a reality.

Communication Is the Key

One of the major problems in life insurance today is basic communication. If the agent/client relationship has faults, consumers are going to be affected, either by purchasing a plan that doesn't suit their needs, by failing to understand how their insurance needs change, by paying too much for what they have, or simply by being left in the dark when new and different plans become available. Without consistent interaction between client and agent, the value of life insurance can be misinterpreted. Peace of mind and security may be lost, and all parties will suffer as a result.

Don't let an agent work for you unless you trust him or her completely. Educate yourself so that you will understand what your agent is talking about. While you cannot become an expert in the field, it is imperative that you be able to understand your agent's explanations.

Keep involved in the ongoing planning. Don't sit back. Review your policy needs periodically, as you would review your investments. Make sure you are benefiting from the latest trends in life insurance. Nothing should be taken for granted.

Generalization

There is a tendency to generalize about life insurance needs. Consumers, agents, friends, your lawyer, and your accountant all do it. Everybody does it. It's a fact of life in the life insurance industry.

During a discussion of insurance options one of my client's remarked, "Oh, I've talked to some of my friends and they said that when it comes to estate taxes, they're so large anyway, that there is really no purpose in doing anything about them!"

Now this man was very wealthy and could well afford insurance to cover what looked like a half-million dollars worth of estate tax obligations that would affect him and his wife. Yet, based on the generalization of a friend, he was ready to throw up his hands and say, "What's the use?" Whether from ignorance or plain impatience, that man had not taken the time to investigate his friend's assumption. There was a chance that he was referring to an entirely different income and estate tax bracket, or simply generalizing when he didn't have any real knowledge at hand. On the subject of life insurance, everyone has an opinion, and there is always one more option. When you're dealing with a sizable sum of money, no statement should be taken at face value, especially from opinionated friends. Research and find out the real answers. Ask your agent. And if he doesn't have the right answers, ask someone else. There is too much at stake to base your life insurance plan, or any plan, on a possible generalization. In the end, only *you* can determine whether there is a true option available or if you are being taken advantage of by another agent trying to introduce his or her products.

Another frequent generalization is the "keeping up with the Jones's" syndrome. This occurs when someone finds that his friend has a particular type of policy and immediately he wants the same policy for himself. He may say, "Your child has a policy? I should have one on my child too!" You may not know, however, that the man had completely taken care of himself and his wife before he used his extra money to buy a small policy for his child—something you may not have done.

Agents and Generalization

Do agents generalize? Yes, they do.

I would say in many instances agents actually go out on a campaign, saying, "This month I think I'll sell Split Dollar, R.L.R., or I'll sell as much Section 79 as I can." So instead of selling to a specific *need*, the agents will generalize their approach. Of course, they may not cause immediate harm and it may just be their way of entering into a relationship. But if agents are professional, they will adjust their approach as they see their client's needs. Those agents who fail to see the client's needs properly have no creativity. The consumer should learn to avoid agents with such limited abilities.

A client should beware of an agent who keeps harking back to one specific plan. You might be dealing with an agent who isn't sure about the new plans, and feels more comfortable staying with the "old tried and true." Let the agent know that you want to see different options, regardless of cost, and that you want to shop around for the right plan.

When you gain the initiative, be sure you keep it. Never relax to the point where you're sitting there constantly nodding and saying, "That's right," when what you really mean is, "Is that true!" or "I don't understand, but because I'm in a hurry, I'll take your word for it." After the proper rapport has been established and you are satisfied with your agent's credibility, then you can relax a little.

If generalizations hurt because they don't apply to specific needs, they can also hurt when they become *too* specific. Don't let yourself be pigeonholed into buying something specific like "cancer insurance" when there is a good chance you may not die from cancer. It might give you a false feeling of security and preclude the total coverage you need.

Don't develop a false sense of security when you buy accidental death insurance through your gasoline credit card. And, certainly, don't wait to buy your life insurance when you get to an airport vending machine.

If you feel that you're worth a certain amount of money to your heirs, why don't you have the right kind of insurance right now? Why develop protection and peace of mind in such a manner? Remember: there is no such thing as an average amount or normal kind in life insurance.

Getting Past Generalizations

As the public begins to understand the difference between a salesperson who is selling insurance, and a salesperson who is trying professionally to suit the needs of the client, the need to generalize will diminish. The consumer will learn which questions need to be asked and how to pin down specific needs. Consumers must be willing to invest the time this requires for them to receive the maximum return.

Insurance agents are going to have to take the time to look into a client's financial history and outline an approach that will best suit the situation. And the client must be ready to participate in a proper fact-finding discussion and know which specifics are applicable.

So, forget what your friend said yesterday, or what your brother-in-law is going to tell you tomorrow. Keep an open mind. Look at the facts that the agent is presenting to you and listen to what he or she has to offer.

The educational process begins with you.

"I'll Never Understand in a Million Years": — The Need for Better Communication in the Life Insurance Industry

WHAT CAUSES THE breakdown of communications between a consumer and an agent?

Technical Experts and Communications

First, the relationship is hampered by the fact that life insurance is a very technical subject, very difficult to explain "on the run." I mention "on the run" because life insurance agents are usually given a very limited amount of time to present their case. In fact, it can safely be said that life insurance agents get the shortest shrift of any salespeople.

There are some very technically oriented agents who know their subject flawlessly. But can they relate technical details to the layman in a situation where communication skills and sales ability are of utmost importance? Walking encyclopedias are fine in the research division creating charts and actuarial surveys, but if they venture in front of a client, usually nothing happens.

Conversely, there are sales persons who are excellent communicators, but who lack the technical expertise to explain their product in the best light. However wonderful their communications skills are, if they trip themselves up and fail to defend their product from a technical point of view at a key moment, their credibility is sacrificed. No layman likes to do business with a salesperson who doesn't understand the product. Without knowledge, communication is wasted.

It is rare for an agent to have both technical prowess and communications skills. The rare person who does possess both is usually the most effective salesperson and a leader in the company and, most important, the agent you are looking for.

Sometimes it's impossible to turn a technician into a communicator. On the other hand, many typical salespersons often have no patience for learning the business properly. In fact, there are many "over night" salespersons who feel that they can fake their knowledge and compensate with their proven sales ability. This can be a disaster for you.

True Communication

True communication is very important and yet so rare. It not only involves explaining a complicated subject in easy terms, but also takes an ability to present an explanation so it won't be wasted. A plan must be presented in terms of being the right plan and offering the right benefits for the right cost. But it must also be acceptable to you according to your particular mood on a particular day.

To adapt a sales approach to moods and psyches is an art form that only the most dedicated professional agent can master. Such qualities are common to good salesmen in other businesses, but they are especially vital in the world of life insurance with its technical nuances and where rejection can come quickly and unexpectedly.

Agents never really know where your saturation point is. They may approach you with a command of their business that allows you to see facts gradually. They make constant use of visual aids and examples, allowing you to see similar plans at work. Only when you can identify with the experience of others like yourself, will you begin to see how a plan can be to your benefit.

Clear communication is difficult to master by itself, without further complicating the picture with a super-technical subject. Add to that the unavoidable suspicion or apathy on the part of consumers who don't want to hear about the subject of life insurance in the first place. Now, even if they do listen, bad communication will make it impossible to comprehend.

Salesmen who communicate well also motivate well. They present the facts in such a way that you are prone to action. You will buy because you understand.

You give many buying signals that an agent must be aware of: when to sell, when to close or when to change approaches in your best interest. Unless the salesperson picks up on these signs, they can be passed over until you are ultimately bored, disgusted, or demotivated out of whatever you might have purchased.

To avoid "missing the boat" with a prospect, the agent is taught to listen and to be alert at all times. It isn't only listening; it's feeling, grasping, understanding, reading between the lines, and then saying things that will put you at ease. It is understanding not only what you said, but what you didn't say, as well.

Urgency and Your Agent

How does an agent overcome preconceived notions? By gaining the prospect's attention, by realizing that nothing is taken for granted, and by carefully detailing all of the necessary information.

Ironically, the sale always begins with "No!" In terms of

helping the potential client, the agent who walks away after that first "No!" has done a terrible job. A "No!" is just the beginning of the selling process.

Agents must be persistent with a prospect who is likely to benefit from the product once it is understood. They must also attach a sense of urgency to the sales approach. Otherwise, the consumer's apathy or procrastination will destroy any motivation to purchase.

It's difficult to ignore the fact that many people consider insurance the lowest of their priorities. The reason is obvious. No one expects to die and certainly not in the near future. Insurance is something to be taken care of tomorrow, like the will and the children's trusts. It can wait. Only, tomorrow may never come.

You might lose your health. Insurance would then be more expensive or unavailable. In fact "you pay for insurance with money, but you buy it with good health."

The new lower prices are an inducement because they encourage consumers to consider plans which they originally thought too expensive. But lower prices are certainly not the only reason to buy insurance. Don't buy a policy just because it's cheap, but rather buy it because you have a need and you find a policy to fulfill that need.

You are the consumer. You should find the right agent with the right technical knowledge, who can communicate properly with you in order to serve your best interests.

10

The Agent/Client Relationship: Adviser or Adversary?

WE ARE IN a revolution, and every day the pressures are increasing on insurance agents who continue to live in the past, selling products and services that have been by-passed by the new prices and practices of the Eighties.

One frequently encountered problem that plays an important part in the agent/client relationship is the way in which an agent approaches the client's current insurance coverage. Many agents will look at a previous policy and say, "I can do better for you" or "Did you *really* buy that?"

Comments like these not only insult the previous agent, but in most cases insult the client as well. In effect, the agent is really saying, "You were stupid to buy this policy in the first place."

By improperly pointing out a previous agent's failings, the new agent can only hurt his or her chances for developing a good relationship with the client. Agents must learn how to point to a client's needs without knocking previous coverage. Price changes are really no one's fault. Error occurs when no one makes an attempt to understand and take advantage of new opportunities. If replacement is called for, the proper recommendations should be made.

Ethical or Unethical

When discussing a previous policy, the agent must handle the situation very carefully. The suggestion that replacement of a current policy was necessary, in many cases, undermined the credibility of the new agent. The word "replacement" carried the connotation that agents were interested only in replacing the current in-force policy for their own benefit and a new commission.

Agents who acted in this manner were called "twisters," in that they were "twisting" (turning out) policies to the detriment of the client, the implication being that they were acting unethically and, in many cases, illegally. The true definition of a twister is one who replaces a policy by using deceptive and misleading methods, to the detriment of the client.

However, there were many situations where policies were properly and professionally analyzed and the analysis without question, proved that replacement would be in the client's best interests. The thin line between "replacer" and "twister" was ignored when it served the purpose of outraged agents who were really not concerned with the client's best interests, but were more interested in preserving and retaining their in-force policy and/or future commissions.

Therefore, a replacement in the best interest of the client is legal, ethical, and moral, if the agent's purpose is to truly satisfy the client's needs.

The following is quoted from an address on the future role of C.L.U.'s presented before some 900 American Society of CLU Chapter officers at 10 conferences held coast to coast in the spring of 1980:

"The ethics involved in replacement is another situation which could be included under the broad category of consumerism. Are there increasingly situations where some replacement is not only ethical but also other situations where not making such a suggestion would be unethical?"

Many states and replacing companies require that complete comparison forms be filled out in order to protect the client in a replacement situation. The client should request comparable papers and a letter of explanation from his current company stating why they would want him to retain a policy that is clearly not in his best interest.

Loyalty

When the subject of replacement comes up and a dialogue begins with a new insurance agent, the question of loyalty to the old agent can arise. Loyalty can sometimes get in the way when new pricing tests old relationships.

When a client tells me that he is anxious to stay with his original agent, because he feels this strong loyalty to him, even though he may be saving $600,000 over the course of his lifetime with a new policy, I immediately suggest that he sit down and write out a check to his old agent for $300,000, so that the agent will be taken care of! The client still comes out ahead $300,000.

The client laughs and states that the savings is not instant and is over the period of a lifetime. I will tell him to write a check for at least the savings on the annual premium, because even with that figure, it will compensate the old agent for most of the loss of renewals he might have obtained over the next few years. I think *that* puts the question of loyalty into the proper perspective.

No person should give loyalty to an agent, unless that agent is returning the favor. If a professional agent is loyal, and is to deserve your loyalty, then that agent is going to point to the new agent's figures and agree that they're better and that you should consider a replacement.

The agent might say to you that the new agent is correct but that he too can buy the policy from the new company directly. The question then is what loyalty do you owe to the new agent who has done the work, created the new approach, and made the tremendous savings possible in the first place. More importantly, if you stay with the old agent, who will do the necessary creative thinking the following year?

Adversary or Ally?

Agents reveal their true motives when they fight the new agent down the line and go so far as to state that the savings are incorrect and attempt to convince the client that he or she is making a mistake by considering replacement. Yet this is exactly what is done in many cases. The current agent suddenly becomes an adversary—fighting off the new agent and the new plan, and alienating the client as well.

Ideally, a company with an inexpensive product tries to appeal to all agents from other companies who are selling more expensive products. They advise them that until their own companies produce a more competitive product, they can broker the business by bringing their clients to the lower pricing. In this way agents still retain their own clientele while serving their best interests.

Sometimes, though, this doesn't work. Some clients tend to shut themselves off from any possible competition and potential savings. This is when an agent needs to be creative. Agents who feel strongly about what they are selling, and how it is going to save the client a great deal of money, will not be put off by the stubborn loyalty the client gives to another agent. They will continue to make their point clear, until the client listens.

Certainly, insurance agents must be the most resilient of

all salespersons, considering the amount of rejection they undergo. Most successful agents possess this "alligator skin" and will not give up until every selling option is closed to them. Even though they lose the sale, the consumer may be disturbed enough to check the new pricing with his previous agent. At least the consumer will have benefited by the new agent's dogged persistence.

The most important point to be reemphasized is that agents are not adversaries but advisers. They cannot serve the client's best interests unless they inspire complete confidence. This will allow them to be creative and of great benefit to the consumer. Choose your agent well and then let your agent work in *your* behalf.

11

—— Agent versus Agent: Client Loses! ——

LET'S TURN NOW from the agent/client relationship and discuss the "behind the scenes" world of agent versus agent.

Consumers' insurance portfolios often reveal that they have five or six different policies bought from five or six different agents. While there can be many reasons for this, in most cases it indicates that the original agent did not follow through and build the necessary client/adviser relationship. Or, the client may have dismissed the previous agent for lack of knowledge, improper service, or for simply failing to develop mutual rapport.

In many instances, the consumers themselves did not truly understand the value of having one agent who would act in their best interests. Instead, they might have bought from whoever would appear on their doorstep, such as a friend, family member, or anyone to whom they may have owed a favor—thus doing a great disservice to themselves.

When consumers decide to deal with a new agent, they most likely will have to deal with a former agent as well. Any policy changes, reevaluations, or service of any kind will prompt the client's current company to send back its own agent to the scene. That agent will attempt to find out what the changes are and why they are being made, and very likely will extol the advantages of his or her own company.

The consumer dealing with two agents can come out the greatest loser. Therefore, consumers should know how agents deal with each other.

Agent Relationships

Agent relationships develop on two levels: between agents of the same company, and between agents of different companies. Within an agency, if agents don't think they can handle a particular case on their own, they will bring in a senior agent to help. That senior agent may communicate well or have more technical knowledge of the subject. Or two agents simply may decide to work together for the purpose of combining their skills.

If an agent feels that the company doesn't have the correct plan, that agent can often broker the insurance to another company that has the desired product. However, the brokering of an alternative company's insurance plan is a controversial issue in the life insurance industry. Some companies don't allow their agents to sell the product of other companies. It is very likely a question of sophistication. Those agents who understand the different rates find that brokering is vital, especially if their own company doesn't have the right policy or the right price, or if the parent company refuses to insure a person beyond a certain amount (for instance, the client wants $10 million in insurance but the parent company will issue only $5 million).

The brokering of different company policies, also known as surplus business, is important for the agent who does not want to appear limited in the eyes of a potential client. An agent wants to be able to say, "If there's a different product you need, I can get it for you."

Most agents are only trained to explain their own products, but they really should learn as much as possible about the products of other companies too. It's a very large industry and of course it's impossible to stay on top of everything. But they should try to know all of the competing plans, especially now when prices are rapidly changing. The public is learning the importance of cost comparison, especially when the figures show that there is a vast difference in price among insurance companies.

This type of competition doesn't extend to all situations. There are a lot of agents working with essentially smaller policies who don't run into great competition. However, their lack of knowledge does leave something to be desired for the client. Obviously, the bigger the policy, the more aware the agent must be of the competition, especially when attorneys and accountants sometimes advise their clients to seek competitive bids.

In the past, agents rarely competed with each other. But through the years, more agents began fighting for bigger business. Now, because of multi-media advertising and promotional campaigns, the public is more aware of the changing prices: they recognize the need to shop around. As a result, more and more agents find themselves in competition.

Certain companies will not allow their agents to sell competitive products. If they find out that this is going on, it's often grounds for immediate dismissal, or contract cancellation. But there are also more sophisticated companies that will say, "You must show us all of your business, and if we can't underwrite it, then you can go elsewhere." In fact, experience shows that the most successful agents are doing so much business for their company that just by virtue of who they are and the leverage they have, the company isn't going to stop them if they go outside.

Agent versus Agent

Once several agents are in the picture, the situation can be complicated for the consumer, particularly when agents are invited to sit down and discuss the relative merits of their respective plans. The confusion that follows can be destructive to the client.

It is important to know what to do if you find yourself in such a situation. You *should* have the facts presented to you, because every agent will be saying the same thing to you: "I'm the best!" "I'm with the best company!" "We're the top agency!" "We have the best product!"

Tell your agent that the most effective means of communicating with you is by being clear and straightforward. You want only the facts. The agent who makes the case understandable is one who clarifies every aspect of what he or she is trying to accomplish, with point-by-point analysis of every detail of the other submitted plans.

The most common error made by the nonprofessional consumer is to analyze the three programs and come up with an incorrect conclusion based upon an inability to truly understand what is being analyzed. This is why it is so important to have one agent that you can completely trust, who knows what he is doing and who can assist you in making the most important decision.

Another problem comes up when a client shops around and doesn't get the same *type* of quote from another company. For example, an agent might submit a proposal with dividends that will reduce the premium. This might seem very clear. You have the basic numbers. But the next agent might look at those figures and put those dividends to work doing something else like building up additions and buying increased coverage. Someone else might show you a minimum deposit plan. You are stuck with attempting to compare one agent's apples to another agent's oranges.

The most effective approach is for you to demand to see one basic policy compared to another company's basic policy. Then you can truly see the difference between the two products. The product is the product, and utilizing different options for merchandising cannot change the character or quality of that basic product.

Agent Competition and You

What really happens when one agent discovers that another agent has just sold, or is in the process, of selling his client a new plan?

Usually, the old agent will call the client—you—and ask what the story is. Why haven't you paid the premium, or why have you allowed another agent to service your old policy? When the client explains that he purchased a new policy from this new agent because the premiums seemed considerably lower and he wishes to effect those savings on a new plan, the old agent will suddenly appear on the scene and explain that he has been your agent for years and that he can really now find a product that is comparable to what you are buying.

How does a client react to this? For one thing, he's upset. He wonders, why didn't this man think of him *before?* Why did it take another agent to spark him?

Secondly, a consumer is wary of sales people who shift arguments, starting in one area and shifting to another when the first one doesn't work. A client should ideally buy from an agent who is direct and honest, not from someone who is telling him too late something he should have known in the first place.

Sometimes, it's a question of education. Some agents simply don't realize that there are companies selling lower-priced product. We found that the pricing revolution actually started five years ago, but very few knew about it. The companies that had the new product were simply not announcing it to any great extent.

We contacted these companies and agents and asked why they weren't selling their Extralife-Economatic policies. In some cases the agents didn't even realize they had the new type policies. Even if they did know, many told us they believed in high cash value, high premium insurance, and didn't feel that the new product was important for them or their clients.

What to Do

It's hard to avert a panic on the part of an agent when he finds a policy's being replaced, even though it is to the benefit of his client. Obviously, monetary compensation is his first thought. He is also concerned with the loss of a client and the possible contacts this client has brought him over the years. Since the average man buys life insurance about six times in his life, if the agent loses him, he's going to lose more than just one future policy.

To prevent this from happening, and yet avoid the panic reaction, an agent who finds his prices are being beat should not confuse the client, but rather admit, immediately, that the prices are lower, but, because, he's done a job over the years, he would like to continue doing the business. The agent who has been honest and forthright can then ask the client whether he wants him involved in the new transaction.

It's up to you, then, to determine whether you want to do business with this man. The agent can possibly continue to maintain the relationship, and still bring the best pricing and savings available. After all, the client isn't demanding anything unreasonable—only honesty.

12

—— Agent versus Investment Broker: ——
Client Loses Again!

AMERICAN CONSUMERS invest an incredible amount of money in life insurance each year. According to the 1980 *Insurance Fact Book* published by the American Council of Life Insurance, the total income of United States life insurance companies in 1979 was $119 billion. That figure, they point out, is approximately the same as that spent by the federal government for national defense in that year, and more than twice as much as the total income of the entire farm population of the United States.

Further, the *Fact Book* informs us that over 72% of the adult population of this country—and over 90% of all husband-and-wife families—own some form of life insurance. In 1979, Americans purchased $527 billion of *additional* life insurance coverage from U.S. companies, bringing the total life insurance coverage in force to almost $3.2 trillion.

Insured families paid an average of over $300 a year in premiums and had approximately $44,800 of insurance coverage in force. In the same year, Americans paid $28 billion in premiums for 146 million ind vidual life insurance policies.

Insurance or Investment

Not surprisingly, investment brokers are finding it to be good economic sense to try to lure some of that money their way.

Investment seminars on many subjects often devote some time to how to save thousands of dollars on life insurance. More often than not, term insurance is strongly suggested as the best buy. New books or brochures prepared by investment brokers always refer to the advantages of term insurance, while frequently playing down permanent insurance.

Many consumers are understandably displeased with paying insurance premiums and lend a willing ear. It is much more interesting to hear of the fortunes one will make with a particular investment, rather than the benefits from the guarantees of permanent life insurance policies.

There also may be a family member, friend, attorney, or simply someone who has made good investments who will laud those investment experiences and point out that there are far better things to do with money than to put it into life insurance. It is rare that anyone will hear of that person's investment losses.

Intelligent insurance agents tell their clients that permanent insurance is for protection and that the cash values in the policy are just a way of keeping the premiums level, but certainly not the purpose for which the insurance was bought.

When you compare life insurance with any investment, you're back to comparing apples with oranges, because you're dealing with two absolutely different financial tools.

However, investment brokers are often hard pressed when asked how to protect consumers' money from tax encroachment or a turn for the worse in the investment marketplace, during the client's twilight years.

As inflation has grown, investment brokers have been discouraging fixed assets like savings accounts and cash value insurance. They have suggested that with inflation hovering at around 10 and 12%, keeping money in these mediums, earning 6 and 7% interest, could be self-defeating.

Nonetheless, it is *guaranteed* money. A savings account or permanent insurance policy earning interest, even below the inflation rate, will end up buying more bread at any price in an emergency than a mutual fund that went totally sour.

The minute you introduce risk in an investment, you eliminate the guarantees. And since life insurance has a guarantee written right into the policy, it should never be compared with nonguaranteed investments. Such differences are crucial.

Preparing colorful charts that show how life insurance compares negatively with the gains of "buy term and invest the difference" ignores a number of key factors that could affect the consumer's entire investment program.

Theoretically, if you make the large sum of money predicted in the "buy term and invest the difference" program, you have to sustain that investment program over the years by continuing to make the right financial moves—something that cannot be taken for granted. When things begin to go wrong with your investment program, panic can set in. Anything can go wrong in a risk situation, and a huge sum of money can disappear overnight.

And what happens when personal emergencies come up that affect your monthly investment plan? Will you ever catch up?

Remember, also, that these investments must be cultivated over a period of years, years when the market may be down and you might find your investments are not panning out the way you had hoped. You might even find yourself after ten years back at square one, as most people have and as Dow Jones averages have indicated.

When risk is introduced, all of this is possible.

Diversify!

It is indeed important to diversify your holdings. You should have fixed assets as well as equity assets. Guaranteed assets can be supplemented by nonguaranteed assets. The object is to protect your financial situation against all possibilities.

As one grows older and perhaps wealthier, it becomes more evident that investments can go wrong. When they do, it's best not to have all the investment eggs in one vulnerable basket. Investments should include some savings, some bonds, some real estate, and some stocks when affordable. Some assets should guarantee you cash when it is needed; these can include a savings account or permanent cash value insurance, which can be borrowed against in times of emergency or great need. Diversification provides the flexibility to deal with an emergency without destroying your financial position.

Permanent insurance also allows you to protect the value of any great gains you have achieved with your investments at a critical time when estate taxes may be eating away at the money you have striven for years to build.

Some investment counselors have a tendency to overlook that possibility, thinking that large cash buildups and well-developed investment portfolios will carry the consumer's family through the loss of a breadwinner. It is the responsibility of those involved in the life insurance revolution to counter such misconceptions and instead prepare the consumer for a more practical approach toward the future.

The preceding pages are not intended as a defense of permanent insurance as an investment, for it is *not* an investment per se. It is my intent to put into proper perspective what purpose investments serve in comparison with the purposes of life insurance, without comparing the investment qualities of the two totally different products.

In the final analysis, investment brokers must fully understand the need for a diversification that includes permanent insurance. They should work cooperatively as part of a team in your behalf. This way, you will never find yourself in the middle of the agent-versus-investment-broker controversy—a conflict in which you, the client, can only lose.

13

———— The Real Story Behind ————
Agent Commissions

THE TRUE STORY of agent commissions has often been shrouded in mystery. Ordinarily, the subject of agent commissions is not treated in insurance articles or books. If it is mentioned, it is only in the most general and uncomplicated terms: a premium is paid and the agent makes a commission on the sale.

But today, consumers are seeking more direct information on insurance policies. Often they want to know in detail what is motivating the agent to make the sale. "Is the agent selling this policy to me from a desire to help me or is it only for his personal profit?"

Most people do not disclose the amount of money they make on selling their products. However, there are formulas that can determine the return produced by any product's sale, and the normal commission result to the salesperson.

While insurance agents should not be forced to disclose how much money is made on any sale, they may have backed themselves into that corner. Because of misinformation and the multitude of production figures that have been advertised and promoted, the consumer is under the impression that agents are making much more money than they actually do receive.

What Commission Does an Agent Get?

Many agents speak in terms of the amount of insurance they've sold, rather than the premiums that will be paid or the commissions they will receive. So much emphasis is put on volume sold that consumers often mistakenly associate those numbers with the agents' income. It should also not be overlooked that many agents are running a business with personnel and other expenses, and their income must pay those expenses.

There is so much ego rejection involved in the sale of life insurance that the agent falls back on production figures for a sense of security and often blows them out of proportion, not realizing that they do not reflect a true income.

For many years, agents simply did not disclose their commissions. There was no pressure on them to do so.

It is surprising that the commission system of the life insurance industry should raise so many eyebrows, but it continues to do so. There is often a general resentment towards successful agents and the amount of commission they earn.

As life insurance agents are treated more professionally, like attorneys, doctors, or accountants, they are becoming more public with their commission structures. Today, honest and straightforward communication precludes agents from being less than open with their clients.

It is easier for an agent to secure facts from a prospect who knows all about the agent. As the agent reveals information about himself, he finds clients responding with comparable facts and much more willing to reveal their true position. It is, therefore, wise for an agent to reveal amounts of commission earned as a way of being open and honest with a client. Quoting success is a form of marketing as apparent in the life insurance industry as it is anywhere else in the business world. If the agent sells a great deal of insurance and he makes a great deal of money, it's up to him to promote himself to his future clients, capitalizing on his success so that they will be more inclined to do business with him. Success does beget success, and people like to develop relationships with winners.

Agent publicity has always been common in the life insurance industry where the Million Dollar Round Table was created to honor those agents who sold the most insurance and performed a service. Most of the successful agents were not afraid to promote their success. They offered their commission structures freely.

There is much talk about the agent not being entitled to renewals or high commissions in the first year. If the commissions are averaged over ten years, it will reveal that the commission is very much in line with that received by salespersons of any product line who sell the same product repeatedly every year. If you buy paper or light bulbs every year, there is a commission to that salesperson every year. Why should the insurance agent be any different?

Although commissions on permanent insurance policies are high the first year (usually 50 to 55% of the premium in New York companies), after the first year, the agent only gets a 5% renewal commission. When averaged over a ten-year period, the commission amounts to only 10% a year.

The size of the first-year commission is used to keep the backbone of the industry alive. To stay in business the average insurance agent needs to make at least $15,000 a year, like any other salesperson. A higher commission is given in the first year as an incentive and to offset rejections and non-sales.

When you realize how many prospects the agent must contact before being granted an interview, and how many times a return is necessary, as well as the many rejections received before a sale is consummated, you can see that an agent is not receiving an inordinately high commission. This is the cost of the distribution system.

Do Agents Make More If They Sell Permanent Insurance?

One of the major misconceptions concerning commissions is that agents make more money from permanent insurance than from term. However, you should know that agents who sell term insurance make a new commission on every new sale of term. Over the period of a lifetime, when you compare the commissions between a term and permanent insurance policy, in most cases the term insurance would offer a very small commission in the beginning, compared to the permanent insurance commission. But the commission would rise for every year the term insurance is renewed, until, finally, the commission is more substantial than that of the permanent insurance.

As in most misconceptions, no one took the time to figure this out. Since consumers have been incorrectly directed to be concerned with price in the early years, they forget how the passage of time affects the cost of term and that the relationship between the term and permanent insurance commission changes considerably over the course of a lifetime.

If the consumer needs $100,000 worth of insurance, the agent is going to find it easier to sell him or her term. Even though only a third of the initial potential permanent insurance commission for an equal sale will be earned, there is a good chance the agent will sell more term policies than permanent policies.

Furthermore, as term prices have continued to be reduced, there has been a tendency for the agent to keep changing the policy every few years. While the client is, of course, benefiting, the agent is also making a new first-year commission on each and every change. This is in contrast to the regular stability of a commission earned from a permanent insurance policy that is purchased and retained. Permanent insurance actually does *not* make more money for the agent in the long run. But, because a few people saw the larger figures in the beginning, they erroneously assumed that profits were higher for the agent.

High Commissions

Insurance companies that are licensed in New York State cannot grant a commission higher than 55% of the first-year premium. However, many other companies have commission structures approaching 90% of the first-year premium, and some even in excess of 100%. In competing for the agent's business, these companies have had to carve out their commission figures from somewhere. In most cases it comes out of the policy's values, so higher commissions produce lesser policies.

Many agents flock to those high-commission banners, but if the products are no longer competitive and the consumer is made aware of that fact, there will have to be changes. Quality agents are looking beyond the commission dollars, demanding quality in their company's product. They realize that the quality product may produce a lower commission, but this will be made up for by the competitiveness of a product that will be of tremendous benefit to clients.

It is vitally important for an agent to be with a company that provides a good product. If agents are going to be successful, they have to build a business based on satisfied clients. If they satisfy their needs, they will receive the referrals which are the lifeblood of the insurance industry and will continue to sell more insurance. If they have not performed in the best interests of their clients, their whole "client house" will come down like the proverbial house of cards.

Agents who fail to understand this long-range view may gravitate to the company that provides the highest commission. Unfortunately, these salespersons hurt the image of the life insurance industry for the rest of the professional and knowledgeable agents, for they seldom service the client's needs before their own pocketbooks.

How the Life Insurance Revolution Affects Commissions

The life insurance revolution has made a dramatic effect on reducing the cost of premiums. It has also dropped agent commissions, causing a panic among those agents who do not understand the benefits to the consumer and ultimately to themselves. All agents see is that they now have to sell twice as much product just to stay even. They don't recognize that the lower price will produce much larger sales based on the greater needs for insurance resulting from inflation.

As a consumer, do not be afraid to ask agents about their commissions. There shouldn't be anything mysterious about them. Commissions are statutory; they're built right into the policy like the premiums and cash value tables. It is a good idea to compare the commission rates of different companies. If you discover that the commission rate is high, you may also discover that the premiums are high.

In the search for honesty in the life insurance industry, I feel that consumers should be granted any information they desire in order to determine which agent and which company can best service their needs.

14

— Saying It Straight Through Advertising — and Public Relations

CAN YOU REMEMBER the last time you saw a life insurance commercial on television? Whichever commercial you saw, it most likely did everything but explain what life insurance really is: protection for your family when you die.

Now imagine a different type of commercial, one that reflects the life insurance revolution of the 1980s. We are near the Pearly Gates of Heaven. A group of the recently departed are waiting in line for their angels' wings, which are being distributed by the Keeper of the Gates—in this case, a beautiful young angel.

When one of the angels-to-be expresses worry, the Keeper reassures him, pointing out the fact that since he bought his life insurance plan from the right company, which guaranteed maximum value at some of the lowest prices, there was no reason to worry.

The new angel, however, continues to mop his brow, producing the policy out of his pocket, "But I brought the policy with me," he whispers.

"You can't bring it with you," exclaims the Keeper of the Gates.

"I know," moans the angel-to-be, "my wife is going to kill me!"

Insurance Advertising

Nowhere is the life insurance revolution more apparent than in the preparation of new advertising and promotional campaigns. Life insurance, that perennial "sleeping giant" when it comes to competitive advertising, is undergoing a profound transformation.

More than at any time in its history, the life insurance industry is talking about cost and how the consumer can save money. Even the subject of "replacement" is appearing in advertisements. We're entering a new era, a time when life insurance agents will not have to whisper about the benefits they offer.

Such creativity and openness have been a long time in coming. Like many professions that offer a product and a service to prospective clients, life insurance has gone through several phases in terms of advertising and promotion. Some of them are still viable, but many have been replaced with the "up-front" approach that consumers are now demanding.

In the past, advertising in the life insurance industry emphasized the strength of the individual companies, their assets, their stability, and the history of their service. For example, "so and so has four billion dollars' worth of insurance in force." Or, another company "represents two hundred fifty thousand happy policyholders," or this company "owns all of these buildings on Park Avenue."

What the companies failed to emphasize was the fact that, for the most part, those assets belonged to the policyholders. Whether intentional or not, such a campaign gave the consumer the impression that insurance companies were huge corporate giants who own whole city blocks and control the destinies of thousands of people while growing in an unchecked and unstoppable manner. Such an approach can foster the idea of the insurance company as "adversary," unfeeling, unknowing, and uncaring.

Another prevalent form of advertising and promotion concentrated on citing the achievements of the individual agent, his agency, or the carrier, such as "State Mutual is proud to announce that Joe Smith will receive the President's Cup for selling the most insurance this year," or a company saying it is "proud to announce that its Seattle office once more took top prize in its annual sales competition, selling $45 million last year." Companies utilize such an approach to build credibility. Advertisements that reveal the success of an agent will indicate that this may be the agent that can be trusted.

Another form of advertising that has been very popular over the years is the folksy approach, where the life insurance company is described as one big happy family that wants to adopt you into the clan. Such an advertising campaign emphasizes tradition and the old-fashioned order, describing the agent as a father figure who wants to "help you get Howard through college," etc. These attempt to show that the insurance company does "care" and that when you're gone, someone will always be around to provide for your loved ones.

Although it is doubtful that insurance companies will ever engage in a full-blown "price war," price is now creeping into advertising copy. It is also apparent that more and more emphasis is being placed on the education of the public. More candor and directness is being shown in the advertising and promotional concepts of today.

Advertising is important not only to promote a product, but also to create a basis for understanding the application of that product. For example, an ad features twin pictures of antiques, describing identical items of value (e.g., two ceremonial Ming vases). The ad states that when you die, because of the possibility of major estate taxes, one of those vases stays in your home, and the other goes to Uncle Sam. Such an analogy helps immensely in explaining the ramifications of estate tax. When this is used, the public identifies with the symbolism, and the ad becomes an effective educational selling approach.

Informing the Public

Insurance companies have a certain responsibility to inform the public when new developments occur in their business. This is very important. The rise of inflation and the fluctuation of the economy is forcing government and business to reexamine priorities, and new tax rulings and laws are written continuously. The average businessperson often lacks the time to comprehend the ramifications of these new laws, but he or she needs to understand these developments.

For instance, in the fall of 1974, President Ford signed into law the complex ERISA Pension Reform Act, which substantially changed all tax-sheltered retirement plans. This law would have a major impact on the life insurance industry. I realized the importance of this event, and only one day after the President signed the bill into law, our advertisements appeared, stating, "New Pension Reform Act of 1974 Is One Day Old. We can help you save taxes this year for your later retirement! President Ford signed into law yesterday . . ."

It was apparent from the beginning that we had scooped our competition by alerting the public to this new law. I vowed that we would always provide the latest information for our clients through the mode of advertising.

Now that prices and practices are changing radically, we again are informing our clients and the public about these revolutionary developments. This type of advertising is the only type that will serve any purpose in the 1980s. The consumer wants to know how our product will benefit *him*, and nothing more.

PART TWO

THE BASICS

Part Two of this book is for those who feel they need more knowledge of insurance and yet do not want to get bogged down in technical explanations.

This part is more than the ABCs of Life Insurance. It is specific in its approach, addressing the problems of family men and women, businesses, young people, wealthy estate owners, children, and even grandchildren. It also includes discussions of the key life insurance controversies of today, such as "Term versus Permanent," "Non-Par versus Par," and "Interest-Adjusted Cost Index."

I hope it treats the basics of life insurance in a way that you will find interesting and provocative, as well as easy to understand. This is not a textbook for students of insurance; it is a comprehensive guide for consumers who want to save money.

15

Non-Par versus Par: A Question of Dividends

IN ADDITION to the other mysteries of life insurance you are now learning to unravel, there are different types of policies available, and different types of companies as well. While plans may be administered by fraternal organizations, religious groups, and savings banks, we are concerned here with the two principal types of insurance companies common in America: mutual and stock.

The two key words to look for are *par* (for "participating") and *non-par* (for "non-participating"). The mutual company offers a "participating plan," which pays dividends to its policyholders. The stock company offers a "non-participating plan," which provides no dividends but guarantees that its premium on permanent insurance policies will stay the same for a lifetime.

The traditional difference between mutual and stock companies is now itself going through a major transformation. Many of the non-par companies include participating, dividend-paying policies in their portfolio. Some of them are offering new products with premiums that can be raised or lowered, based on their investment results. Some of these policies state that the ultimate death benefit is tied to their realizing the improved interest levels they are predicting.

This proliferation of new products completely changes the traditional par and non-par structure that has previously existed in the industry. However, it is important to understand the historical differences between par and non-par, and their particular advantages, before any further basic information is discussed.

Mutual Life Insurance ("Participating") Companies

The theory of the mutual life insurance company is that the consumer participates in all the profits of the company. The nature of the product and government legislation required that a portion of the profits be used to create reserves and surpluses to keep the company stable. Therefore, any "dividend" the consumer receives is merely an overpayment of premium, and as such is not taxable. This has been a point of criticism from insurance antagonists; in fact, they have been stating a truth. Many insurance agents and companies attempt to defend what doesn't have to be defended, instead of agreeing with these antagonists and saying "So what? The end result is a lower net premium each year!" It doesn't matter what you call it, it still reduces the premium.

Even though these "dividends" are not guaranteed, they have been paid regularly since the 1840s by some companies. Over the last thirty years a great many dividends have been increasing, reflecting the lower mortality factors and the increased profitability of insurance company investments in a period of high interest rates.

The stock companies that have participating policies have also been declaring "dividends," but consumers must understand that the first loyalty in a stock company is to the stockholders, and if there is a profitability in that company, it is possible that most of the profits will go to the stockholders. So, in comparison, participating companies usually offer a better dividend and a resulting lower net cost.

The fact that non-participating companies had lower going-in premiums, even though they experienced higher net costs, has now been affected by the ongoing revolutionary changes in the participating companies. Certain mutual companies, utilizing the Extralife-Economatic approach, have brought the premium down to dramatic levels—actually lower in both the going-in premium and the net cost.

Stock ("Non-participating") Companies

If net costs are usually better in participating/mutual companies, then how did the non-participating/stock companies secure a foothold in the life insurance marketplace? For many years, the key advantage of a non-par policy was its lower beginning outlay, plus the fact that it guaranteed that the premiums would stay level for a lifetime. (Remember, participating policy "dividends" are never guaranteed; they simply reflect the profitability of the company.) Though companies have been paying larger dividends for years, there is always the possibility that par company profits could be affected.

Over the past thirty years, as government reports have indicated, the participating policies have been the better buy. In many cases, however, non-par rates over a lifetime were far more expensive than par, which used the "dividend" to reduce premiums. Today, with the many available cost-comparison charts, consumers are realizing that even though non-par policies may in some cases look less costly going-in, it is much wiser to purchase a par policy that can utilize "dividends" to eventually reduce the premium below non-par levels.

"Dividends"

Since "dividends" are the basic difference between par and non-par policies, let's discuss how they actually work in a policy. The various uses of "dividends" indicate why they are so valuable.

The first option is to take the dividend in cash, and utilize it outside the insurance environment.

The second option is to utilize the dividend to reduce the premium, so that eventually your dividends will be paying the premium and you won't have to utilize as much cash flow for your insurance.

Third, many people have chosen to let their dividends accumulate at interest in the policy, building up a sizable amount of cash. However, as interest rates in banks have soared, more and more policyholders are taking their dividends in cash and investing them elsewhere. Also, in the 1960s, when investment counselors began attacking permanent insurance, those who kept their dividends in accumulation were told that they were losing money and that those dividends had better be used in some other way.

The fourth option was to buy additional insurance; the paid-up adds approach. The "dividend" itself purchased each year—at net cost, with no commission to the agent, and no examination for the client—a paid-up policy. The paid-up add had a paid-up death benefit, its own cash value and dividend. This option guarantees additional insurance through the years and is particularly beneficial to the client who has a health problem, since he can buy this insurance at standard rates in spite of any future health deterioration.

The fifth dividend option allowed the consumer to purchase one-year term insurance each year from the dividend, once again with no agent commission or health examination. This term insurance is used to cover the amount of the cash value in the policy. In this way, when the insured dies, his beneficiaries not only collect the face amount of the policy, but the cash value as well. Such an option is extremely popular in "minimum deposit" plans in which the insured is borrowing from the cash value to pay the premium.

While the fifth dividend option is effective in minimum deposit plans, the cost of term insurance increases to the point where the dividend is no longer large enough to purchase term insurance to equal the cash value in the policy. After a certain number of years, the death benefit is going to deteriorate.

Dividends Today

Today, dividends are best utilized to reduce premiums.

The value of this is evident in the following example. Let's say the par premium is $3,100 a year, compared to $2,600 for the non-par. By using the dividends to reduce the premium, by the sixth year the par company premium is usually down to the level of the non-par. Shortly thereafter, the par policy would actually go *below* the non-par policy premium.

But you did not buy this policy for only six years. We assume that you bought this permanent insurance for your lifetime. Twenty or thirty years from now that dividend is going to offer you even more savings over the non-par policy, which is still continuing at $2,600 a year.

Again, it is a question of sophistication. As more and more agents realized the value of dividends, non-par companies began to suffer. The non-pars looked cheaper in the beginning, just as term insurance looks cheaper, but within six years, it wasn't cheaper. Also, the cash values on the quality par policies (since they were derived from a larger premium) are higher, so that by the sixth year not only is the premium lower, but the cash values are considerably higher, thus resulting in a lower net cost for the par policy.

In response to these facts, non-par company agents have historically questioned the par dividends, pointing to the fact that they aren't guaranteed. There was a time, particularly in the 1930s and 1940s, when the guarantee of non-par premiums was an important factor. This was an era in which people didn't foresee the coming growth of the country, with its resulting increase in values of equity investments and real estate from which the insurance companies would derive considerable profit.

Recent findings of the Federal Trade Commission indicate that non-par policies, particularly those written in the '50s and '60s—before the stock companies began creating more competitive products—were in most cases in need of serious review and possible replacement.

Nevertheless, there are still many consumers who appreciate the lower going-in outlay, and non-par policies are still being sold. Non-par salesmen point out that their premiums are never going to be more than the $2,600 (in our example) and that if anything went wrong with the par company, you, the consumer, would still be stuck paying the $3,100.

Of course, these salesmen fail to mention the fact that by utilizing the dividend to reduce the premium or to buy additional paid-up insurance, you would have a paid-up policy in a shorter time span, and once that occurred, those dividends could be working in other useful ways. Thus, you have a great deal of flexibility with that dividend. And despite what the non-par agents say about the non-guarantee of par dividends, those dividends continue to be paid by the par companies, allowing consumers to bring their premiums down to very manageable levels.

The Difference Counts

While non-par agents continue to promote the value of non-par policies, their own companies are creating new products to better answer the par company competition.

In the past, very few consumers understood the difference between par and non-par companies. They usually bought their insurance from the agent who got to them first, and the fact that he was with a stock or mutual company usually didn't matter. He was there and he was selling insurance. If the consumer was in the mood to buy insurance that day, this was the agent he was going to buy it from.

However, today, with cost comparisons more necessary than ever, consumers are beginning to understand how important the difference is between par and non-par. Much of the change brought about during the life insurance revolution is bringing these differences into sharper focus.

One final point summarizes the past difference between the two types of companies and the motivating force behind many of the new product developments. Quoting Page 43 of the recent FTC report, "The challenge facing the industry was succinctly stated by (actuary) Mr. E. J. Moorhead:

"If interest rates stay up, companies with non-par policies on the books will be in the same untenable position that many of them are in today: their informed policy holders still in good health will drop their policies or buy term policies. Only their ignorant or impaired-in-health (or lazy) policy holders will keep their policies..."

16

What's Your Type?
Insurance Policies Available Today

ONCE YOU UNDERSTAND the basic types of policies available—term and permanent—all the variations on them suddenly become easy to understand. We shall discuss their particular advantages in the next chapter; for now, we shall simply outline how each plan works and give some idea of its possible variations.

Term Insurance

Term insurance is simply life insurance for a specific period. This may be one year, five years, ten years, term to (age) 65, etc. If you die within that period of time, the insurance company will pay your beneficiaries the face amount of the policy (this is the amount the insurance company guarantees to pay upon your death). Once the term is up, you can buy new insurance, usually at a more expensive rate. Annual renewable term insurance rates increase each year as you age, because the chance that you will die (the "mortality rate") increases.

If the term insurance is renewable, you can purchase a new term plan without going through a medical examination to determine your insurability. Such a system may carry you with term insurance until you are 65 or 70; recently, companies have introduced term insurance policies that go beyond that age, even to age 100. However, term insurance becomes prohibitively expensive in one's later years, so that few people can afford to carry their term insurance that far. Some choose to buy convertible term that allows them to convert to permanent insurance later on.

Non-renewable term insurance means that once the term policy ends, the insured must undergo a new medical examination in order to purchase a new term policy. *Non-convertible term insurance* means that you can never convert to a permanent policy without another health examination. The rates for term insurance are higher when you build in the option to renew a policy and/or convert a policy.

The form of life insurance that is initially cheapest is a one-year *renewable term* policy, which covers the insured for the period of one year. At the end of the year the insured has the option of renewing that policy for a larger premium. One-year renewable term insurance provides the most protection for the smallest initial cash outlay, and is especially designed for families with small children, a number of liabilities, and only a small amount of cash available for life insurance. It is also suitable for new businesses that have yet to make a profit and therefore need a type of insurance that does not reduce their cash flow too much.

Gradually, however, most families and businesses get to the point where they have more cash available, and they may decide to convert their term insurance into a permanent insurance policy. The type of insurance that permits this is *convertible term insurance*. Most term policies are convertible. In most cases, the longer you wait to convert, the higher will be the premium you pay at the time of conversion to the permanent policy.

Often people who have the cash available purchase term insurance anyway, not realizing that when they convert they will have thrown away all the previous term premiums, built no equity, and caused themselves to pay a higher premium for permanent insurance, since they will be older by the time they convert their policies.

Another variation of term insurance is *five-year renewable term*, which insures the policyholder for a longer period of time at a level premium. Obviously, five-year renewable term is more expensive than one-year renewable term because the insurance company averages the cost of term insurance over five years and it rises each year in accordance with mortality tables.

The most expensive type of term insurance is *term to 65*, which averages a term premium over a very long period of time, including the years when term insurance becomes prohibitively expensive.

Decreasing term insurance and mortgage insurance is bought with a level premium for a steadily decreasing amount of protection that can coincide with the decreasing amount of your mortgage. At first, decreasing term might look cheap. But you must remember that it gives a decreasing amount of coverage each year, so that the rate per thousand really goes up each year. While this type of coverage may be appropriate for a mortgage or other type of loan, it is not suitable for other needs. Most people eventually achieve a better standard of living and therefore have more income to protect for their families. That and the increasing need for money to offset inflation, makes it clear that there will be a need for more insurance over the years, not less. Therefore, decreasing term insurance is diametrically opposed to most people's requirements and objectives.

Investment counselors often comment that investments will offset the need for insurance. However, successful investments (assuming that they are indeed successful) will themselves bring about an additional need for insurance, in order to meet the estate tax liability they create.

Permanent Insurance

For those who want to have insurance for the course of their entire lifetime, there is *permanent insurance*, which is essentially level-premium insurance to age 100. Permanent insurance is also known as *whole life, ordinary life, straight life, level premium life*, or *cash value insurance*. It has been the predominant form of life insurance in America.

Permanent insurance is designed to help consumers handle the high cost of insurance in later years, when premiums are prohibitively expensive. This is done by averaging out premium costs, so that the high cost of premiums for later years is transferred to earlier premiums.

There are permanent insurance plans that can be paid off faster than by age 100. These are called *limited pay whole life* plans and are usually available in 10-Pay, 20-Pay, 30-Pay, or Paid-up at Age 65 forms. Each plan features a higher premium that creates a higher cash value and allows the consumer to pay off his insurance policy in a shorter period of time. These plans are designed for those who want to be free of premium payments at a specific period of time. However, you have to pay dearly for the privilege.

Another form of permanent life insurance is *modified whole life*, which brings the insured into the policy at a lower premium rate the first few years, and then raises the premiums up to normal levels when the consumer can afford them. Unfortunately, the modified plan creates very small cash values in the early years, so that most consumers would be far better off if they bought term insurance and then converted when they could afford the permanent premiums.

Extralife-Economatic

A popular type of permanent insurance is *Extralife-Economatic*, which we discussed in an earlier chapter. Extralife-Economatic lowers the price of permanent insurance while paying far less than the whole amount of the policy, the balance being made up by a combination of additional paid-up insurance and one-year term insurance purchased from the dividends, which provides the total face value purchased. As the paid-up additions grow, less term insurance is purchased until finally there is no term insurance at all (usually within twelve to twenty years). Eventually, when the policy reaches its crossover point, the dividends can either be taken in cash or used to purchase more insurance.

The Extralife-Economatic plan is particularly effective in minimum-deposit plans. It allows the insured to pay the absolute minimum by borrowing, if necessary, from the policy's cash value each year to pay the premium. Since the premiums on Extralife-Economatic policies are so much cheaper, the insured has to borrow less than in similar programs on older policies. Eventually, all he or she is paying is tax-deductible interest.

According to Eliot Janeway, a permanent policy on the minimum-deposit plan "allows you the right to borrow back your premiums from the insurance company at tax deductible below-market rates."

Minimum deposit is a good way to purchase large amounts of permanent insurance without paying out large amounts of cash. However, in later years, the face amount of the policy will eventually deteriorate, particularly with the old type of policies.

Endowment Policies

A third form of life insurance, which was at one time quite popular, but has lost its popularity over the years, is the *endowment policy*. Endowment policies are really a variation of the limited pay permanent insurance plan.

There are 20-year endowments, endowments at age 65, and other variations. Each guarantees a certain sum of money at a specific time, but, if the insured should die prematurely, the face amount would be available immediately.

Endowments were usually bought by parents who wanted to give their children a certain amount of cash for college tuition, and so forth. An endowment could also be utilized as retirement money.

The problem with endowments, and the reason that fewer are being sold these days, is their exorbitant cost. It takes a very large cash value to get to $20,000 in twenty years, and a larger premium must be paid to create that high cash value.

Because of this larger-than-necessary premium, endowments are not held in high regard, and are of value only to those who need a form of forced savings, since the premiums are disproportionate to the death element of the policy.

You are now armed with information about the basics of life insurance, and ready to come face to face with the greatest myth ever perpetrated on the American public.

17

The Myth of Term Insurance: The Level Premium versus Increasing Premium Dilemma

IMAGINE CARPENTERS at work in their wood shops, surrounded by many tools: machine saws, planes, sanders, files, screwdrivers, vises, and levels. However, because of a myth that has been circulating, they have been told not to use anything except for one file. And there they sit, perplexed, with one file in hand, contemplating the work around them that must be finished.

And then imagine bartenders, surrounded by every possible type of liquor, from exotic Italian and French wines to tropical mixes and the more common scotches, bourbons and vodkas. Another myth is circulating, telling them that they must dispose of everything in their liquor cabinets except for Bombay rum. So there they stand, polishing their glasses, with a wall of rum bottles behind them. Rum becomes the sole survivor of a large portfolio that was originally designed to meet their clientele's every need—which rum cannot do. It serves the purpose of the rum drinker and certainly the rum distiller, but it cannot possibly satisfy everyone. Eventually, those bartenders are going to lose business, en masse.

Now let's take the insurance agents' situation. Sitting on their desks are many different insurance plans, designed to

121

cover every possible need. Permanent policies, level and decreasing term policies for special short-term needs, retirement policies, Split Dollar, Section 79, Retired Life Reserve, pension plans, and a myriad of others. Suddenly the agents are told that term insurance is the only product they need keep in their portfolio. All of the others can be put aside, for term insurance will accomplish every task in every situation.

The agents appear baffled, but because their clients also hear the same myth, they are forced to put their other policies aside and sell only term insurance. Things are a lot simpler now. For them, as for the carpenter and the bartender, there is no longer a choice. It is impossible for agents to discharge their responsibilities, for they have now been limited to one product in an increasingly complex world where there can never be one answer to everything.

The myth, which started with a half-truth, has been repeated and repeated until the half-truth has now become the whole truth. Overzealous reporters as well as consumer advocates, not realizing how or why the myth originated, repeat its message. At last the truth is buried, and the myth totally prevails—to the complete detriment of the consumer.

Fighting Off the Myth

Of course, the carpenters and the bartenders have not really been deprived of their tools. Neither have the insurance agents, really. However, the pressure to confine themselves to one kind of insurance policy—pressure originating with investment counselors who naturally have their own interests at heart and have successfully spread their point of view to accountants, lawyers, and financial advisers—is such that the essential functions of the insurance industry are threatened. Many people still buy permanent life insurance; many others are confident that term insurance can be the cheapest and most effective way to buy life insurance. That confidence has a very insecure foundation.

Insurance companies have been trying to counter with arguments for permanent insurance, such as: "But you may need this insurance when you're older"; "Term insurance becomes prohibitively expensive in later years"; "You might need an emergency fund of cash at an unforeseen time"; or "Your investments may not pan out the way you hope." However, these arguments for permanent insurance have been delivered too softly.

The insurance industry has no effective counterattack to offset the term insurance myth in one fell swoop. Word is generated too slowly in the ranks. It is time to take a much stronger tack. Making term insurance the sole product in the insurance portfolio is as silly as sticking only rum bottles on every shelf of a bar. Someone is going to have a strong need for something else. And then what are they to do?

Finally, the investment industry and its stockbrokers will no longer propose municipal bonds, convertible bonds, common stocks, new offerings, preferred stocks, commodities, money market funds, etc. Instead, they will offer only mutual funds, due to a myth—started outside of their own industry by unknowledgeable people with their own vested interests— which will be repeated over and over until finally the total answer for the entire investment industry and its clients will be mutual funds, and only mutual funds.

Term insurance must be returned to its proper place in the insurance portfolio. It can be of legitimate use in certain prescribed cases. But it cannot be the panacea that investment people would have us believe.

The myth of term insurance has also reached the insurance agent who generally has a difficult time selling insurance in the first place. But, because term allowed him to take the line of least resistance, he was suddenly able to sell his policies, even if they were to the disadvantage of his clients.

Not one to turn away business, he continued to sell term if the client wanted it, regardless of the client's true needs. In any case, the client's investment broker, his financial adviser, and his uninformed friends had already convinced him that permanent insurance was too expensive, so why shouldn't the agent accept the order and make the commission.

Defending permanent insurance in the face of tremendous odds becomes more and more difficult for agents and therefore they accept the easier way to sell term insurance and its resulting profits. For this type of agent, it doesn't matter how much his home office president talks about the values of permanent insurance, nor how many magazine articles written by fellow agents point out the deficiencies of term insurance, nor how many times he, himself, points out to the client that there may be a strong need for permanent insurance in the future: that agent is still succumbing to "term fever." Since the agent is trying to make a living, he feels he must catch that fever or perish.

This "giving-in" is going to stop and it's going to stop in a very dramatic way. Consumers are already beginning to understand the difference between term and permanent insurance, and as the prices of permanent insurance come down dramatically (as they have done in the new Extralife-Economatic series), more and more agents are going to be developing a counterattack capability to quash the term insurance myth, once and for all.

What Term Insurance Is Good For

Term insurance has its purposes. It was designed for young people who need a lot of insurance at a specific point in their lives in order to protect their family needs. By purchasing term insurance when they do not have too much cash available, for possible conversion later to permanent insurance, they protect their insurability.

Term insurance is also very important in a new business. If my partner and I, for example, are the vital links in a new business, it is logical to buy insurance to protect each other. We're not sure how the business, or our relationship, is going to work out, so we buy term insurance that is convertible. When our business gets well established, we can then purchase the permanent insurance we need.

Term insurance provides a valuable service when we use it to indemnify a loan or mortgage. A banker may give you a loan of $100,000 because he knows how creatively you can handle that money, but he also knows that money is good in your hands only as long as you're alive; if you die before that money begins to pay off and deliver a return, the banker is never going to get his money back. So to protect yourself and the banker against that situation, you take out a term insurance policy to cover the amount of the loan.

What Term Insurance Is Not Good For

Now that we have shown how term insurance can be a useful part of the insurance agent's portfolio, let us show why it cannot be anything else.

Because of its very nature, term insurance eventually expires, leaving the insured without any protection. If one is resolved to continue renewing a term policy, what would happen?

Take as an example one of the lowest-priced term products in America. At age 70, the renewal premium on that policy is $72 per thousand; if you purchased a million dollars' worth of insurance, you are going to spend $72,000 that year. If you should live to be 75, you're going to spend $100,000 that year for your term insurance; at age 80, you're paying $167,000 for the million.

Just think of the predicament you're in when you've been buying term insurance all these years and you had the good fortune of making it to 80, but the bad fortune of having just spent the $167,000 and not getting any money in return because you lived.

What do you do next year when you turn 81? Do you pay $180,000 for that million? And if you do, you've given the insurance company $347,000 in the last two years alone, not to mention the moneys you've spent in the last ten years for the same policy, with nothing to show for it—not to mention what you would spend if you lived another ten years.

Such a predicament is common for those who decide that term insurance is going to provide them with long-range coverage or estate-tax relief.

Yet if you had bought a permanent policy for $1 million at age 35, it would have cost only $11,000 a year and the policy would have long since been paid up (twenty-two years, age 57). It would have developed a substantial cash value asset that could have been used over your lifetime. And there are dividends, if it was a par policy, that you would be receiving every year with no premium payments to be made.

Term insurance proponents counter that argument by saying that the client could have bought term insurance at age 35 for only $2,000 a year. However, it should be remembered that the differential between $2,000 and $11,000 is going to close up yearly as the term premium increases, until finally at age 75, term costs $100,000, as we have described.

The result is that the client who was originally told to buy term and invest the difference in outside investments is going to have to start converting those investments into cash to pay the exorbitant term rates, until the available capital is exhausted and the client is left without protection of any kind.

The inflexibility of term insurance is also an important consideration. You buy insurance because you may die now. But the odds say that you're not going to die until your seventies, so it is prudent to consider an insurance policy that will last your entire lifetime. While you can understand your insurance needs now when you're physically and financially healthy, you have absolutely no knowledge of your future circumstances. At the age of 35 years, you can scarcely picture what it's going to be like to be 55, let alone 70. You have to plan for the future in a way that cannot be done with term insurance.

Term insurance has no cash value and allows you no emergency fund for later use. Without a cash value, you do not have the option to borrow at guaranteed low interest rates. With term insurance you cannot take a paid-up policy at retirement age, and you certainly can't use the nonexistent cash values to provide yourself with retirement income for life. With term insurance, because of the cost, you may not be able to continue your life insurance as long as you wish. You will also never have the piece of mind of knowing that the level of your premium is not going to increase. And should you lose your health and your job, you will never be able to keep your term policy from lapsing, whereas permanent policies allow you to borrow the cash value to pay the premiums.

It is easy to show the person with substantial income and property the advantages of permanent insurance as a tax shelter, since the cash values accrue on a tax-free basis. However, permanent insurance is no less important for those who have less income, as a useful means of supplementing social security retirement benefits.

Level Premium versus Increasing Premium

One of the major problems of the insurance industry over the years is that permanent insurance has been too often referred to as insurance protection plus a savings account, giving the investment industries a convenient opening to launch their attack on permanent insurance.

Cash value is not a savings account; it is an asset that you can borrow against. It is a reserve that can be used in later years to keep the premium level, and if you cancel your policy, you will be entitled to that reserve in cash.

By eliminating references to savings in life insurance, we can put everything into its proper perspective. You can buy insurance in two different ways—level premium or increasing premium. You can buy level premium insurance, which costs you more in the early years and less in the later years. Or you can buy increasing premium insurance, which is cheaper now but is going to be very expensive later.

Once consumers and their advisers realize this, the myth of term insurance will be set to rest.

Term Versus Permanent Comparison Tables

As you can see in the following tables, permanent insurance is more expensive than term only during the beginning years.

Based on a male age 45, the term premium will exceed the permanent premium from the seventeenth year on. If you compound the premium savings difference between term and permanent insurance at 8% interest, the total policy values of the permanent policy will exceed the 8% cumulative difference in premium from the seventeenth year on.

Furthermore, the 8% cumulative difference in premium that you saved with the excess premium of permanent over term, would be completely eliminated in the thirty-third year resulting in additional out of pocket outlay for the term from then on. If you live to normal life expectancy, the cost of term will be exorbitant and much more expensive than permanent insurance.

The above figures are based on a male age 45. We have also included tables for ages 25, 30, 35, 40, 50, 55, and 60 so that you can compare the cost difference at these ages as well.

TABLE 3.
CUMULATIVE COST COMPARISON
between
TERM INSURANCE AND PERMANENT INSURANCE

$1,000,000　　　　　　　　　　　　　　　　　　　　　　　　　AGE: 25M

AGE	YR	TERM ANNUAL PREMIUM	PERMANENT ANNUAL* PREMIUM	YEARLY PREMIUM DIFF.	CUMULATIVE DIFFERENCE IN PREMIUM (8%)	TOTAL POLICY VALUE	CUMULATIVE NET COST OF PERMANENT OVER TERM	YR	AGE
25	1	1,305	6,925	5,620	6,070	720	5,350	1	25
26	2	1,405	6,925	5,520	12,517	1,169	11,348	2	26
27	3	1,575	6,925	5,350	19,296	1,816	17,480	3	27
28	4	1,605	6,925	5,320	26,585	5,877	20,708	4	28
29	5	2,275	6,925	4,650	33,734	12,824	20,910	5	29
30	6	2,325	6,925	4,600	41,401	20,291	21,110	6	30
31	7	2,375	6,925	4,550	49,627	28,314	21,313	7	31
32	8	2,425	6,925	4,500	58,457	36,924	21,533	8	32
33	9	2,475	6,925	4,450	67,939	46,166	21,773	9	33
34	10	2,525	6,925	4,400	78,126	56,076	22,050	10	34
35	11	2,575	6,925	4,350	89,074	67,226	21,848	11	35
36	12	2,725	6,925	4,200	100,736	79,125	21,611	12	36
37	13	2,825	6,925	4,100	113,223	91,794	21,429	13	37
38	14	3,025	6,925	3,900	126,493	105,267	21,226	14	38
39	15	3,225	6,925	3,700	140,608	119,586	21,022	15	39
40	16	3,425	6,925	3,500	155,637	134,798	20,839	16	40
41	17	3,725	6,925	3,200	171,544	150,895	20,649	17	41
42	18	4,025	6,925	2,900	188,399	167,931	20,468	18	42
43	19	4,325	6,925	2,600	206,279	185,954	20,325	19	43
44	20	4,575	6,925	2,350	225,319	205,045	20,274	20	44
45	21	4,975	6,925	1,950	245,450	223,797	21,653	21	45
46	22	5,375	6,925	1,550	266,676	243,609	23,151	22	46
47	23	5,775	6,925	1,150	289,252	264,530	24,722	23	47
48	24	6,175	5,046	-1,129	311,173	284,629	26,544	24	48

Age	Age							Age	Age
52	28	8,375	-2,438	-10,813	380,065	344,446	35,619	28	52
53	29	9,075	-2,856	-11,931	397,585	360,041	37,544	29	53
54	30	10,025	-3,313	-13,338	414,987	375,857	39,130	30	54
55	31	11,025	-3,771	-14,796	432,206	319,883	40,323	31	55
56	32	12,025	-4,232	-16,257	449,225	408,124	41,101	32	56
57	33	13,025	-4,729	-17,754	465,989	424,518	41,471	33	57
58	34	14,125	-5,216	-19,341	482,380	441,073	41,307	34	58
59	35	15,525	-5,730	-21,255	498,015	457,744	40,271	35	59
60	36	17,025	-6,260	-23,285	512,708	474,494	38,214	36	60
61	37	18,525	-6,780	-25,305	526,395	491,321	35,074	37	61
62	38	20,525	-7,324	-27,849	538,430	508,189	30,241	38	62
63	39	22,825	-7,874	-30,699	548,349	525,057	23,292	39	63
64	40	25,325	-8,427	-33,752	555,765	541,901	13,864	40	64
65	41	28,025	-8,991	-37,016	560,249	558,678	1,571	41	65
66	42	31,025	-9,554	-40,579	561,244	575,319	-14,075	42	66
67	43	34,025	-10,114	-44,139	558,473	591,766	-33,293	43	67
68	44	37,025	-10,651	-47,676	551,661	607,991	-59,330	44	68
69	45	40,325	-11,217	-51,542	540,128	623,919	-83,791	45	69
70	46	44,025	-11,770	-55,795	523,080	639,533	-116,453	46	70
71	47	49,025	-12,294	-61,319	498,702	654,848	-156,146	47	71
72	48	53,025	-12,788	-65,813	467,520	669,896	-202,376	48	72
73	49	61,025	-13,218	-74,243	424,739	684,749	-206,010	49	73
74	50	67,025	-13,593	-80,618	371,651	699,468	-327,817	50	74
75	51	72,925	-13,944	-86,869	307,564	714,062	-406,498	51	75
76	52	78,925	-14,283	-93,208	231,504	728,483	-496,979	52	76
77	53	84,925	-14,607	-99,532	142,530	742,680	-600,150	53	77
78	54	91,925	-14,962	-106,887	38,494	756,521	-718,027	54	78
79	55	99,925	-15,313	-115,238	-82,883	769,934	-852,817	55	79
80	56	108,925	-15,685	-124,610	-224,092	782,845	-1,006,937	56	80
81	57	118,925	-16,046	-134,971	-387,788	795,222	-1,183,010	57	81
82	58	129,925	-16,361	-146,286	-576,800	807,082	-1,383,882	58	82
83	59	141,925	-16,616	-158,541	-794,168	818,503	-1,612,671	59	83
84	60	154,925	-16,845	-171,770	-1,043,213	829,509	-1,872,722	60	84

TABLE 4.
CUMULATIVE COST COMPARISON
between
TERM INSURANCE AND PERMANENT INSURANCE

$1,000,000   AGE: 30M

AGE	YR	TERM INS. TERM ANNUAL PREMIUM	PERMANENT ANNUAL* PREMIUM	PERMANENT INSURANCE YEARLY PREMIUM DIFF.	8% CUMULATIVE DIFFERENCE IN PREMIUM	TOTAL POLICY VALUE	CUMULATIVE NET COST OF PERMANENT OVER TERM	YR	AGE
30	1	1,325	8,725	7,400	7,992	910	7,082	1	30
31	2	1,465	8,725	7,260	16,472	1,598	14,874	2	31
32	3	1,635	8,725	7,090	25,447	3,267	22,180	3	32
33	4	1,725	8,725	7,000	35,042	11,608	23,434	4	33
34	5	2,525	8,725	6,200	44,542	20,580	23,962	5	34
35	6	2,575	8,725	6,150	54,747	30,188	24,559	6	35
36	7	2,725	8,725	6,000	65,607	40,458	25,149	7	36
37	8	2,825	8,725	5,900	77,228	51,426	25,802	8	37
38	9	3,025	8,725	5,700	89,562	63,123	26,439	9	38
39	10	3,225	8,725	5,500	102,667	75,588	27,079	10	39
40	11	3,425	8,725	5,300	116,604	89,430	27,174	11	40
41	12	3,725	8,725	5,000	131,333	104,105	27,228	12	41
42	13	4,025	8,725	4,700	146,915	119,693	27,222	13	42
43	14	4,325	8,725	4,400	163,421	136,216	27,205	14	43
44	15	4,575	8,725	4,150	180,976	153,764	27,212	15	44
45	16	4,975	8,725	3,750	199,504	172,384	27,120	16	45
46	17	5,375	8,725	3,350	219,083	192,053	27,030	17	46
47	18	5,775	8,725	2,950	239,795	212,841	26,954	18	47
48	19	6,175	8,725	2,250	261,733	234,808	26,925	19	48
49	20	6,575	8,725	2,150	284,994	258,032	26,962	20	49
50	21	6,975	8,725	1,750	309,683	281,129	28,554	21	50
51	22	7,675	8,725	1,050	335,592	305,515	30,077	22	51

52	23	8,375	2,177	-6,198	355,746	324,246	31,500	23	52
53	24	9,075	-1,179	-10,254	373,131	340,335	32,796	24	53
54	25	10,025	-1,643	-11,668	390,380	356,651	33,729	25	54
55	26	11,025	-2,117	-13,142	407,417	373,191	34,226	26	55
56	27	12,025	-2,603	-14,628	424,212	389,946	34,266	27	56
57	28	13,025	-3,116	-16,141	440,717	406,861	33,856	28	57
58	29	14,125	-3,629	-17,754	456,800	423,924	32,876	29	58
59	30	15,525	-4,148	-19,673	472,097	441,122	30,975	30	59
60	31	17,025	-4,704	-21,729	486,398	458,396	28,002	31	60
61	32	18,525	-5,249	-23,774	499,634	475,746	23,888	32	61
62	33	20,525	-5,808	-26,333	511,165	493,136	18,029	33	62
63	34	22,825	-6,383	-29,208	520,514	510,515	9,999	34	63
64	35	25,325	-6,951	-32,276	527,297	527,879	-582	35	64
65	36	28,025	-7,529	-35,554	531,082	545,177	-14,095	36	65
66	37	31,025	-8,127	-39,152	531,285	562,310	-31,025	37	66
67	38	34,025	-8,682	-42,707	527,664	579,270	-51,606	38	67
68	39	37,025	-9,253	-46,278	519,897	595,992	-76,095	39	68
69	40	40,325	-9,845	-50,170	508,305	612,399	-104,094	40	69
70	41	44,025	-10,412	-54,437	489,097	628,474	-139,377	41	70
71	42	49,025	-10,951	-59,976	463,451	644,245	-180,794	42	71
72	43	53,025	-11,450	-64,475	430,894	659,752	-228,858	43	72
73	44	61,025	-11,897	-72,922	386,611	675,064	-288,453	44	73
74	45	67,025	-12,308	-79,333	331,859	690,215	-358,356	45	74
75	46	72,925	-12,657	-85,582	265,979	705,240	-439,261	46	75
76	47	78,925	-13,002	-91,927	187,977	720,095	-532,118	47	76
77	48	84,925	-13,354	-98,279	96,874	734,708	-637,834	48	77
78	49	91,925	-13,706	-105,631	-9,457	748,969	-758,426	49	78
79	50	99,925	-14,094	-114,019	-133,354	762,758	-896,112	50	79
80	51	108,925	-14,452	-123,377	-277,270	776,049	-1,003,319	51	80
81	52	118,925	-14,820	-133,745	-443,896	788,792	-1,232,688	52	81
82	53	129,925	-15,151	-145,076	-636,896	800,996	-1,437,086	53	82
83	54	141,925	-15,415	-157,340	-856,904	812,745	-1,669,649	54	83
84	55	154,925	-15,651	-170,576	-1,109,678	824,065	-1,933,743	55	84

*DIVIDENDS ARE NOT GUARANTEED, BUT ARE BASED ON THE 1980 DIVIDEND SCHEDULE WHICH MAY BE CHANGED AT ANY TIME.

TABLE 5.
CUMULATIVE COST COMPARISON
between
TERM INSURANCE AND PERMANENT INSURANCE

$1,000,000   AGE: 35M

AGE	YR	TERM INS.	PERMANENT INSURANCE				8%		YR	AGE
		TERM ANNUAL PREMIUM	PERMANENT ANNUAL* PREMIUM	YEARLY PREMIUM DIFF.	CUMULATIVE DIFFERENCE IN PREMIUM	TOTAL POLICY VALUE	CUMULATIVE NET COST OF PERMANENT OVER TERM		YR	AGE
35	1	1,365	10,895	9,530	10,292	910	9,382	1	35
36	2	1,655	10,895	9,240	21,094	1,644	19,450	2	36
37	3	1,975	10,895	8,920	32,416	7,448	24,968	3	37
38	4	2,265	10,895	8,630	44,329	17,861	26,468	4	38
39	5	3,225	10,895	7,670	56,159	28,966	27,193	5	39
40	6	3,425	10,895	7,470	68,720	40,788	27,932	6	40
41	7	3,725	10,895	7,170	81,961	53,364	28,597	7	41
42	8	4,025	10,895	6,870	95,938	66,729	29,209	8	42
43	9	4,325	10,895	6,570	110,708	80,911	29,797	9	43
44	10	4,575	10,895	6,320	126,390	95,965	30,425	10	44
45	11	4,975	10,895	5,920	142,895	112,558	30,337	11	45
46	12	5,375	10,895	5,520	160,289	130,100	30,189	12	46
47	13	5,775	10,895	5,120	178,641	148,689	29,952	13	47
48	14	6,175	10,895	4,720	198,030	168,355	29,675	14	48
49	15	6,575	10,895	4,320	218,538	189,170	29,368	15	49
50	16	6,975	10,895	3,920	240,255	211,226	29,029	16	50
51	17	7,675	10,895	3,220	262,953	234,466	28,487	17	51
52	18	8,375	10,895	2,520	286,711	258,974	27,737	18	52
53	19	9,075	10,895	1,820	311,613	284,859	26,754	19	53
54	20	10,025	10,895	870	337,482	312,198	25,284	20	54

55	21	11,025	10,895	-130	364,340	339,618	24,722	21	55
56	22	12,025	7,590	-4,435	388,698	365,020	23,678	22	56
57	23	13,025	-900	-13,925	404,755	382,640	22,155	23	57
58	24	14,125	-1,439	-15,564	420,326	400,417	19,909	24	58
59	25	15,525	-2,004	-17,529	435,021	418,305	16,716	25	59
60	26	17,025	-2,555	-19,580	448,676	436,309	12,367	26	60
61	27	18,525	-3,146	-21,671	461,166	454,366	6,800	27	61
62	28	20,525	-3,730	-24,255	471,863	472,463	-600	28	62
63	29	22,825	-4,330	-27,155	480,285	490,549	-10,264	29	63
64	30	25,325	-4,914	-30,239	486,050	508,629	-22,579	30	64
65	31	28,025	-5,537	-33,562	488,687	526,624	-37,937	31	65
66	32	31,025	-6,150	-37,175	487,633	544,464	-56,831	32	66
67	33	34,025	-6,740	-40,765	482,617	562,103	-79,486	33	67
68	34	37,025	-7,337	-44,362	473,316	579,494	-106,178	34	68
69	35	40,325	-7,943	-48,268	459,052	596,576	-137,524	35	69
70	36	44,025	-8,546	-52,571	438,999	613,308	-174,309	36	70
71	37	49,025	-9,120	-58,145	411,323	629,708	-218,385	37	71
72	38	53,025	-9,635	-62,660	376,556	645,837	-269,281	38	72
73	39	61,025	-10,108	-71,133	329,857	661,753	-331,896	39	73
74	40	67,025	-10,526	-77,551	272,490	667,508	-405,018	40	74
75	41	72,925	-10,902	-83,827	203,756	693,130	-489,374	41	75
76	42	78,925	-11,255	-90,180	122,662	708,582	-585,920	42	76
77	43	84,925	-11,624	-96,549	28,202	723,784	-695,582	43	77
78	44	91,925	-12,013	-103,938	-81,793	738,598	-820,391	44	78
79	45	99,925	-12,398	-112,323	-209,646	752,944	-962,590	45	79
80	46	108,925	-12,793	-121,718	-357,873	766,749	-1,124,622	46	80
81	47	118,925	-13,168	-132,093	-529,163	779,991	-1,309,154	47	81
82	48	129,925	-13,507	-143,432	-726,403	792,689	-1,519,092	48	82
83	49	141,925	-13,798	-155,723	-952,696	804,888	-1,757,584	49	83
84	50	154,925	-14,033	-168,958	-1,211,386	816,661	-2,028,047	50	84

*DIVIDENDS ARE NOT GUARANTEED, BUT ARE BASED ON THE 1980 DIVIDEND SCHEDULE WHICH MAY BE CHANGED AT ANY TIME.

TABLE 6.
CUMULATIVE COST COMPARISON
between
TERM INSURANCE AND PERMANENT INSURANCE

$1,000,000   AGE: 40M

AGE	YR	TERM INS. TERM ANNUAL PREMIUM	PERMANENT ANNUAL* PREMIUM	YEARLY PREMIUM DIFF.	PERMANENT INSURANCE 8% CUMULATIVE DIFFERENCE IN PREMIUM	TOTAL POLICY VALUE	CUMULATIVE NET COST OF PERMANENT OVER TERM	YR	AGE
40	1	1,825	13,805	11,980	12,938	1,220	11,718	1	40
41	2	2,475	13,805	11,330	26,209	2,223	20,986	2	41
42	3	3,065	13,805	10,740	39,905	12,653	27,252	3	42
43	4	3,635	13,805	10,170	54,081	25,612	28,469	4	43
44	5	4,575	13,805	9,230	68,376	39,366	29,010	5	44
45	6	4,975	13,805	8,830	83,383	53,940	29,443	6	45
46	7	5,375	13,805	8,430	99,158	69,386	29,772	7	46
47	8	5,775	13,805	8,030	115,763	85,720	30,043	8	47
48	9	6,175	13,805	7,630	133,265	102,985	30,280	9	48
49	10	6,575	13,805	7,230	151,734	121,221	30,513	10	49
50	11	6,975	13,805	6,830	171,249	141,153	30,096	11	50
51	12	7,675	13,805	6,130	191,570	162,188	29,382	12	51
52	13	8,375	13,805	5,430	212,760	184,388	28,372	13	52
53	14	9,075	13,805	4,730	234,889	207,848	27,041	14	53
54	15	10,025	13,805	3,780	257,763	232,650	25,113	15	54
55	16	11,025	13,805	2,780	281,386	258,869	22,517	16	55
56	17	12,025	13,805	1,780	305,819	286,509	19,310	17	56
57	18	13,025	13,805	780	331,127	315,640	15,487	18	57

58	19	14,125	13,805	-320	357,272	346,371	10,901	19	58
59	20	15,525	13,805	-1,720	383,996	378,867	5,129	20	59
60	21	17,025	8,737	-8,288	405,765	406,220	-455	21	60
61	22	18,525	-265	-18,790	417,933	425,251	-7,318	22	61
62	23	20,525	-874	-21,399	428,257	444,340	-16,083	23	62
63	24	22,825	-1,509	-24,334	436,236	463,427	-27,191	24	63
64	25	25,325	-2,158	-27,483	441,454	482,468	-41,014	25	64
65	26	28,025	-2,796	-30,821	443,483	501,443	-57,960	26	65
66	27	31,025	-3,453	-34,478	441,726	520,245	-78,519	27	66
67	28	34,025	-4,088	-38,113	435,902	538,838	-102,936	28	67
68	29	37,025	-4,720	-41,745	425,690	557,166	-131,476	29	68
69	30	40,325	-5,371	-45,696	410,393	575,155	-164,762	30	69
70	31	44,025	-5,998	-50,023	389,200	592,789	-203,589	31	70
71	32	49,025	-6,607	-55,632	360,253	610,075	-249,822	32	71
72	33	53,025	-7,168	-60,193	324,065	627,062	-302,997	33	72
73	34	61,025	-7,667	-68,692	275,803	643,828	-368,025	34	73
74	35	67,025	-8,111	-75,136	216,720	660,424	-443,704	35	74
75	36	72,925	-8,504	-81,429	146,115	676,889	-530,774	36	75
76	37	78,925	-8,905	-87,830	62,947	693,155	-630,208	37	76
77	38	84,925	-9,291	-94,216	-33,769	709,153	-742,922	38	77
78	39	91,925	-9,697	-101,622	-146,222	724,756	-870,978	39	78
79	40	99,925	-10,108	-110,033	-276,756	739,868	-1,016,624	40	79
80	41	108,925	-10,540	-119,465	-427,919	754,403	-1,182,322	41	80
81	42	118,925	-10,942	-129,867	-602,408	768,352	-1,370,760	42	81
82	43	129,925	-11,308	-141,233	-803,133	781,724	-1,584,857	43	82
83	44	141,925	-11,627	-153,552	-1,033,220	794,561	-1,827,781	44	83
84	45	154,925	-11,880	-166,805	-1,296,027	806,947	-2,102,974	45	84

*DIVIDENDS ARE NOT GUARANTEED, BUT ARE BASED ON THE 1980 DIVIDEND SCHEDULE WHICH MAY BE CHANGED AT ANY TIME.

TABLE 7.
CUMULATIVE COST COMPARISON
between
TERM INSURANCE AND PERMANENT INSURANCE

$1,000,000 TERM INS.   AGE: 45M

AGE	YR	TERM ANNUAL PREMIUM	PERMANENT ANNUAL* PREMIUM	YEARLY PREMIUM DIFF.	CUMULATIVE DIFFERENCE IN PREMIUM 8%	TOTAL POLICY VALUE	CUMULATIVE NET COST OF PERMANENT OVER TERM	YR	AGE
45	1	2,595	17,375	14,780	15,962	1,830	14,132	1	45
46	2	3,595	17,375	13,780	32,121	3,660	28,461	2	46
47	3	4,625	17,375	12,750	48,461	18,860	29,601	3	47
48	4	5,535	17,375	11,840	65,125	34,770	30,335	4	48
49	5	6,575	17,375	10,800	81,999	51,550	30,449	5	49
50	6	6,975	17,375	10,400	99,791	69,180	30,611	6	50
51	7	7,675	17,375	9,700	118,251	87,730	30,521	7	51
52	8	8,375	17,375	9,000	137,431	107,210	30,221	8	52
53	9	9,075	17,375	8,300	157,389	127,700	29,689	9	53
54	10	10,025	17,375	7,350	177,918	149,210	28,708	10	54
55	11	11,025	17,375	6,350	199,010	172,590	26,420	11	55
56	12	12,025	17,375	5,350	220,709	197,200	23,509	12	56
57	13	13,025	17,375	4,350	243,063	223,120	19,943	13	57
58	14	14,125	17,375	3,250	266,018	250,420	15,598	14	58
59	15	15,525	17,375	1,850	289,298	279,240	10,058	15	59

60	16	17,025	17,375	350	312,820	309,680	3,140	16	60
61	17	18,525	17,375	−1,150	336,603	341,690	−5,086	17	61
62	18	20,525	17,375	−3,150	360,130	375,470	−15,339	18	62
63	19	22,825	17,375	−5,450	383,054	411,150	−28,095	19	63
64	20	25,325	15,550	−9,775	403,142	446,970	−43,827	20	64
65	21	28,025	904	−27,121	406,103	467,250	−61,146	21	65
66	22	31,025	206	−30,819	405,308	487,350	−82,041	22	66
67	23	34,025	−473	−34,498	400,474	507,230	−106,755	23	67
68	24	37,025	−1,166	−38,191	391,265	526,820	−135,554	24	68
69	25	40,325	−1,866	−42,194	377,000	546,050	−169,049	25	69
70	26	44,025	−2,545	−46,570	356,864	564,890	−208,025	26	70
71	27	49,025	−3,208	−52,233	329,001	583,360	−254,358	27	71
72	28	53,025	−3,802	−56,824	293,948	601,520	−307,571	28	72
73	29	61,025	−4,357	−65,382	246,850	619,430	−372,579	29	73
74	30	67,025	−4,827	−71,852	188,997	637,160	−448,162	30	74
75	31	72,925	−5,275	−78,200	119,661	654,740	−535,078	31	75
76	32	78,925	−5,686	−84,611	37,854	672,130	−634,275	32	76
77	33	84,925	−6,134	−91,059	−57,461	689,220	−746,681	33	77
78	34	91,925	−6,561	−98,486	−168,424	705,890	−874,314	34	78
79	35	99,925	−7,022	−106,947	−297,401	722,030	−1,019,431	35	79
80	36	108,925	−7,494	−116,419	−446,926	737,560	−1,184,486	36	80
81	37	118,925	−7,937	−126,862	−619,692	752,450	−1,372,142	37	81
82	38	129,925	−8,337	−138,262	−818,590	766,730	−1,585,320	38	82
83	39	141,925	−8,683	−150,608	−1,046,734	780,460	−1,827,194	39	83
84	40	154,925	−8,977	−163,902	−1,307,487	793,690	−2,101,177	40	84

*DIVIDENDS ARE NOT GUARANTEED, BUT ARE BASED ON THE 1980 DIVIDEND SCHEDULE WHICH MAY BE CHANGED AT ANY TIME.

TABLE 8.
CUMULATIVE COST COMPARISON
between
TERM INSURANCE AND PERMANENT INSURANCE

$1,000,000   AGE: 50M

AGE	YR	TERM ANNUAL PREMIUM	PERMANENT ANNUAL* PREMIUM	YEARLY PREMIUM DIFF.	CUMULATIVE DIFFERENCE IN PREMIUM (8%)	TOTAL POLICY VALUE	CUMULATIVE NET COST OF PERMANENT OVER TERM	YR	AGE
50	1	3,475	22,465	18,990	20,509	3,200	17,309	1	50
51	2	5,315	22,465	17,150	40,671	8,360	32,311	2	51
52	3	6,965	22,465	15,500	60,665	27,490	33,175	3	52
53	4	8,255	22,465	14,210	80,865	47,410	33,455	4	53
54	5	10,025	22,465	12,440	100,770	68,260	32,510	5	54
55	6	11,025	22,465	11,440	121,187	90,040	31,147	6	55
56	7	12,025	22,465	10,440	142,157	112,800	29,357	7	56
57	8	13,025	22,465	9,440	163,724	136,570	27,154	8	57
58	9	14,125	22,465	8,340	185,830	161,380	24,450	9	58
59	10	15,525	22,465	6,940	208,191	187,320	20,871	10	59
60	11	17,025	22,465	5,440	230,722	215,360	15,362	11	60
61	12	18,525	22,465	3,940	253,435	244,820	8,615	12	61
62	13	20,525	22,465	1,940	275,805	275,820	-14	13	62
63	14	22,825	22,465	-360	297,480	308,510	-11,029	14	63
64	15	25,325	22,465	-2,860	318,190	343,040	-24,849	15	64

16	65	-41,988	379,630	337,641	-5,560	22,465	28,025	65	16
17	66	-62,802	418,210	355,407	-8,560	22,465	31,025	66	17
18	67	-87,674	459,030	371,355	-11,560	22,465	34,025	67	18
19	68	-116,640	483,760	367,119	-31,430	5,595	37,025	68	19
20	69	-150,269	506,430	356,160	-37,342	2,983	40,325	69	20
21	70	-187,474	526,930	339,455	-41,850	2,175	44,025	70	21
22	71	-231,791	547,020	315,228	-47,578	1,447	49,025	71	22
23	72	-282,741	566,770	284,028	-52,240	785	53,025	72	23
24	73	-345,214	586,260	241,045	-60,839	186	61,025	73	24
25	74	-417,991	605,550	187,558	-67,379	-354	67,025	74	25
26	75	-501,775	624,670	122,894	-73,767	-842	72,925	75	26
27	76	-597,500	643,560	46,059	-80,246	-1,321	78,925	76	27
28	77	-706,051	662,150	-43,901	-86,708	-1,783	84,925	77	28
29	78	-829,429	680,280	-149,149	-94,200	-2,275	91,925	78	29
30	79	-969,829	697,810	-272,019	-102,719	-2,279	99,925	79	30
31	80	-1,129,697	714,710	-414,987	-112,228	-3,303	108,925	80	31
32	81	-1,311,637	730,900	-580,737	-122,732	-3,807	118,925	81	32
33	82	-1,518,528	746,420	-772,108	-134,177	-4,252	129,925	82	33
34	83	-1,753,520	761,340	-992,180	-146,577	-4,652	141,925	83	34
35	84	-2,019,987	775,740	-1,244,247	-159,901	-4,976	154,925	84	35
36	85	-2,321,578	789,710	-1,531,868	-174,148	-5,223	168,925	85	36
37	86	-2,661,167	803,330	-1,857,837	-188,351	-5,426	182,925	86	37
38	87	-3,042,942	816,720	-2,226,222	-203,479	-5,554	187,925	87	38
39	88	-3,470,352	830,000	-2,640,352	-218,547	-5,622	212,925	88	39
40	89	-3,947,134	843,320	-3,103,814	-233,550	-5,625	227,925	89	40

*DIVIDENDS ARE NOT GUARANTEED, BUT ARE BASED ON THE 1980 DIVIDEND SCHEDULE WHICH MAY BE CHANGED AT ANY TIME.

TABLE 9.
CUMULATIVE COST COMPARISON
between
TERM INSURANCE AND PERMANENT INSURANCE

$1,000,000   AGE: 55M

| TERM INS. | | | PERMANENT INSURANCE | | | | | | |
AGE	YR	TERM ANNUAL PREMIUM	PERMANENT ANNUAL* PREMIUM	YEARLY PREMIUM DIFF.	8% CUMULATIVE DIFFERENCE IN PREMIUM	TOTAL POLICY VALUE	CUMULATIVE NET COST OF PERMANENT OVER TERM	YR	AGE
55	1	4,745	28,775	24,010	25,930	5,120	20,810	1	55
56	2	7,345	28,775	21,410	51,128	13,710	37,418	2	56
57	3	10,085	28,775	18,670	75,381	37,560	37,821	3	57
58	4	12,055	28,775	16,700	99,448	62,180	37,268	4	58
59	5	15,525	28,775	13,230	121,692	87,760	33,932	5	59
60	6	17,025	28,775	11,730	144,096	114,280	29,816	6	60
61	7	18,525	28,775	10,230	166,672	141,810	24,862	7	61
62	8	20,525	28,775	8,230	188,894	170,420	18,474	8	62
63	9	22,825	28,775	5,930	210,410	200,150	10,260	9	63
64	10	25,325	28,775	3,430	230,948	213,090	-141	10	64
65	11	28,025	28,775	730	250,212	264,540	-14,327	11	65
66	12	31,025	28,775	-2,270	267,777	299,580	-31,802	12	66

67	13	34,025	28,775	-5,270	283,508	336,310	-52,801	13	67
68	14	37,025	28,775	-8,270	297,257	374,960	-77,702	14	68
69	15	40,325	28,775	-11,570	308,542	415,760	-107,217	15	69
70	16	44,025	28,775	-15,270	316,734	459,050	-142,315	16	70
71	17	49,025	16,055	-32,970	306,465	490,980	-184,514	17	71
72	18	53,025	7,217	-45,808	281,510	514,600	-233,089	18	72
73	19	61,025	6,502	-54,523	245,147	538,140	-292,992	19	73
74	20	67,025	5,827	-61,198	198,666	561,640	-362,973	20	74
75	21	72,925	5,221	-67,704	141,440	582,850	-441,409	21	75
76	22	78,925	4,696	-74,229	72,588	603,810	-531,221	22	76
77	23	84,925	4,157	-80,768	-8,833	624,440	-633,273	23	77
78	24	91,925	3,594	-88,331	-104,936	644,560	-749,496	24	78
79	25	99,925	3,008	-96,917	-218,001	664,040	-882,041	25	79
80	26	108,925	2,401	-106,524	-350,486	682,780	-1,033,266	26	80
81	27	118,925	1,835	-117,090	-504,982	700,750	-1,205,732	27	81
82	28	129,925	1,311	-128,614	-684,284	717,970	-1,402,254	28	82
83	29	141,925	861	-141,064	-891,375	734,540	-1,625,915	29	83
84	30	154,925	471	-154,454	-1,129,495	750,510	-1,880,005	30	84
85	31	168,925	172	-168,753	-1,402,107	766,010	-2,168,117	31	85
86	32	182,925	-74	-182,999	-1,711,916	781,110	-2,493,026	32	86
87	33	197,925	-222	-198,147	-2,062,868	795,990	-2,858,858	33	87
88	34	212,925	-327	-213,252	-2,458,210	810,750	-3,268,960	34	88
89	35	227,925	-383	-228,308	-2,901,440	825,520	-3,726,960	35	89

*DIVIDENDS ARE NOT GUARANTEED, BUT ARE BASED ON THE 1980 DIVIDEND SCHEDULE WHICH MAY BE CHANGED AT ANY TIME.

TABLE 10.
CUMULATIVE COST COMPARISON
between
TERM INSURANCE AND PERMANENT INSURANCE

$1,000,000   AGE: 60M

AGE	YR	TERM ANNUAL PREMIUM	PERMANENT ANNUAL* PREMIUM	YEARLY PREMIUM DIFF.	CUMULATIVE DIFFERENCE IN PREMIUM	TOTAL POLICY VALUE	CUMULATIVE NET COST OF PERMANENT OVER TERM	YR	AGE
		TERM INS.	PERMANENT INSURANCE 8%						
60	1	7,245	38,535	31,290	33,793	6,250	27,543	1	60
61	2	10,865	38,535	27,670	66,380	21,830	44,550	2	61
62	3	15,405	38,535	23,130	96,671	50,230	46,441	3	62
63	4	19,425	38,535	19,110	125,043	79,810	45,233	4	63
64	5	25,325	38,535	13,210	149,313	110,830	38,483	5	64
65	6	28,025	38,535	10,510	172,609	143,030	29,579	6	65
66	7	31,025	38,535	7,510	194,529	176,350	18,179	7	66
67	8	34,025	38,535	4,510	214,962	210,840	4,122	8	67
68	9	37,025	38,535	1,510	233,790	246,550	-12,759	9	68
69	10	40,325	38,535	-1,790	250,560	283,600	-33,039	10	69

70	11	44,025	38,535	-5,490	264,675	323,580	-58,904	11	70
71	12	49,025	38,535	-10,490	274,520	365,600	-91,079	12	71
72	13	53,025	38,535	-14,490	280,833	410,100	-129,266	13	72
73	14	61,025	38,535	-22,490	279,010	457,650	-178,639	14	73
74	15	67,025	24,066	-42,959	254,936	492,520	-237,583	15	74
75	16	72,925	14,146	-58,779	211,850	518,260	-306,409	16	75
76	17	78,925	13,254	-65,671	157,874	543,650	-385,775	17	76
77	18	84,925	12,565	-72,360	92,356	568,790	-476,433	18	77
78	19	91,925	11,867	-80,058	13,283	593,560	-580,276	19	78
79	20	99,925	11,122	-88,803	-81,560	617,870	-699,430	20	79
80	21	108,925	10,382	-98,543	-194,510	639,190	-833,700	21	80
81	22	118,925	9,711	-109,214	-328,022	659,650	-987,672	22	81
82	23	129,925	9,081	-120,844	-484,775	679,230	-1,164,005	23	82
83	24	141,925	8,547	-133,378	-667,604	698,060	-1,365,664	24	83
84	25	154,925	8,096	-146,829	-879,587	716,230	-1,595,817	25	84
85	26	168,925	7,737	-161,188	-1,124,036	733,880	-1,857,916	26	85
86	27	182,925	7,413	-175,512	-1,403,512	751,070	-2,154,582	27	86
87	28	197,925	7,213	-190,712	-1,721,761	767,990	-2,489,751	28	87
88	29	212,925	7,055	-205,870	-2,081,842	784,760	-2,866,602	29	88
89	30	227,925	7,003	-220,922	-2,486,984	801,570	-3,288,554	30	89

*DIVIDENDS ARE NOT GUARANTEED, BUT ARE BASED ON THE 1980 DIVIDEND SCHEDULE WHICH MAY BE CHANGED AT ANY TIME.

18

—— "I Don't Need Any Life Insurance!" ——
True or False?

MOST OF THE OPINIONS you have heard on the topic of life insurance have probably been those of counselors, lawyers, accountants, your friends and family, and perhaps some of your co-workers. To give a different perspective to the subject, a group of senior citizens I interviewed and asked for their opinions on the subject of life insurance. I felt that here were people who could speak from experience in telling what insurance had meant to them over the course of their lifetime.

What follows are exact quotes from seniors who were asked the question, "How has life insurance affected you?"

Female, Age 66

"We had a policy, but we lost it during the Depression when we were wiped out and had to cash it in. My husband felt it was a good benefit, and he didn't want to give it up, but we really didn't have any choice. We needed the money."

Female, Age 70

"I'm grateful for my policy. When my husband died, I had a chunk of money. On Social Security alone, I could have never survived."

Female, Age 67

"Very few people ever ask me about my insurance. Frankly, very few people talk to me altogether. They're afraid of talking about death."

Male, Age 70

"I bought a policy for my grandson so that when he was ready for college, he could cash it in, which he did. The money came in handy."

Male, Age 72

"I regret that I didn't buy more insurance when I was young. But people generally don't believe in it. We never think about getting old."

Female, Age 65

"My husband believed in life insurance, but he believed in the stock market more. So he sold his policy to buy stocks, and eventually we lost everything."

Male, Age 67

"Insurance is good for people who can't save. I first started buying it for 10¢ a week in New York, when you could provide a child with $1,000 for her thirteenth birthday."

Male, Age 65

"Personally, I'd rather leave my money in the bank. With life insurance, you're just paying for the agent's commission. The higher the premium the bigger the commission."

Female, Age 52

"My insurance policy for me was a good investment. I cashed it in and used the money to travel around the world. While you have the policy, you never know when you might need the money. And when you need the money, it's always there."

Female, Age 62

"I cashed in my policy to take a trip. The insurance was always a convenient nest egg. I gave the benefits to my son, as well. My mother always told me that life insurance was a good idea."

Male, Age 67

"I believe strongly in life insurance. It's security against bad times. You can borrow on your policy during sick times. For a young man with a family, it's vital."

Male, Age 70

"We cashed in all of our policies when we got to age 65, and we used the money to put a down payment on a house."

Male, Age 71

"During the Depression, life insurance was a forced savings, when many people couldn't save money because they didn't have any."

Female, Age 67

"I have a daughter whose husband believed strongly in life insurance and he protected his home and his life with it, and he actually died at age 34. That insurance was a godsend."

Male, Age 60

"I took out a policy because it was actually cheaper than the one I got in the army."

Female, Age 64

"Women were never told to buy insurance. They would eventually marry and it was natural for the husband to handle the insurance needs. In other words, let him worry about it."

Female, Age 69

"When I married, my mother cashed in her policy to get me started. My husband and I got $12,500, which was a beginning."

Male, Age 67

"Life Insurance is important for protecting your property. Don't get into a position where you have to say, 'Why didn't I take advantage of life insurance?'"

Female, Age 70, who insisted on responding to the questions by telling a story.

"Two women are at an unveiling. One woman is listening while the other is sobbing over a tombstone. The sobbing woman keeps repeating, 'He wanted to, but I wouldn't let him. He wanted to, but I wouldn't let him. He wanted to, but I wouldn't let him.' Finally, the other woman walks over and asks the crying woman, 'What did he want?' To which the crying woman replied, 'He wanted to take out another insurance policy for $50,000, but I wouldn't let him.'"

Male, Age 65

"My son-in-law doesn't believe in life insurance. He doesn't want to leave his money to his wife's next husband."

Female, Age 63

"Life insurance should be tailored to the individual, but you definitely need it when you're young. As you get older and you have other sources of income, life insurance becomes secondary."

Male, Age 60

"Life insurance certainly helps, like when it pays for burial expenses. That can be an exorbitant expense of several thousand dollars, especially if you're in a lower income bracket. I used my wife's insurance to help bury her. That money was put to good use."

Female, Age 63

"Life insurance is advantageous when you're young, but when you're older, it's more difficult to keep up the payments."

Male, Age 67

"All I have is a term insurance policy which I bought through the Veterans Administration. I never converted it. It's now too expensive and I have to give it up."

Male, Age 65

"Young people should buy insurance when they're young. The rates are very low, and they shouldn't be passed up."

Male, Age 64

"I used to pay smaller rates. But my term insurance goes up every year. It's not a good deal. I should have bought permanent insurance."

Female, Age 66

"If I had to do it all over again, I would take out the maximum and I'd try to borrow to keep it going. Especially in these times when inflation makes investments so risky."

Female, Age 63

"Life insurance is a luxury for the future, and you naturally have second thoughts about buying something like that, but you can't pass it up."

While our poll of Santa Monica Bay seniors was merely a random sampling, the results were quite extraordinary. Of the fifty persons who were questioned, five would not participate. Of the forty-five respondents, everyone had had some form of life insurance coverage over the course of their lifetime, and forty-one had something positive to say about their coverage. In general those who questioned the need for life insurance in their early years began to see its real advantages as they grew older.

Insurance or No Insurance?

But what about those who say, "I don't believe in life insurance"? What is their reasoning? First of all, life insurance is not something to be believed in. Life insurance is a method. You don't believe in a method, you believe in the end result. Life insurance provides a method for compensating for human life value, for replacing lost family income, for covering estate taxes, for funding a stock redemption agreement, for providing a college fund and so forth. It is one of the ways, and in most cases the most effective way, to perform those functions. To say, "I don't believe in life insurance," is totally illogical.

There *are* people who don't need life insurance. They have no obligations, no responsibilities. They don't intend to have any debts, no mortgages, no borrowed money, and in many cases, they feel totally self-sufficient.

But, if you have any idea of self worth that you would like to estimate, or any thought of getting married and having children, or starting a business, or borrowing money from the bank, or any other of the many purposes for life insurance, then you will eventually see the need. With foresight, you might start your program at an early age, when life insurance is inexpensive, and when you are theoretically in the best of health and at your most insurable rating.

You will thus be protected against the unexpected. Young people have died prematurely; some have developed sicknesses that can make them uninsurable in later years. You don't buy at a young age because you think you're going to die, which is highly unlikely, but because you might develop a physical impairment that could prevent you from buying much needed coverage in later years.

For example, let us consider two men both in their thirties, both making $30,000 a year and both having a spouse and two children. One man is insured and the other is uninsurable, because of an automobile injury suffered when he was a young man.

The insurable man has $200,000 of insurance and is secure in the knowledge that should anything ever happen to him his family will be taken care of, his children can remain in their home and be educated, and his spouse can look forward to having money for survival.

With this security, he can begin to utilize his excess money in outside investments, investing wisely, but with some risk, realizing that the greater the risk, the greater the potential. He knows that his $30,000 a year is money to live on and that only through wise investment will he have the opportunity to better his present life style.

Meanwhile, the uninsurable man has no insurance to fall back on, no rainy day money for his children's education should he die unexpectedly, no survival money for his spouse. With this in mind he conservatively pours every extra dollar he makes into a risk free savings account. He cannot risk his money in investments; he cannot take the chance of sacrificing his family's well being on such ventures.

How much would it have been worth to that uninsurable man to have bought life insurance at a younger age when he was insurable? As one of the seniors said, "Don't get to the point where you have to say, 'Why didn't I take advantage of life insurance when I could?'"

Those who understand the value of life insurance can derive some interesting benefits. I know of one young man who was determined to build a multi-million dollar business and he desperately wanted a self-worth of a million dollars. It meant very much to him. And I remember that after he bought a million dollars of term insurance from me many years ago, he actually carried the policy around with him.

He told me, "I have been here too short a time to build my estate, but should I die, that money will go to my mother, whom I love dearly, so I know that someone will receive the million dollars I wanted to make over the course of my lifetime. If I go tomorrow, at least I feel I shall have accomplished something."

That man is now worth millions of dollars. Perhaps that one policy gave him the time and confidence he needed to make his first million. Life insurance can provide benefits that cannot be estimated in dollars alone.

What Are Your Needs?

Times change. What doesn't seem like a need now, may become a strong one in ten years. To keep in step with the times, you should constantly review your financial position and the need for protection. You may not have needed insurance five years ago, but today your situation could be entirely different.

Time eradicates misconceptions. Eventually, people find the time to sit down and listen to a professional. They realize that perhaps they don't know all of the answers. Whether realization of the need for life insurance advice comes naturally or through the intervention of an event or crisis, people wake up to the real facts.

The need is there. How you assess that need is the vital factor.

19

────────── "How Much?" ──────────
Insurance Needs for the Family

NEXT TO BUYING A HOME, your life insurance may be the
biggest single purchase you will ever make. The type of
insurance that best suits your situation will be determined
by how much you need and, of course, by your budget.

There are four ways to figure the amount of your insurance
needs. These are: (1) the price-earnings ratio, (2) the human
life value, (3) the principal-and-interest approach, and (4)
the programming method.

Price-Earnings Ratio

The *price-earnings ratio* considers you, the breadwinner, as
a stock and your dependents as stockholders.

A company's stock may sell on the stock exchange for ten
times its yearly earnings. If that company made $100,000, on
a ten times earnings ratio the company's stock would be
worth $1 million. A stock may sell at a conservative five
times earnings, or have a great growth potential and sell at
twenty times earnings.

You can be considered in the same manner. You too are
selling out. You are going to die some day and you want the

insurance to buy you out. If you make $30,000, you are not going to ask for a mere $30,000. That will protect your dependents for only one year. You may figure you need at least five years of earnings for them, and, utilizing a price-earnings ratio approach, you determine that you need $30,000 × 5, or $150,000 worth of insurance. If you would like to apply a ten times earnings ratio approach, you would buy $300,000 of life insurance. The insurance agent may put it in even simpler terms, by asking you how many years of income you would like to leave for your dependents.

Human Life Value

The second way to compute the amount of insurance to be bought is through the *human life value* method, in which an actual value is put on your life.

Many people put values on their possessions—their house, their car, their jewelry—and they buy the appropriate casualty insurance to protect them. However, they often fail to think of themselves as having a specific value, too. Here are all the golden eggs nicely protected, and yet the goose that laid those eggs is vulnerable.

This is immediately apparent when you consider your automobile insurance. If there was an accident and you and a pedestrian were killed, and you had liability insurance but no life insurance, your insurance company might be paying the other person's family $500,000, while your family would receive nothing. It is alarming to think that many people, in reality, take out insurance on everybody but themselves.

The value of human life can also be seen from another perspective. Let's say you are a successful playwright with two plays produced on Broadway and one being made into a feature film, giving you a current worth of well over $2 million and income of $400,000 yearly. *You're still in your thirties, so you figure you have forty productive years left.* If you were killed in a plane crash, your spouse's attorney would sue the airline company not for your current income of $400,000 but for the present value of your projected income over forty years.

There are, however, other ways to die. Would your spouse think you were worth $16 million if you went down in a plane, but some lesser amount if you died, for example, in a hurricane? In matters of life insurance, you don't go about it halfway; the policy must cover all eventualities of death.

How do you establish the value of human life? Let's appraise you. Suppose you make a conservative $30,000 every year (which is unlikely because inflation alone will make your salary grow) and **like that playwright**, you are thirty years old, with forty good, productive years left. That equals about $1.2 million over your lifetime (40 x $30,000 = $1.2 million).

You now discount that $1.2 million with interest; that is, you figure that $400,000 put at interest would equal $1.2 million over a period of forty years. Therefore, the present value of your life is $400,000. And you take out a $400,000 policy on your life. That is human life value.

Principal and Interest

The third way to compute the amount of insurance you should buy is based upon *principal and interest.*

There are only two ways to make money: a person at work, or money at work. Either you are working, making your $30,000 a year, or you receive $30,000 a year by having $300,000 in the bank at 10% interest.

So you can equal your earnings by placing $300,000 in the bank; with a 10% interest return, you would collect $30,000 a year in perpetuity. If you die, your family can apply the same approach if they have $300,000 worth of life insurance. They will not have to touch any other assets, and their economic situation, at least, will remain stable.

One final demonstration of principal and interest at work: A man puts $1 million into a college trust fund to establish ongoing scholarships. At 10%, that million will provide $100,000 in scholarships yearly in perpetuity. The original $1 million need never be touched. Many people establish charitable trusts through life insurance in this manner.

Programming

The fourth way to calculate the amount of insurance required is called *programming*. This is the method most commonly used by insurance agents. It is so simple that you can do it yourself with a worksheet.

You determine your needs, then calculate your assets and subtract your liabilities (including the needs you estimated); the difference will be the amount of insurance you require.

Here is a typical example. Let's start with your two children. You would like to establish a college fund for them, so that if you die, they will have enough money to finish college. Four years of college could cost $10,000 a year, per child. That's $80,000 (we'll call it A) you must figure into your liabilities.

For your funeral and any medical expenses not covered by insurance, you might allow $5,000 (B).

Another liability is your $100,000 mortgage (C). We'll assume here that you would like your mortgage paid off and your house free and clear for your family at your death.

You must further provide for your spouse, who is taking care of the children while they are growing up. You are currently making $2,500 a month in salary. After taxes it might be only $2,000. There will be an additional savings of approximately $500 a month on the cost of your clothes, food, and expenses, resulting in a family need of only $1,500 a month or $18,000 a year. To produce that figure (using the principal-and-interest method) your spouse is going to need $180,000 (D).

Your total needs are now $365,000 (A + B + C + D). This figure may also be increased if you want to settle any other outstanding debts, or create any moneys for future contingencies and emergencies that may arise for your surviving spouse and children.

Now let's look at your assets. You have $20,000 (E) in your bank accounts. You also have stocks totaling $35,000 (F). Your Social Security benefits to your spouse may be $500 a month, which, until the children are 22, comes to $5,000 a year, or $50,000 over ten years (G). Since you have chosen to have your family retain your home, it is no longer a usable asset. In addition, your group insurance at work is $20,000 (H) and you have $40,000 (I) of personal life insurance policies. Your total usable assets are $165,000 (E + F + G + H + I).

Subtracting your total assets of $165,000 from the required $365,000 of liabilities gives you a $200,000 deficit, which is the amount of additional life insurance you will need.

This is a typical example of programming. While it is simplified, it does show you how required amounts of life insurance can be figured in detail.

Once their children have passed college age, some people might want to reduce their coverage by the appropriate amount. I am against this, because I generally don't adjust the amount of insurance purchased for an inflation factor, and this additional insurance coverage will take up the slack. In addition, there is always going to be, contrary to uninformed opinion, an increasing need for insurance, not a lessening one. The idea that you need less insurance as you grow older is erroneous. It contradicts the theory used in the sale of stocks and mutual funds that you must buy them in order to accommodate inflation in future years. If inflation is going to create a larger need for these funds, it will also create a greater need for life insurance. Finally, as your standard of living improves, you need more insurance, not less.

How to Figure Your Needs

We have considered the four different methods of arriving at the amount of insurance that should be purchased. The price-earnings ratio method arrived at the conclusion that one consumer earning $30,000 a year required between $150,000 and $300,000 of insurance. The human life value method arrived at approximately a $400,000 figure; the principal-and-interest method arrived at $300,000; and, finally, the programming approach arrived at a $200,000 figure. While you may favor one of these methods as a means of arriving at how much insurance you require, most professional agents will work from an average of these various methods, taking into consideration any other factors affecting your particular needs.

During the programming phase, the agent also determines how you can afford the insurance you need and what type. If you cannot afford $200,000 of permanent insurance, the agent will advise you to buy a combination of term and permanent insurance that you can afford. The term insurance is convertible so that at a certain future point you can buy the whole sum in permanent insurance if it is a lifetime need. If the only way you can accommodate this need is through the purchase of term insurance, then term obviously is the appropriate buy.

Your insurance needs should be based totally on what you require, but you must also take into consideration what you can afford. In this way you will not overspend. Your insurance will remain in your portfolio, protecting you as you grow in financial stature.

20

"How Much?"
Insurance Needs for the Business

LIFE INSURANCE is a wonderful tool for use in business. While many people understand the benefits of "key man" and group insurance, there is a much more complex and vital side to business insurance. In fact, the survival of business often depends on the proper use of insurance by key executives. Without such protection, an untimely death could disrupt the cohesiveness of a thriving business, forcing a liquidation that could have been easily avoided.

In the business world, the death of a key executive can have grave repercussions. Such a loss may affect productivity, morale, and the entire credibility of a company. Many companies have been completely devastated in this way. The profits this employee was responsible for can disappear; others will suddenly be burdened with increased responsibility and a larger share of the work load. There is also the problem of how to utilize existing staff, offices, and floor space without that executive's leadership. Finally, there is the need to find a suitable replacement and to offset the loss of potential profits.

What Insurance Is Needed?

What kind of capital is needed to insure the continued productivity of the company during this transitional period?

First, one has to estimate the executive's worth to the company. As a key executive, he or she might be directly responsible for as much as $50,000 in annual profit and, by freeing other associates to secure even more business, indirectly responsible for an additional $50,000. Let's use that $100,000 figure and go back to price-earnings ratio.

How many years does the company need before it replaces those lost profits? Would it take three years to replace this key executive's impact with a new key executive? If so, then the company is going to need $300,000 to replace those profits.

However, profits are not the only worry. One has to figure on expenses that have to be paid during the transitional period. The deceased executive's allocated expenses may be $30,000 a year, a figure we must add to the $300,000. So, for the three-year period, we now have a total of $390,000 that the company needs to cover the profit and expenses until the new executive gets the sales team into operation.

This is where key-man insurance prevents major problems. Whether it is three years and $390,000, or any other formula-produced figure, insurance that the company has purchased on that person's life will provide the liquidity to survive the transitional period.

Many of the same approaches outlined in the previous chapter describing principle and interest, human life value, and price-earnings ratio can be applied on a business basis. You can even program the business expenses and profits lost to determine the insurance needs.

Key-Man Insurance

Obviously, certain employees are more important to the company than others.

If you are the inventor or chemist who created the company's unique products, your loss might mean total disaster for the company, so you would be protected by a correspondingly large amount of insurance.

If you are the financial officer and thus responsible for securing all necessary banking, your loss must be offset by appropriate insurance to compensate for the difficulty in securing money without your ability and know-how.

If you are the "inside" person and your loss brings about a total slowdown in production, then all the goods sold will not be delivered, and additional compensation must be provided.

If you are fortunate enough to find immediate replacements in any of these situations, which is highly unlikely, then you must have substantial money available in order to pay generous salaries and bonuses to entice this talent away from where it is now working.

Key-man insurance is often used in the entertainment world, especially in motion pictures and television, in which the key actors are insured for large amounts of money. If they are injured or killed, millions in production expenses and millions more in profits could be jeopardized. Insurance policies are very common in an industry where personalities are vital to the success of such ventures. It is hard to imagine NBC not insuring Johnny Carson's life.

The same is also true in the world of sports. The assets of a team are its players, and they must be protected by insurance. The loss of a key player may destroy the team's chances, and if the team loses, other losses follow, including attendance figures, concession sales, even souvenir revenue. The fate of an entire franchise may depend on the availability of a single player.

Key executives must be protected at all costs.Yet the cost for the insurance that provides that protection is a small part of the overall expense pattern of the company.

Protecting Investments

Insurance is also utilized in the business world to protect investments, including expensive equipment, floor space, or even an entire building. This is not a question of casualty insurance, but of life insurance to insure that, if you die prematurely, your family or partner will not be saddled with the debts and liabilities that may have been incurred in the purchase of those investments.

Let's consider a man who has just leased an entire floor of an office building for $200,000 a year for ten years. That's $2 million over that period. Should he die any time during that ten years, his family will be responsible for those lease payments. If the economy turns around and the inflation rate drops along with real estate values, the deceased's family may not be able to get rid of that premium floor space. If there is a need for capital and reorganization, the dependents will be trapped with a business expense they neither need nor can afford. Only business life insurance can protect that family from the burden of that lease.

The Attractions of Business Life Insurance

Life insurance not only protects key executives, it can also attract them to the company fold. You attract employees to your company by providing them with benefits, such as reasonable group insurance. As they move up the company ladder, they will receive more benefits through their profit-sharing or pension plans. As you begin to deal with the upper strata of company officers, you might start talking about stock options, bonuses, or—perhaps the most advantageous method of retaining the employee—the deferred-compensation program.

There are many variations of deferred-compensation programs. You might give your key person a plan that offers 50% of salary to his or her dependents for ten years upon premature death. If he or she lives to retirement age, the same plan would continue to pay 50% of salary for ten years.

Many companies recruit key executives by providing them with deferred-compensation programs, funded by life insurance policies on those executives' lives.

In smaller companies, such plans have still other uses. The death of an owner can mean the end of a business unless there is some incentive for the key executive to stay on and continue running the business, instead of leaving the company to join a rival or starting a new rival company.

By means of a life insurance plan, you can give that executive the right to buy 50% of the business upon the owner's death. This can be accomplished with a tax deductible salary increase that will allow payment for that insurance. This helps in three ways: first, it gives a strong incentive to continue with the company; second, the money the executive pays to buy that 50% interest is going to go to the owner's dependents, providing much needed funds; third, if the executive stays in the company, the deceased's family will continue to make 50% of the company's profits. Fifty percent of a going business is a wonderful nest egg. Without insurance, there may be no key man left, and then no business to produce any nest egg.

Maintaining such an insurance program for key personnel not only assures a continuing relationship between your family and the business, but also makes those employees happy and ambitious while you are still very much alive, since they know they have security.

Life Insurance and Partnerships

Life insurance plays an important role in partnerships.

Suppose you and I are partners. If I die, I would like my estate to take my half of the money out of the business. I don't want my family to be dependent on you because I know how important I was to this business. And I don't want to impede your progress either. You never liked my spouse, who, furthermore, may marry one of our competitors, which is very likely since most of our social relationships were within our business.

Because of all this, your lawyer draws up a buy/sell agreement, and each partner buys an insurance policy on the other's life. Without such an agreement, there will be great difficulty in the disposition of the business at death. Without life insurance to fund the buy/sell agreement, there will be no money and little purpose for the agreement.

When one partner dies, the other partner can use the insurance to purchase the deceased partner's half of the business. That money goes to the deceased's dependents. The remaining partner now owns the company in total.

But you're stubborn and you know there is another way, so let's examine the possibilities. For argument's sake, let's say it will take a million dollars to buy out the other partner. How do you get it?

1) You can make the money yourself. But if your business returns 10% on sales, it's going to take you $20 million in gross sales to make $2 million in profits, leaving $1 million after taxes for the buyout. And to make $20 million in sales, it might take you a long time, depending on the type of business. And don't forget the uncertainty of a business under new management.

2) You can use money you have invested elsewhere, in real estate, in a buried savings account, or stocks. But you do not

really want to liquidate all of your holdings and invest them in a business that may have some definite risk involved. You can't afford to leave yourself with nothing to fall back on in case of emergency.

3) You can borrow from the bank, if you are able to secure a loan. Remember, the company is no longer as stable as it once was, and the loan officer might question your ability to repay that loan with your partner no longer alive. In any event, the interest payments on a million-dollar loan could be $150,000 a year (depending on the prevailing interest rate). How are you going to afford that? Insurance premiums are much lower than the after-tax cost of interest as well as the after-tax repayment of the loan.

It is a lot simpler to have insurance pay for that company without sacrificing your own capital, going out on a limb with a huge loan, or waiting for profits to increase.

Another form of the buy/sell agreement is the stock redemption plan in which the dependents of the deceased can cash in his or her stock. This is a nice arrangement if the company has the liquidity to purchase what might be a huge block of stock. To achieve that liquidity, a life insurance policy is bought by the company on the owner so that when he dies, the company can use the death benefit to redeem the deceased's stock. The company does not have to dissolve its assets to buy back the stock, and the dependents receive the value of the business to continue their lives.

Tax-Deductible Life Insurance

It may not be widely known that it is possible to buy life insurance in a tax-deductible manner through a company pension or profit-sharing plan. It is the best tax shelter ever created, and it is important that all consumers who have these plans look into the possibility of purchasing their insurance in this manner.

When a wealthy person needs insurance to pay his estate taxes, he may find purchasing that insurance through his pension plan is most beneficial, since all assets in the plan can be arranged to be estate-tax free.

Many times I find that clients have purchased large policies that end up in their estate, actually *increasing* the estate taxes unnecessarily. One client was paying for $1 million of insurance; in his 50% estate tax bracket, his family would receive only $500,000 after taxes. By purchasing that policy through his already existing profit-sharing plan, his family would receive the full $1 million. Furthermore, his million dollars of insurance cost $17,000 a year. Since it was in his profit-sharing plan, it was tax deductible, costing him only $8,500, plus a recoverable economic-benefit tax.

In his income-tax bracket (50%), he had to make $34,000 to have $17,000 to pay his premium for $1 million of insurance; and, given his estate-tax bracket (50%) this would result in his family receiving only $500,000. Would he not have been better off using his pension or profit-sharing plan to pay the $17,000 premium? It would cost only $8,500 after income tax, and would be subject to no estate taxes, therefore producing for his family the full $1 million at his death. Why spend $17,000 for $500,000, when for $8,500 a year, you can buy $1 million? I may have been redundant, but how do I emphasize this point enough for the many people who are not taking advantage of this exciting and most meaningful program?

This insurance policy has created one million dollars for the businessman's family. Ordinarily, it would take $40 million in gross sales to create that same one million dollars.For this example, let us say that it is a small closely held corporation and we strip the corporate veil and say the corporation is this individual, and he is the corporation. He is in a 50% income and 50% estate tax bracket.

For a business returning ten percent on sales, $40 million in sales equals $4 million in profits. After income taxes, he has earned $2 million, and should he die, that $2 million is further subject to estate taxes which would bring the figure down to $1 million for his dependents. Why should his family wait for $40 million in sales, when life insurance can do the job, when he buys a million dollars in protection for as little as $8500 net a year?

Consumers should always investigate the possibility of buying insurance through their pension and profit sharing plans, where the tax advantages are enormous. This method of buying insurance also avoids the substantial after-tax impairment of cash flow to any individual or his corporation.

Insurance Protects!

Whichever way the business insurance is bought, it is the most viable means to protect the key executive. Whether that person heads a 60,000-employee automobile corporation or a mom-and-pop grocery store, he or she is going to need that protection. Although the insurance is designed to protect the business, ultimately it will be used to benefit the breadwinner's family and dependents.

In the next chapter, I will be discussing estate taxes. You may notice an overlapping and redundancy in some intances, because I have attempted to reinforce previous statements. These three chapters take us from the family man to his business, and to his ultimate estate-tax problems. All three are interwoven, since estate tax problems affect the family, and the best way to resolve those problems, in most cases, is through the breadwinner's business.

21

—— "Estate Taxes Are Expensive!" ——
Let the Insurance Company
Pay Them for You

THIS CHAPTER is for consumers who have a substantial estate—
$1 million or more—and are beginning to think about the
impact estate taxes will have on their heirs. Life insurance
can help.

This chapter outlines some general concepts. However,
almost every estate is a special case, so that planning should
be discussed only with an attorney who can implement all
the necessary legal procedures and, since life insurance can
be a useful—almost essential—planning tool in this respect,
with an insurance agent who specializes in estate analysis.

Life insurance really has two purposes. It can be used to
create or conserve an estate. People who have obtained a certain position and wealth in life must do everything they can to
preserve their fortunes. It is too hard earned over too long a
period of time to see it dissipated by our system of taxation.
After all of the most sophisticated estate-tax approaches,
trusts, and other systems of tax deferral have been imple-
mented through the attorney, there will probably still remain
estate taxes to be paid. These people and their advisers must
understand that other substantial, knowledgeable people have
found that the least expensive way of paying those taxes is to

let the insurance company pay them. This method avoids forced liquidation of stocks, real estate, and other holdings, and total devastation to existing bank accounts.

A man may take a lifetime to build his fortune. The same intelligence must prevail in the preservation of that fortune.

Recently, a thirty-five-year-old man came to my office. He was divorced, had two children, and an estate of $9 million, mostly concentrated in real estate. Because of estate taxes, state inheritance taxes, probate costs, and other miscellaneous expenses, it is quite probable that, without adequate protection and estate planning, when this man dies 70% of his estate is going to disappear. It's rather disheartening to think that after all the work, the risk, and the heartache that went into building that fortune, it's going to erode because adequate precautions were not taken.

Optimize Your Money

It has been said many times that while tax evasion is illegal, tax avoidance is something incumbent on every citizen. It is each person's right to avoid any tax that he can legally; in all probability, it's in the best interests of this country that he does. Imagine if there were no incentives for investment, no reason to put capital to work, no dream of the tremendous potential that risk can bring. If people knew they couldn't keep the money, there would be no new businesses, no new buildings, no new jobs, no progress and eventually no America as we know it. Therefore, it is absolutely imperative that every citizen optimize his money and make sure that he can pass on as much as possible, intact, to his family.

There are various steps that can be taken to prevent the erosion of wealth by estate taxes. One that is frequently recommended is that portions of a person's wealth should be given while he is alive to prospective heirs—gifts *inter vivos*— so that at the time of death the estate will be smaller and thus less liable to estate taxes, although they would already have been subjected to gift taxes. This is a practical and logical approach, but it has drawbacks. First, a person's future life span and hence future requirements are unknown factors; the wealth that has been given away may turn out to be needed. Second, of an emotional but no less real nature: persons of great wealth, especially those who have worked hard to acquire it, can have justifiable doubts about giving away wealth to persons who may after all turn out to be bad custodians. It would be very galling to have to stand by and watch the wealth one has acquired being frittered or perhaps gambled away.

Paying Estate Taxes

There are four ways to pay estate-tax obligations.

First, you can utilize cash reserves and pay the taxes outright. This makes the assumption that a wealthy person has a large sum of money sitting in the bank. Very few people do, because if you have a lot of money, you have that money at work, not in a bank account. Nonetheless, if you have cash in the bank and you take it out to pay taxes, then you lose not only the principal but the return you make on that principal annually.

The second option is to borrow the money to pay the taxes. This may be difficult to do with the principal family provider no longer there. But assuming you are eligible to borrow the tax money from a bank or the government, you will have to pay it back, with all the additional tax ramifications I have mentioned in previous chapters.

The third—very frequent—method of dealing with the tax problem is liquidation of real property or even an entire business. The problem with liquidation is that it often becomes a forced liquidation that does not realize the true value of the property. Business liquidations may be impractical, particularly if your intention is for your sons or daughters to continue in that business.

Many people have built substantial fortunes based on real estate. This probably is the most nonliquid of all assets. The ramifications of real estate liquidation can be far reaching, particularly if your estate is forced to liquidate when the market is soft. If the taxes are $1 million, the estate may find itself selling property with a $1.5 million net equity in order to realize that $1 million.

And that is assuming you can realize a full $1 million from the sale of that property. Did the taxes truly cost only $1 million? NO! Real estate people say that property appreciates 10% to 15% a year, so that that property will be conservatively worth $2 million in ten years. The property also probably yields 10% income per year, meaning an additional loss of $1 million to the estate over the ten-year period. Thus, the true cost of the taxes ten years later will be $3 million.

Let us go one step further. Many people have $1 million in equity in a property that is worth $5 million. (There is a $4 million mortgage.) Now if $1 million in equity doubles in ten years, a $5 million property will be worth $10 million over the same period. If you subtract the original $4 million bank loan, you have a $6 million equity in ten years. And now if you add the income on your investment, which could be an additional $1 million, that $6 million becomes $7 million— lost because of a $1 million estate-tax bill.

It is bad enough to lose $7 million over the course of ten years, but your children and grandchildren will continue that family unit for at least another fifty years. How would that property have grown over their lifetime? The figures are almost inconceivable: even if we cut the growth to 8% annually and eliminate *any* yearly income, fifty years from now, the $7 million will have grown to $328 million. Taxes are more expensive than you may ever have realized.

Later in this book you will find a chapter on the interest-adjusted net cost index. This is a method that the government requires insurance companies to use to show the true cost for any life insurance purchased. It simply adds an interest factor to whatever is spent. The theory is if you do not spend that dollar and invest it at a stated return, it will have grown to X plus that return. We have applied that government formula to the original $1 million in taxes, and have found that the true cost, over a sixty-year period, would be $328 million on an interest-adjusted basis. Wouldn't it be easier to buy a $1 million life insurance policy?

Let Insurance Pay the Tax

We now come to the fourth and most logical way to pay estate taxes: through life insurance. Let the insurance company pay those estate taxes in a "pay as you go" plan.

In other words, the insurance company tells you, "We will put a million dollars away for you, and when your estate needs it because you died and your taxes have to be paid, we'll pay them for you."

What will they charge you for that million dollars? If you are 35 years old, they will charge you $11,000 annually (the Extralife-Economatic rate), which is equivalent to 1.1% of that million dollars.

Would you rather borrow money later and pay it back with after-tax dollars paying an interest rate of 10%, 15%, or even 20%, or would you rather start paying now at a cost of one percent? And *is* it a true cost of one percent? Actually it's not, because by the third or fourth year, depending on your age, the cash value of the policy is equivalent to the premium outlay. Once the acquisition cost is paid, your life insurance is simply a transfer of assets. And if you buy the insurance in a certain manner, you may even be able to make it tax deductible.

Either you pay the insurance company now or you pay the government later. Which is less costly?

If you are 45 years old, the Extralife-Economatic premium for $1 million is approximately $17,000 or 1.7%. At age 56, the premium is $31,000 or 3.1%; and at age 64, it's $50,000 or 5%. In most cases, particularly at the younger ages, you finish paying at the end of twenty-two years and you need divert no additional capital to your insurance.

The 35-year-old man with a $9 million estate will retain his $9 million for his children if he buys $6 million of insurance to cover his taxes. If he doesn't buy the whole amount necessary, any protection is at least a step in the right direction.

Sometimes a man will not buy as much as he needs because he can't see himself making such a large first purchase. It is important for the consumer not only to buy the correct amount of insurance, but to purchase it properly so that it does not become part of the taxable estate. This can be accomplished by having another member of the family buy the life insurance on your life so that the death benefit is not subject to estate taxes. If the family member who bought the insurance dies first, the only thing that would be taxable in his or her estate would be the cash value.

There are other ramifications, particularly in community-property states like California where property is usually owned jointly by spouses. Under those circumstances, if the wife were to die before the husband, he would pay taxes on her estate. Some men feel that when they die they don't care if taxes are paid with their estate assets. However, when their wife dies, they don't like the idea of dissipating estate assets and their working capital to pay substantial taxes at her death. This is where we find wife insurance most prevalent.

There's one additional technical situation that I will touch upon here. It is called "income in respect of a decedent," and it is a problem for anyone with an expected future income, such as composers and writers with royalties, and insurance agents with renewals and so forth. The government says that you will have this future income, and though you have not yet received it, there is a present value to it. As a result, it is included as part of your estate, and your family actually pays estate taxes on these moneys they haven't even received. In such a situation, insurance is urgently needed.

One final example. I own a large business and my son is in the business with me. I want him to continue the business when I die, not only for himself, but as a continuing source of income for my wife. I don't want estate taxes to force him to liquidate. If I do not buy enough insurance to pay estate taxes when I die, my son and my wife will have no business and no income. In this case, insurance bought nominally to preserve the business is really bought to preserve the family unit that uses the business as an economic base.

Talk to a Professional

There are too many uninformed consumers who have been ill-advised as to their estate tax obligations. They have been told that their liquidity will offset the tax. Most qualified estate-planning attorneys and tax accountants are familiar with and make use of insurance in their estate planning. Certain advisers, however, have biases and may not recommend insurance for their own personal reasons. It is unfortunate that someone else's misconceptions can affect the large estate owner. It is the responsibility and obligation of every professional insurance agent to explain all details of estate protection to his client. The client who is fully aware of all options available can then make the appropriate decision.

There is a definite problem in getting the public to understand the value of insurance as an estate preserver. Many people still need estate tax protection and yet have never met a tax attorney or a professional insurance agent. They have been so busy working and building their fortune that they don't find time for this advice; their success makes them so independent that they are difficult to reach. Incompetent advisers have not been their problem—just a closed door. It is vital for the large estate owner to plan for his estate with the help of an insurance agent who has not just technical book knowledge, but also the experience of working with the substantially wealthy, so that they can identify immediately with their needs. Moreover, you will only respect and work with the kind of agent who represents to some degree the type of success you have personally enjoyed.

Not long ago, I had a meeting with an attorney, during which we discussed my speaking before his estate-planning group. He asked me what my topic would be, and I said, "How to save a fortune on your life insurance." He replied that the subject did not seem technical enough for his advanced group. I asked, "What is the purpose of the meeting?" He said it was to discuss the various methods of estate planning. I then asked, "What is the purpose of estate planning?" to which he replied, "To save money."

It is amazing how often substance is sacrificed for form.

22

—— "I'm a Woman. What do I Need?" ——

WHAT HAS BEEN SAID so far in this book probably applied in the past rather more to men than to women. It was often thought that a woman did not need insurance, and that only when she married and had a family was it necessary to protect her life. Insurance questions, in any case, were usually left to husbands. Often a husband simply bought a small policy or added a term insurance rider to his own policy. Today the subject of life insurance for women can no longer be so neatly categorized.

The needs of a woman are no different from those of a man, especially if she is the breadwinner.

Insurance for Today's Women

Women today are as aggressive and intent on establishing their own identity, both social and financial, as are men. If we tell young men that they need life insurance because of their future needs, a future commitment to a family or an estate, we must tell women the same thing.

Security and a self-appraised sense of self-worth can be appreciated by women as well as men, and many are realiz-

179

ing that such security and peace of mind can begin with life insurance. One day a woman may find herself with a business, and with loans, debts, and a partner; and because of ill health, she may not have the ability to buy insurance. Because of that lack of health, she may be unable to consummate a portion of her business plans. If she had made the proper arrangements, by buying life insurance at a younger age when insurable, she would be able to proceed without reservation.

A client of mine walked into a bank and asked for a loan to start a business, telling the banker, "There is only one way I'm not going to be able to pay back this money and that is if I die. In order to protect against that one factor I've purchased a life insurance policy to cover the amount of the loan, which I will pledge to you as collateral."

With that kind of message, she was well received by the banker; he was very impressed with her conviction to pay off the loan at all costs, even in death.

In addition to a business incentive, women recognize the value of life insurance as retirement security. Many women truly understand the fact that cash values in permanent insurance policies are a form of security against all emergencies. And, if the woman does not build an estate that needs insurance for death purposes, in later years, her cash values can be surrendered to create a retirement reserve. Women are often more conservative than men in planning for retirement. They look more to diversification, seeing the retirement advantages of the cash value.

Insurance for Wives

In today's economy, many families have two breadwinners. With this comes the need for life insurance protection.

Specifically, if a man has an income of $30,000 a year and his wife also has an income of $30,000 a year, a death to either spouse would have a tremendous impact on the family's life-style. When a man is accustomed to sharing the support of his family, how long will it take to find someone not only to marry but also to help provide a similar amount of income to guarantee that family's continued standard of living?

It is therefore wise to buy an insurance policy to replace the wife's $30,000 in the event of her premature death. You could also discount her $30,000: after taxes, it would really be $20,000. Because she is not there, the husband would not need to allocate money for her clothes, traveling expenses, and share of the food; these factors could discount the income perhaps another $10,000. With that, the *net loss* to the family unit would only be $10,000—which, based on a 10% return, could be protected by a $100,000 policy. This certainly is not an unreasonable expense; it will at least avoid adding financial stress to the considerable stress associated with the loss of a spouse.

Even if the wife is not a fellow breadwinner, there are other factors that call for similar insurance coverage. A woman is many things to a man beyond simply a mate. He may begin to realize these things in financial terms once she is gone. For example, he may have to hire a maid to replace her housekeeping ability. He may have to go to a tailor where before she did all of the sewing in the family. If she was the cook in the family, he might have to adapt to eating out in restaurants. If the man wants to decorate his house, he might have to go outside to hire an interior designer, while his wife, had she been alive, might have done the same job. Also, when it comes to taking care of children without a wife, the cost of day-care centers, nurses, and baby-sitters would also have to be absorbed. Finally, being single also means larger income taxes.

Reviewing these expenses, a man begins to realize why his wife should be protected by life insurance.

In substantial estates, since a portion of the estate may be in the wife's name or be community property, life insurance is needed to cover estate taxes. A man could not protect his estate with insurance on himself alone. But even if the estate was not in her name, it eventually will be if he dies before her, and there will be a need for insurance at that time.

Aside from the fact that insurance for women has lower rates actuarially because women live longer than men, there are no special insurance plans for women. Anything female-oriented would thus be strictly a marketing approach. This reinforces the idea that insurance is a basic need for either sex, and that the woman must also buy as intelligently as possible.

Unfortunately, men generally don't sell life insurance to women. And, since even women agents do not yet fully understand the great market of potential women buyers, there has not been a strong effort to approach, educate, and service this large interest group. Considering that women make up almost half of the work force in this nation, bringing home an annual income of close to $400 billion, this is one knowledge gap that will have to be filled.

Since so many men die prematurely, women are left to become the heads of many households. As they assume all the responsibilities of the former breadwinner, they must be protected for the benefit of the children. The lack of insurance is far more perilous for the surviving children in case of the wife's death, since there would be neither father nor mother remaining.

As in all life's affairs, women are assuming more responsibilities and one of those responsibilities is the purchase of life insurance for *herself*.

23

— "Am I Too Young for Life Insurance?" —

IT IS CRUCIAL that young people learn the basics of finance—something that is going to affect them for the rest of their lives. It's never too soon to grasp the meaning and importance of life insurance.

I believe strongly that in high school there should be a "life" class taught to seniors, which would educate them in the worlds of finance, philosophy, psychology, communications, and basic social relationships—studies that could be applied to life beyond high school. It would be a course in everyday living, dealing with such subjects as savings accounts, the stock market, investments, buying clothes and food, job hunting, marriage, and so forth.

Learning about money would be a vital part of this class. The student would become acquainted with the principles of banking, loans and mortgages, house buying, credit, and the meaning and value of insurance. Students would learn the reasons for taxation, putting basic political science and economics to practical use.

What Life Insurance Can Mean to a Young Person

Most young people are uneducated about the meaning and value of life insurance. They may not realize the worth of their current policies taken out for them previously by their parents, policies that may have developed sizable cash values.

A recent example concerned the son of a Los Angeles businessman. This was during the period when municipal bonds issued by the city of Long Beach were priced to yield 12% tax-free interest. The son, now 15, had a policy for $100,000 with an annual premium of $1,000. The policy was eleven years old and had approximately $10,000 in cash value. We took a look at the policy and compared it to the new Extralife-Economatic policies, finding that for an additional $390—or a total of $1,390 annually—we could multiply his insurance by 2½ and purchase $250,000.

This we did. Then we surrendered his old policy, which had $10,000 in cash value, and bought 12% Long Beach municipal bonds, which guaranteed a yearly interest return of $1,200. We netted the $1,200 tax-free interest against the $1,390 new premium. The bottom line was that the outlay by the client was now $190, versus the previous $1,000; and instead of $100,000, the client had $250,000 of insurance, plus another $10,000 invested in the tax-free bond.

This policy will be completely paid up in twenty-five years. It will have its own larger cash value because of the larger premium, and the young man will begin receiving, in cash, a dividend before age 40, since the dividends will be larger than the yearly premium. Finally, if you compound that $810 savings ($1,000 versus $190) over the young man's next fifty years, you will find that he will be saving hundreds of thousands of dollars, besides having a larger life insurance policy.

That is just one example. There are millions of policies like it for which families are paying unnecessarily exorbitant premiums. Because young people are uneducated in finance and compound interest, and even ignorant as to their actual insurance protection, many cannot properly review their policies alone.

"Jumping Juveniles"

In the old days, children's insurance was always a matter of merchandising. The insurance agent came in and sold the proud parents of a newborn child a very unpractical policy like the expensive limited-pay whole life. While it may have been difficult to sell a policy on the father, agents were very successful in selling a policy on the new child. They would tell the parents to look ahead and see that if the policy was bought now on this baby, by the time the child was twenty years old, the policy would be paid in full and the money would be available for college expenses.

I have always objected to these policies because they were usually purchased before the breadwinner, the father, was adequately insured. Usually the oldest, he was therefore the most likely to die. Certainly, the child was the least likely to die and no family wanted to benefit on the child's death.

One of the more popular insurance plans for youngsters was a progressive plan that started at perhaps $25,000 and could be expanded by increments of $25,000 every three years. Under such a plan, insurance taken out at age 21 could be expanded without examination at ages 24, 27, 30, 33, 36, and 40.

These plans were wonderful because they provided coverage when the child was insurable and guaranteed future insurability. It was also permanent insurance, not limited-pay whole life, and the costs were minimal and easily absorbed by a family that had already taken care of its own insurance needs. Such plans and other marketing approaches that expanded coverage from its original amount were often called "Jumping Juveniles."

Student Insurance

For years, students were victimized by agents selling expensive policies "on time," getting young people into debt from the beginning, offering them exorbitant plans which they did not need, and hurting their financial future rather than helping them.

Students were told that they could pay back the money over a period of years. Because it didn't impair their immediate cash flow, many students bought what they thought was a free lunch.

The problem with that type of insurance was that when the students finally realized what they had done, they tried to unravel the mess and quickly ran into legal difficulties in which large loans were suddenly outstanding. The outcome of that situation was that a very bad taste developed for future discussions of life insurance and that all insurance agents became suspect.

Buying Life Insurance Young

How can younger persons with a very limited budget buy life insurance when it may seem like the lowest of current priorities?

They should take the time to plan with their agent programs that stay within their budget, involving initially very small increments of insurance that could be increased in later years. It is important not to be misled into unnecessary debt to start such a program. This is an elective plan and therefore causes very little drain on available cash.

We may be witnessing the beginning of a new era of life

insurance awareness among young people in this country. The breadwinners of the future are beginning to ask questions. And, like the parents of the young man who reduced his cash outlay from $1,000 to $190, they are beginning to see how life insurance should work. They realize that the time to buy is now when insurance is inexpensive and the opportunity to create a great deal of protection for their future families or business is within their grasp.

Young people have that chance. Whether they take advantage of it will depend on their realizing that the revolution in life insurance is their revolution as well.

24

----- "The Bargain of a Lifetime": -----
Wonderful Gifts for
Your Child and Grandchild

NEW OPPORTUNITIES are available today in the form of insurance "gifts." Because of the dramatic lowering of insurance premiums in the last few years, an insurance policy purchased upon the birth of a child will offer some very substantial benefits by the time that child reaches his early twenties, or college age. Also, because of policies like the Extralife-Economatic, premiums for that very same policy will stop in the child's twenties. The child will have a paid-up insurance policy and no out-of-pocket expenses. No wonder that insurance bought in this way is referred to as the "bargain of a lifetime."

From Grandparent to Grandchild

As I have said, purchasing insurance on infants should not be considered until both parents are adequately insured. In the case of a substantial insurance "gift," if the parents cannot afford to benefit the child in this way, the grandparents may step in and help. They may be in a more stable financial situation, and thus in the best position to help provide such a "gift." In so doing, they may benefit as well.

189

In addition to becoming a straight gift to the child, in certain instances that money transferred from grandparent to grandchild can be used to purchase insurance on the father or mother, so that upon their death, there will be additional money available for the children to pay estate taxes.

This interesting approach is frequently utilized in estate planning. First, such a "gift" takes taxable money out of the grandparents' estate. Second, for those grandparents who are concerned that the money they leave in trust for their grandchildren will be spent by the parents for their own emergencies, such an insurance gift allows an amount of cash eventually to filter down to the grandchildren.

Third, if the insurance policy is bought by the children on their parents, the death benefit is taken out of the parents' estate, leaving the benefits to the children, who, actuarially, are considered the least likely to die.

Finally, such a gift provides a practical way for the parents to be insured, allowing them the luxuries of insurance without the responsibility for the premiums.

Keeping the death benefit out of the parents' and grandparents' estates is a vital reason for having children buy the insurance. If the grandparents can afford such an insurance gift, it is a present that will eventually benefit everyone.

Additionally, insurance gifts allow the grandparents to take advantage of the $3,000 gift tax exemption that the government allows. If both grandparents take advantage of this exemption, $6,000 could be made available for such gifts. In these revolutionary times, $3,000 to $6,000 can buy a great deal of life insurance, especially on an infant's very insurable life.

An Insurance Gift

Let us take a look at a typical insurance gift purchased

through the Extralife-Economatic plan on a one-year-old infant for a $1 million policy (see Table 11).

The premium for the policy is $3,775 annually, until the twentieth year. In that year dividends, which are used to reduce the premium, bring the premium down to $511, followed by $373 in the twenty-first year, $302 in the twenty-second year; until by the twenty-sixth year, no more premiums need be paid. In that same twenty-sixth year, in addition to his $1 million in insurance coverage, that young person now has $120,312 in cash available at 8% guaranteed simple interest. This sum could be used to help buy a house, or finance extra college expenses. All of these opportunities are now available at absolutely no cost. In fact, because of the size of the dividends, this policy is already returning cash to the fortunate policyholder.

There are other exciting approaches to this program, requiring only six payments and then no more payments for the rest of the individual's life. However, through the miracle of compound interest, hundreds of thousands of dollars will be made available over a lifetime (see Table 12).

The Benefits of a Life-Insurance Gift

Although grandparents do create other financial gifts for their grandchildren, including the usual stocks, mutual funds, savings accounts, trust funds, and different types of investment bonds, they often prefer life insurance as a practical gift, because it provides for their grandchildren much more than a supply of money that could be spent carelessly. No other gift can provide the protection of the life insurance gift.

Obviously, the impact of the insurance revolution is felt quite strongly here because the lower rates allow grandparents to buy quite substantial amounts of insurance as gifts. Should the grandparent die before completing premium payments on the infant's policy, the child can be protected by a payor provision in which the insurance company continues to pay premiums—a kind of insurance policy on the insurance policy. It is similar to the waiver of premium benefit, which will be discussed in a later chapter.

Although it is not recommended for most insurance situations, grandparents who would like to pay off their premiums sooner can purchase limited-pay whole life policies that are paid up in five or ten years, or even shorter periods of time if so desired. Grandparents might utilize a limited-pay approach if they are buying the insurance gift in their seventies or eighties, because they certainly do not want to pay premiums for more than a few years. If they have the money to provide the insurance gift, it is perfectly natural to pay the premiums quickly so that the grandchild or his parent has the benefit of a policy that needs no additional premium dollars.

Inflation and the reduction in premium costs are making the effect of these insurance gifts even more dramatic. Twenty years ago, certain life insurance plans would barely double their cash values over a child's lifetime. Now, utilizing plans like the Extralife-Economatic, larger face amounts are actually quadrupling in certain cases, creating astonishing cash values for their policyholders, all at no future costs.

The fact that a child will have such an amount of available cash some day, plus the protection of a substantial insurance policy that has long since been paid for, cannot help but benefit his parents, who now have one less insurance worry.

And for grandparents who would like to spend their twilight years confident that their grandchildren's need for the future will be adequately met, there is nothing more wonderful than the insurance gift. It is truly the "bargain of a lifetime."

Table 11. Extralife Illustration

DEATH BENEFIT:

YEAR ONE	1,000,000

YEAR TWO AND THEREAFTER

Sum Insured	615,000
Supp. Insurance	385,000
TOTAL Insurance	1,000,000

POLICY: Extralife
DIVIDEND: Supplemental Ins. Benefits Until
OPTION: Crossover then reduce premiums

AGE/SEX: 1 MALE	
TELEPHONE: 277-9374	
ANNUAL PREMIUM:	3,775.00
PREMIUM WAIVER:	150.00

POLICY YEAR	ANNUAL PREMIUM (1)	PREVIOUS* YEAR DIVIDEND (2)	TOTAL PREMIUMS PAID (3)	TOTAL* POLICY VALUE (4)	TOTAL* PREMIUMS PAID LESS TOTAL VALUE (5)	TOTAL* DEATH BENEFIT (6)	PAID-UP* INSURANCE (7)
1	3775		3775	510	3265	1000000	9708
2	3775	510	7550	928	6622	1000000	17202
3	3775	910	11325	1440	9885	1000000	25948
4	3775	981	15100	2060	13040	1000000	36021
5	3775	1061	18875	2804	16071	1000000	47503
6	3775	1150	22650	3884	18766	1000000	63654
7	3775	1450	26425	5178	21247	1000000	81984
8	3775	1606	30200	7761	22439	1000000	113182
9	3775	1734	33975	11995	21980	1000000	159726
10	3775	1903	37750	16577	21173	1000000	207279
11	3775	2045	41525	22080	19445	1000000	261027
12	3775	2207	45300	27964	17336	1000000	315173
13	3775	2334	49075	34255	14820	1000000	369898
14	3775	2490	52850	40994	11856	1000000	425463
15	3775	2674	56625	48172	8453	1000000	481458

POLICY YEAR	ANNUAL PREMIUM (1)	PREVIOUS* YEAR DIVIDEND (2)	TOTAL PREMIUMS PAID (3)	TOTAL* POLICY VALUE (4)	TOTAL* PREMIUMS PAID LESS TOTAL VALUE (5)	TOTAL* DEATH BENEFIT (6)	PAID-UP* INSURANCE (7)
16	3775	2833	60400	55828	4572	1000000	632171#
17	3775	3012	64175	63882	293	1000000	696998#
18	3775	3092	67950	72318	+4368	1000000	760293#
19	3768	3119	71718	81267	+9549	1000000	823086#
20	511	3264	72229	87348	+15119	1000000	852096#
21	373	3402	72602	92251	+19649	1000000	866511#
22	302	3473	72904	97385	+24481	1000000	880411#
23	216	3559	73120	102727	+29607	1000000	893491#
24	152	3623	73272	108326	+35054	1000000	906020#
25	81	3694	73353	114194	+40841	1000000	917989#
26	+7	3782	73346	120312	+46966	1000000	929208#
27	+78	3853	73268	126740	+53472	1000000	940044#
28	+188	3963	73080	133429	+60349	1000000	950088#
29	+275	4050	72805	140427	+67622	1000000	959657#
30	+385	4160	72420	147719	+75299	1000000	968552#
31	+486	4261	71934	155340	+83406	1000000	976968#
32	+599	4374	71335	163269	+91934	1000000	984681#
33	+697	4472	70638	171555	+100917	1000000	991954#
34	+816	4591	69822	180212	+110390	1000000	998813#
35	+953	4728	68869	189205	+120336	1000000	1005106#
36	+1096	4871	67773	198549	+130776	1000000	1010923#
37	+1249	5024	66524	208233	+141709	1000000	1016250#
38	+1390	5165	65134	218274	+153140	1000000	1021287#
39	+1585	5360	63549	228586	+165037	1000000	1025671#
40	+1738	5513	61811	239220	+177409	1000000	1029716#
41	+1903	5678	59908	250154	+190246	1000000	1033358#

Age							
42	+2069	5844	57839	261407	+203568	1000000	1036668#
43	+2250	6025	55589	272960	+217371	1000000	1039588#
44	+2417	6192	53172	284833	+231661	1000000	1042209#
45	+2598	6373	50574	297010	+246436	1000000	1044507#
46	+2779	6554	47795	309487	+261692	1000000	1046523#
47	+2956	6731	44839	322267	+277428	1000000	1048310#
48	+3157	6932	41682	335303	+293621	1000000	1049777#
49	+3327	7102	38355	348614	+310259	1000000	1051040#
50	+3510	7285	34845	362194	+327349	1000000	1052140#
51	+3715	7490	31130	375994	+344864	1000000	1052989#
52	+3896	7671	27234	390035	+362801	1000000	1053671#
53	+4085	7860	23149	404277	+381128	1000000	1054132#
54	+4258	8033	18891	418731	+399840	1000000	1054442#
55	+4428	8203	14463	433384	+418921	1000000	1054615#
56	+4607	8382	9856	448196	+438340	1000000	1054619#
57	+4762	8537	5094	463155	+458061	1000000	1054495#
58	+4910	8685	184	478249	+478065	1000000	1054282#
59	+5068	8843	+4884	493426	+498310	1000000	1053920#
60	+5201	8976	+10085	508684	+518769	1000000	1053485#
AGE 60	+5068	8843	+4884	493426	+498310	1000000	1053920#
AGE 65	+5625	9400	+32030	569862	+601892	1000000	1050778#
AGE 70	+6985	10760	63124	645626	+708750	1000000	1048806#

#BASED ON CONTRACTUAL PAID-UP PRIVILEGE.

Note: A number of the figures above include dividends that are not guaranteed but are based on the current dividend schedule, which may be changed at any time.

How the Six-Payment Plan Works

A parent or grandparent can purchase a $1 million death benefit for a 7-year-old child and have costs for only six years. With a 50% tax bracket the after-tax cost beginning in the eighth year is $0.

The program works as follows: The parent will pay four full premiums of $6,422 (A in Table 12) to qualify the policy for tax-deductible interest. In the fifth year there will be no cost (B on the schedule) and in the sixth year the after-tax cost would be $2,812 (C on the schedule). The seventh-year cost after tax would be $412 (D on the schedule). Beginning in the eighth year, a loan will be taken from the policy to pay the premium and reimburse the parent for the after-tax cost of the interest (please note: the parent actually writes a check yearly for the full interest to the insurance company).

Even though the premiums and after-tax interest are being paid with the cash value of the policy, the loan reserve account will continue to grow (e.g., at age 38—or year 31—there will be a loan value available of $110,918 (E on the schedule). The death benefit, since the dividends are purchasing paid-up additions, will never go below $1 million and, as you can see, is constantly growing (e.g., at age 43—year 36—the death benefit has grown to $2,046,207 (F on the schedule).

The proposal projects the yearly premium, loan, loan reserve account, interest, total outlay, after-tax outlay, additional insurance, and total death benefit at age 85.

Table 12. FLEXIBLE DEPOSIT SCHEDULE

$1,587,301 EXTRALIFE

SIX-PAYMENT PLAN

AGE–07F

DIVIDENDS PAID-UP ADDITIONS

BASIC PREMIUM $6,421.82

YEAR	PREMIUM DUE	ANNUAL LOAN	RESERVE LOAN ACCOUNT	INTEREST AT 8.00%	TOTAL OUTLAY	AFTER TAX OUTLAY	TOTAL DEATH BENEFIT
1	6,422	(0)	0	0	6,422	6,422(A)	1,609,523
2	6,422	(0)	1,381	0	6,422	6,422(A)	1,049,205
3	6,422	(0)	3,145	0	6,422	6,422(A)	1,077,777
4	6,422	(0)	5,099	0	6,422	6,422(A)	1,106,348
5	6,422	(6,421)	868	0	0	0(B)	1,131,159
6	6,422	(3,866)	0	513	3,069	2,812(C)	1,160,317
7	6,422	(6,421)	647	823	823	412(D)	1,188,302
8	6,422	(7,090)	1,097	1,336	668	0	1,217,152
9	6,422	(7,373)	1,747	1,904	952	0	1,245,696
10	6,422	(7,668)	2,603	2,493	1,247	0	1,277,097
11	6,422	(7,975)	4,460	3,107	1,554	0	1,309,753
12	6,422	(8,294)	6,600	3,745	1,873	0	1,342,064
13	6,422	(8,626)	9,085	4,409	2,205	0	1,375,605
14	6,422	(8,971)	11,901	5,099	2,550	0	1,410,360
15	6,422	(9,330)	15,122	5,816	2,908	0	1,444,728
16	6,422	(9,703)	18,764	6,563	3,282	0	1,480,280
17	6,422	(10,091)	22,855	7,339	3,670	0	1,515,413
18	6,422	(10,495)	27,380	8,146	4,073	0	1,551,697
19	6,422	(10,915)	32,397	8,986	4,493	0	1,585,941
20	6,422	(11,351)	37,933	9,859	4,930	0	1,619,713
21	6,422	(11,805)	42,044	10,767	5,384	0	1,652,994
22	6,422	(12,277)	46,594	11,712	5,856	0	1,685,766
23	6,422	(12,769)	51,550	12,694	6,347	0	1,718,007

YEAR	PREMIUM DUE	ANNUAL LOAN	RESERVE LOAN ACCOUNT	INTEREST AT 8.00%	TOTAL OUTLAY	AFTER TAX OUTLAY	TOTAL DEATH BENEFIT
24	6,422	(13,279)	56,994	13,716	6,858	0	1,748,109
25	6,422	(13,811)	62,951	14,778	7,389	0	1,777,637
26	6,422	(14,363)	69,414	15,883	7,942	0	1,806,569
27	6,422	(14,938)	76,448	17,032	8,516	0	1,834,881
28	6,422	(15,535)	85,560	18,227	9,114	0	1,862,547
29	6,422	(16,156)	92,389	19,470	9,735	0	1,887,954
30	6,422	(16,803)	101,321	20,762	10,381	0	1,912,664
31	6,422	(17,475)	110,918(E)	22,107	11,054	0	1,938,235
32	6,422	(18,174)	121,183	23,505	11,753	0	1,961,464
33	6,422	(18,901)	132,102	24,959	12,480	0	1,983,907
34	6,422	(19,657)	143,661	26,471	13,236	0	2,005,535
35	6,422	(20,443)	155,831	28,043	14,022	0	2,026,312
36	6,422	(21,261)	168,667	29,679	14,840	0	2,046,207(F)
37	6,422	(22,111)	182,137	31,380	15,690	0	2,066,771
38	6,422	(22,996)	196,295	33,149	16,575	0	2,083,205
39	6,422	(23,916)	211,077	34,988	17,494	0	2,100,232
40	6,422	(24,872)	226,504	36,902	18,451	0	2,116,226
41	6,422	(25,867)	242,571	38,890	19,445	0	2,131,166
42	6,422	(26,901)	259,202	40,959	20,480	0	2,143,382
43	6,422	(27,977)	276,301	43,112	21,556	0	2,156,023
44	6,422	(29,096)	293,956	45,350	22,675	0	2,165,868
45	6,422	(30,260)	312,019	47,678	23,839	0	2,176,044
46	6,422	(31,471)	330,460	50,098	25,049	0	2,183,325
47	6,422	(32,730)	349,200	52,616	26,308	0	2,189,246
48	6,422	(34,039)	368,203	55,235	27,618	0	2,193,753
49	6,422	(35,400)	387,314	57,958	28,979	0	2,196,790
50	6,422	(36,816)	406,523	60,790	30,395	0	2,196,710
51	6,422	(38,289)	425,582	63,735	31,868	0	2,196,627

52	6,422	(39,821)	444,446	66,798	33,399	0	2,191,716
53	6,422	(41,414)	462,923	69,984	34,992	0	2,186,671
54	6,422	(43,070)	480,846	73,297	36,649	0	2,178,250
55	6,422	(44,793)	498,016	76,473	38,372	0	2,167,968
56	6,422	(46,585)	514,335	80,326	40,163	0	2,154,164
57	6,422	(48,448)	529,482	84,053	42,027	0	2,138,348
58	6,422	(50,386)	543,263	87,929	43,965	0	2,120,438
59	6,422	(52,402)	555,397	91,960	45,980	0	2,097,177
60	6,422	(54,498)	565,434	96,152	48,076	0	2,074,827
61	6,422	(56,678)	573,292	100,512	50,256	0	2,050,123
62	6,422	(58,945)	578,882	105,046	52,523	0	2,022,970
63	6,422	(61,302)	582,115	109,762	54,881	0	1,993,271
64	6,422	(63,755)	582,895	114,666	57,333	0	1,960,923
65	6,422	(66,305)	581,126	119,766	59,883	0	1,925,822
66	6,422	(68,957)	576,704	125,071	62,536	0	1,887,855
67	6,422	(71,715)	569,523	130,587	65,294	0	1,846,910
68	6,422	(74,584)	559,475	136,325	68,163	0	1,802,867
69	6,422	(77,567)	546,442	142,291	71,146	0	1,755,602
70	6,422	(80,670)	530,307	148,497	74,249	0	1,704,986
71	6,422	(83,897)	510,946	154,950	77,475	0	1,650,885
72	6,422	(87,253)	488,228	161,662	80,831	0	1,593,159
73	6,422	(90,743)	462,020	168,642	84,321	0	1,531,664
74	6,422	(94,373)	432,183	175,902	87,951	0	1,466,249
75	6,422	(98,147)	398,570	183,452	91,726	0	1,396,757
76	6,422	(102,073)	361,032	191,304	95,652	0	1,323,025
77	6,422	(106,156)	319,411	199,470	99,735	0	1,244,884
78	6,422	(110,403)	273,543	207,962	103,981	0	1,162,156

Note: A number of figures above include dividends that are not guaranteed but are based on the current dividend schedule which may be changed at any time.

25

———— "I Want My Money!" ————
How to Benefit in Life and/or Death

THERE ARE numerous misconceptions about getting your life insurance money. Many people still believe that the only benefit one gets from life insurance comes after death, and that any money put into a life insurance policy will never be seen again. By now, you are probably beginning to get the idea that this is *not* so.

Many consumers have never been informed about surrender values, dividends, cross-over points, borrowing of cash values, and so forth. Insurance does have benefits in life as well as in death, and these benefits, if understood, can make the purchase of life insurance much easier.

There are four basic ways to get your money: (1) by a death benefit, (2) through surrender value, (3) through borrowing on your cash reserves, and (4) through dividends.

Death Benefit

The death benefit is by far the simplest way to get your money. When you die, your beneficiary receives the face amount of your policy. This is the whole purpose of life insurance, and it is virtually the only income-tax-free wind-fall ever created. The death benefit can be paid out in a lump sum, or it can be paid out in installments as in an annuity. However it is paid out, this large sum of cash is made available. The payment of a death benefit is similar in both term and permanent insurance policies.

Surrender Value

In a permanent policy, if you decide to surrender your policy before you die, you receive the amount of cash value in your policy that is being held in reserve to keep the premium level. So if you purchased a $100,000 policy at age 35 and you decide to surrender it at age 50, you will get your cash value back, which in this case is $18,000.

Borrowing on Cash Value

The third way to get your money is by borrowing on your cash value, which is always available for such a purpose. The attractiveness of borrowing on your cash value is the guaranteed interest rate and the fact that you don't have to pay back the loan. It is simply deducted from the face amount of your policy at death. So, if at age 50 you borrow your cash value, instead of surrendering it, you will retain the policy, with a face value of only $82,000 ($100,000 − $18,000). There are ways to keep that face amount level, even after borrowing, and we will discuss them later.

Dividends

In addition to your surrender values, in participating plans, you also have the right to your dividends. There are five ways to utilize dividends: (1) you can receive them in cash annually; (2) you can keep them accumulating at interest; (3) you can utilize them to reduce your premium; (4) you can purchase paid-up adds; or, finally, (5) you can employ the fifth dividend option, which purchases increasing term insurance to the extent of your cash value and will provide at death the face amount plus the cash value of the policy.

Because of the increase in inflation, the reduction in mortality tables, and the increased productivity of insurance companies, dividends have been increasing in recent years. When consumers use them to reduce premiums, they spend even less on their policies, and actually get money back in less time than ever before.

With Extralife-Economatic policies, the dividend can be big enough by the twentieth year to reduce the entire premium substantially. If the dividends continue to be used to reduce the premium, the consumer may find there is nothing left to pay—he actually receives money back from the insurance company.

For instance, Jack S. buys a $100,000 Extralife-Economatic policy at age 29. He is paying $855 annually for the insurance. His policy is from a participating company, and in the twenty-second year he decides to use his dividends to reduce his premium. In the twenty-third year, the dividend is larger than his premium, allowing him a net dividend of $88, after paying the full premium with the dividend. The year after, he receives a net dividend of $134, and so forth.

Because of new policies like Extralife-Economatic and the dividends they offer, many consumers may pay premiums for only a little over twenty years if they eventually use the dividends to reduce the premium. After that, their insurance is paid for automatically and net dividends are on the way. Naturally, these dividends are not guaranteed.

The Fifth Dividend Option

In times of emergency, borrowing on cash reserves in your permanent insurance policy can be a very important option. Usually, you can borrow to the extent of everything but the interest, which your company will hold back in reserve. If you have a 5% interest loan policy, then you can borrow 95% of your cash value. If you have a 8% interest loan policy, you can borrow 92% of the cash value. In this way, the insurance company has retained enough cash value to cover the interest should you decide to surrender your policy.

Rather than reduce their premiums, some consumers prefer to use their dividends to buy term insurance to guarantee their cash values. Thus, even if they do borrow on their cash values, the face value of the policy will always remain level, and the consumer's beneficiary will receive the face value, plus the cash value, less any loan. This is the often mentioned fifth dividend option, which has been popular for many years.

The problem with the fifth dividend option is that the cost of term insurance purchased by the dividend rises every year, so that eventually the dividend is not large enough to pay for the term insurance needed to cover the cash value and guarantee the face amount.

Even if you do not borrow on the cash value, the dividend can still be utilized to buy term insurance, guaranteeing the beneficiary both the face amount and the cash value. However, few agents will now recommend this option, especially those who understand the new types of policies available.

For many years, agents used the fifth dividend option to answer those who claimed you couldn't get your cash value in death. Also, many sophisticated agents saw the value of an option that protected the face amount of the policy if borrowing against the cash value did occur during emergencies.

Insurance Is Money

The most important aspect of benefiting in life and/or death with your policy is having the proper relationship with an excellent insurance agent. If you can communicate what your current and future objectives are, he or she will be able to accommodate them all.

Insurance is money. Money may be too expensive to keep in the bank for future emergency use. Your insurance can provide that money for you and your family in life and/or death.

26

—— "I'm Ready. Bring on the Agent!" ——
Preparing for Your Next Insurance Interview

IN THIS BOOK we have tried to alert you to a number of facts and trends in the insurance industry. We hope that, armed with this information, you will now have the ability to prepare yourself for an insurance interview—to know how to ask the meaningful questions that will get you the answers you need. Now you know what to look for.

You should understand as well how to calculate your business and personal needs, how to plan your insurance objectives, and how to follow insurance agents' discussions objectively and without preconceived notions.

It is important that you express your own needs clearly, and also try to ascertain your agent's intentions and professional qualifications.

Feel Free to Question

Above all, feel free to question agents.

How long have they been in the business? Do they have career positions, or are they moonlighting? What understanding do they have of finance?

If agents are young, their youth may be compensated for

207

by a greater aggressiveness; they may also be more dynamically in tune with the modern insurance world. The older agent may, in turn, have correspondingly greater knowledge and experience.

Make sure that you know something about the companies that agents represent and how they work with those companies—whether as exclusive agents, dealing with only one company, or as brokers who deal with different companies.

Also, how do companies compare in terms of competitive pricing? The better agents gravitate to the better companies.

Don't hesitate to ask about commissions. Be careful of agents who are collecting larger commissions.

It is important to find out whether agents meet your particular insurance needs and whether they suit your personality and type of business. Find out what kind of clientele they handle, and whether they usually deal with estate situations or basic family insurance.

And are they flexible? Be wary of agents who are intent on merchandising only one set plan such as Split Dollar or Section 79. You want to be treated as an individual, not sold a ready-made policy that does not fit your needs.

Ask for Examples

Ask for frequent examples.

Be sure agents show you how particular plans have worked for others. Obviously, it is an advantage if an individual agent has dealt with your friends, because then you can determine what kind of treatment they have received. If the agent is a stranger, ask for similar examples that allow you to see your potential plan at work.

Give an agent a job to do, such as reevaluating your present coverage. Take a careful look at that evaluation and the suggestions that go with it. Even if you presently have an insurance agent with whom you are satisfied and who is completely loyal to you, you ought to double-check your present coverage periodically in order to be sure that you are getting the right figures and the best coverage based on the newest developments in the field.

There is nothing wrong with showing a prospective new agent's work to another agent. If both agents have integrity and have your best interest in mind, you can lose nothing by having the evaluation compared.

Don't Be Secretive

Do not be secretive with an agent who wants to evaluate your situation.

Treat an insurance interview like your annual physical; you must disrobe and subject yourself to the physician's complete examination. You don't say to your doctor, "It hurts—guess where?"

Insurance agents cannot play these games. They must have all of the facts in front of them, in order to make a proper appraisal of your financial situation. Whether it is a copy of last year's tax statement, your present income, a copy of your present insurance policy, or the size of your estate, everything must be revealed.

You should not be frightened of the potential of insurance savings through possible replacement or comparative bidding on new policy purchases. The insurance interview is an opportunity for an enlightening financial review. Because of the changes in life insurance, you can now treat your financial situation as you would your physical condition. And every consumer over age 40 must have an annual checkup.

Screen Your Agent

Obviously, it would be ideal to preinterview every agent that comes your way. In practice, however, insurance encounters are very spontaneous. Someone calls you on the telephone; you turn him down. You get direct-mail letters; you throw them away. Then someone dies in your family, you change jobs, or you simply get motivated for one reason or another. Unless you have an immediate contact, you rarely do more than wait for the next caller, the next letter, or simply the first agent who walks through your door.

Although life insurance is such an important purchase, most analysis by consumers comes down to a question of price. Very rarely is it based on an evaluation of total services, facilities, and the credibility of the agent. Remember, though, that while price is of great importance, it is really only one of many other long-term considerations.

While no one expects you to become an expert on the subject of insurance, it is vitally important to keep an open mind. Your insurance agent is a professional, just as much as your accountant, financial adviser, or lawyer. Deal with him or her as a professional, and you'll find you will get the best insurance service possible.

27

"Customize My Policy": ——— Creative Options in Life Insurance

You HAVE DECIDED to fill a need. You have picked your company, your agent, your type of policy, and the amount you can spend, in accordance with your budget. Now we come to the most important point of all: How do you buy that insurance? How do you customize or individualize that policy and adjust it to your own personal needs?

Questions you should ask include: Do I buy the insurance personally? Do I have my wife or child buy the policy on me so that they own it and, therefore, it is not part of my estate when I die and not subject to estate taxes?

Do I utilize a pension or profit-sharing plan to buy the insurance so that I don't impair my personal or corporate cash flow, utilizing instead an already allocated sum of pension or profit-sharing money? In certain cases, can my life insurance be made tax deductible?

Do I pay for the policy with pretax corporate dollars or do I use any personal funds available? What type of cash flow is best suited to this policy?

These are a few of the many questions that must be answered once the policy is purchased. If the consequences of each of the options are not fully understood, a great part of the objectives and need for the insurance could be neutralized.

The problem many insurance agents have is that once they explain these options, the client may take what proves to be the line of least resistance. Consumers are prone to buy insurance in the easiest and safest way possible. The agent may suggest a plan that involves using pension or profit-sharing moneys, but because the plan may be difficult to understand, the client may eventually have the agent buy the policy with personal funds. Because this is the only way the client feels comfortable with the policy, the agent will go along, knowing that although the client did buy the insurance, satisfying the needs to be met, the policy was not purchased in the most cost-effective way.

Filling the client's need is the most vital factor. While there are various ways to purchase the policy, additional options can further customize the policy to the individual.

How Do You Pay?

One interesting question is: How will you pay for your insurance? Will you pay annually, semiannually, quarterly, or monthly? How you pay for your insurance policy determines how much it actually costs.

Did you know that the cheapest way to buy your insurance is the *single-premium method*? With this method, you might buy a $100,000 policy outright for $32,000, depending on age. In most cases, this is the wrong way. That $32,000 could produce $3,000 in interest alone—which could more than pay the yearly premium. Still you would be paying less for the policy.

Similarly, if you were to pay cash for a $100,000 house, you would be saving a great deal of money over your lifetime, for that house might well eventually cost you $400,000 if you paid monthly payments instead.

An insurance policy is nothing more than money that the insurance company promises to pay your beneficiaries on your death. And because policies are discounted at interest, a $100,000 policy may cost you only $32,000. Most people cannot afford the single-premium method, just as few people can pay cash for their houses. Instead, you may decide to pay $2,000 a year for your insurance, or $575 quarterly, or maybe $175 a month. Because the insurance company calculates an interest figure into the premium, the smaller the amount you pay each period, the larger the total sum you will eventually pay for your life insurance.

There was a time when people did pay a premium in one lump sum. They then borrowed the cash value and *deducted the interest*. Since the interest would usually be enough to pay the entire premium, that was a way to make insurance premiums tax deductible.

However, as is often the case, the government stepped in and determined that when you paid a single premium, you were not entitled to deduct the interest when you borrowed on the cash value. Since consumers do not want to tie up a large amount of cash for no immediate reason, the single-premium method has been all but abandoned. Occasionally, a grandparent may want to provide for the grandchildren with a single payment, but even that type of gift is now a rarity.

Waiver of Premium

Among the additional options available is the *waiver of premium*. A fee for this option is added to the premium.

If you utilize this option and you lose your health and cannot work, the insurance company will pay the premiums for you. You do not owe the insurance company anything for this, and they will continue to pay the premiums until you return to work, in accordance with your waiver-of-premium contract. If you have a permanent policy, the insurance company not only waives your premium, but you continue to build up your cash values and dividends. Thus your insurance policy, in effect, serves to operate like a disability plan. You can actually borrow that increasing cash value, or use the dividend to help pay any additional expenses you may have accrued during your illness.

The waiver-of-premium cost is usually very small and well worth the advantages you can derive from its use.

Double Indemnity

You may be familiar with another common insurance clause. It is called *double* or *triple indemnity*. Like the waiver of premium, this option can also be purchased for an additional fee that is tacked on to your premium. In return, the insurance company will pay twice the face amount of your policy if you die in an accident (double indemnity), and triple the face amount if you die in an accident involving a common carrier, such as a train, plane, or bus (triple indemnity), up to contractual limits.

However, if you have bought enough insurance in the first place, there is no need to add such an option, because you have a specific need for money—and that need is not determined by the way you die. You do not buy insurance as a bet that you may die on a plane. And as you might guess, based on the very low fee involved, double or triple indemnity claims are rare.

Life insurance is not a game. It is a solid product in a solid industry that you, as a solid citizen, should use in a manner that best serves your needs. If you cannot afford all the insurance you need, then perhaps the additional option of double or triple indemnity will be most beneficial to make up the deficit; but don't forget it involves a contingency factor.

Riders

The final form of customizing is adding a rider to the regular policy, like attaching an amendment to a congressional bill. There are different types of riders.

A *spouse rider* is usually a small policy attached to the principal income earner's regular policy. The purpose is to provide coverage for both spouses in one policy.

A *children's rider* is usually a small level-term policy. It is also carried on the principal income earner's policy, and is convertible when the child reaches the age of 25.

A *guaranteed insurability* rider requires you to pay a few dollars extra every year so that over a period of possibly the next twenty years, you can purchase additional insurance without evidence of insurability. For example, if you buy a $25,000 policy when you're 30 and healthy, you can pay an additional fee and be able to purchase an additional $25,000 at ages 33, 36, 39, 42, and 45. You might have these five options to buy another $25,000 each time, regardless of your health.

Guaranteed insurability riders are good options to build into young persons' policies. If they lose their health, they will still be able to purchase additional insurance as their needs grow.

Term riders are simply amounts of term insurance added to a permanent insurance policy, usually without charging a separate policy fee. A term rider is usually convertible so that in later years the entire policy may consist of permanent insurance. It provides a method of purchasing additional insurance to cover your current or future needs at the lowest cash outlay.

28

The Interest Adjusted Index:
Comparing the Cost of Money and Policies

WE FEEL the effect of inflation every day. When we pay for gasoline, when we buy milk and bread, when we see the menu at our favorite restaurant, when we visit the local movie theater. Prices are going up, in most cases dramatically.

But what if, in addition to the inflation factor, we had to calculate another factor into our daily purchases? What if we figured in the amount of the interest we would make if we placed that money in a bank savings account instead? At 5% interest, a $4 lunch would cost us $4.20 this year. If that figure were compounded for thirty years, that lunch might cost close to $50. Would we visit that restaurant again, I wonder?

What would happen if we interest-adjusted our yearly income-tax payments? An annual income-tax payment of only $2,000 every year would amount to $440,000 over the course of a lifetime, if the money had been left to compound in a bank account. We might theorize over what would happen to American spending habits under this system. If people understood the true cost of ta :ation and the cost of an unbalanced budget, maybe the national debt would disappear. Maybe inflation would become ancient history. Maybe a taxpayer revolution would ensue.

217

If $2,000 a year, interest adjusted, produces $440,000 in principal and interest over a person's lifetime, can you imagine the effect on taxpayers paying $5,000, $10,000, and $20,000 in yearly taxes—no less the few who pay in excess of $100,000 yearly. The true cost of income taxes on an interest-adjusted basis easily translates into millions of dollars, over a lifetime, for wage earners making over $40,000 annually, depending on their age.

In the next few years, as consumers wake up to the realities of the life insurance revolution, they will give more attention to the cost of insurance policies and the various methods used to determine those costs, including the interest-adjusted method.

The Interest-Adjusted Net-Cost Index

Interest-adjusted net cost indexes have been in use only since 1970. Prior to the introduction of this index, consumers determined the cost of their permanent insurance policies in the traditional manner: cost of premiums minus cash value (and dividends, if applicable).

If you paid a $1,000 premium for twenty years and you built up your cash value of $20,000 over the same period, it was said, *incorrectly*, that your policy really cost nothing and that you came out even.

Many sophisticated agents realized from the beginning that this was false; they would correctly state that the policy cost you nothing *other than the cost of money*. Since you could borrow from your policy at 5% (in those days), the true cost for money in a 50% tax bracket was only 2.5%, since the interest could be tax deductible. To determine the true cost of that policy, it was decided to add an interest factor. It was simply a method of determining the cost of securing that money.

If a businessman was truly a stock market genius and could make 40% on his money in a stock venture, it would not have been proper to add that 40% figure to the insurance costs. He could have borrowed against his policy at a gross cost of 5% and still have made 35%. Since he still made the 35%, the cost of money was only the cost of borrowing that money from his insurance policy to make it available for his investment.

People who claimed they were earning 10%, 20%, and 40% on their investments were really making smaller amounts, since they seldom took into consideration their tax situation. In many cases, they were losing their investments altogether. In most cases, people with substantial investments are in the 50%-to-70% tax bracket, and their return is dramatically less than they envision.

There are problems with a 5% mandatory interest-adjusted cost index. When individual states established the 5% figure—the theory being that you make at least 5% with your money—they were establishing a very liberal figure, especially for people in the higher tax brackets.

In a 50% bracket, you would have to make 10% to net 5%. Furthermore, if you were in a 70% maximum tax bracket (on invested moneys that can be taxed up to 70% by the federal government), you would have to make 20% on your money. While there have been some very high interest rates of late, there is no historic proof that on a long-term basis you could make 10% clear, let alone 20%. These returns are also subjected to state income taxes in many cases.

The interest-adjusted net cost index is familiar to many sophisticated insurance agents who have been utilizing similar cost indexes on a voluntary basis for years. It is one thing when such a method is voluntary, and another when the government singles out the insurance industry to interest-adjust its policies. This is nothing more than adding a cost of money to our products. Why not all consumer products as well?

Problems with the Index

It concerns me, philosophically, that only one product and one industry is interest-adjusted. When you buy a suit of clothes, did the suit cost you $300, or, because you can no longer make 5% on that $300 for the rest of your life, should we add interest to find the true cost? When you pay your secretary's salary, should you interest-adjust her check to determine your true costs? While I am in accord with the *concept* of interest adjustment, and I use it constantly to show cost comparisons on insurance policies from different companies, I again ask the question: Why isn't everything you can buy subject to the same cost index?

It is important to note that an interest-adjusted cost index is not absolute, especially when state governments demand only a twenty-year index. A twenty-year index does not represent the total picture. If the consumer buys his insurance at age 35, by age 55 his dividends may be nearly as big as his premiums, so that he may choose to use the dividends to reduce his premium, and eventually pay no premium at all. In fact, he may actually receive a check every year for the amount by which the dividend exceeds the premium.

Obviously, this information is not reflected in a twenty-year index. Such an interest-adjusted cost index would have to be extended to cover life expectancy to reflect a true cost.

Lower Figures May Not Mean a Better Buy

An additional problem with interest-adjusted net cost indexes is that a lower interest-adjusted figure may not mean that a particular policy is the best buy.

If you pay a larger premium—and you therefore have a

larger cash value—you will have a lower net cost. However, if the premium was substantially larger than a comparable policy, to produce that lower net cost you would have to put the difference at compound interest to reflect the true cost of both policies. In this manner, we find that, in some cases, you cannot utilize interest-adjusted net cost indexes alone to determine the best buy.

The lowest net cost policy might be a Ten-Pay policy. This squeezes the premium into a shorter period so that the premiums will be much higher, resulting in much higher cash values and a lower net cost. Since Ten-Pay limited whole life insurance policies are not competitive products, their low interest-adjusted net cost doesn't indicate a bargain.

To determine a good policy, you often have to look at the going-in premium. You might prefer a lower premium with a little higher interest-adjusted cost, rather than a higher premium with a very low interest-adjusted cost. Remember, you want only enough cash value to keep the premium level over your lifetime.

For example, a $100,000 policy for a 35-year-old man has a yearly premium of $2,062 and an interest-adjusted cost of $2.29 per thousand. Yet I can show you a similar policy for the same amount of insurance for which you would pay $1,628 a year and have an interest-adjusted figure of $2.95 per thousand.

I submit that the client might be better off paying the lower premium of $1,628 and having the slightly higher interest-adjusted figure, than paying a $2,062-a-year premium, particularly if the $434 difference was put to work at compound interest.

Let us consider a $100,000 Extralife-Economatic type policy and compare it to a conventional permanent policy on a 35-year-old man. A conventional policy has a premium of $2,136 a year, and an interest-adjusted net cost of $3.03 per thousand. An Extralife-Economatic plan for the same face amount has an interest-adjusted figure of $3.14. This is more than the $3.03, but the premium outlay is only $1,413 per year. Why quibble over a few pennies on the interest-adjusted figure when there is $723 difference in the annual premium? One final example for this comparison: we found one policy for a nonsmoker with a premium of $1,112 a year with an interest-adjusted figure of $1.88 per thousand. This policy had the lowest premium as well as the lowest interest-adjusted figure.

Compare Carefully

The public is going to find the interest-adjusted index confusing in many cases where it does not present a clear cost comparison. Bearing this in mind, I believe that consumers should purchase policies that give the lowest cash value to sustain a low level premium for a lifetime. And since consumers want to keep as much money in their own pockets, they should try to keep premium outlay down, even if the net cost is a little higher. Naturally, the ideal policy will have both a lower premium and a lower net cost.

By paying careful attention to compound-interest factors, the difference in premiums, and the interest-adjusted net cost index, consumers can save tens of thousands to hundreds of thousands of dollars over the course of a lifetime. Yet many people ignore these factors, preferring to buy from a friend or a brother-in-law, thinking that the prices are not that different and that all companies are the same. But **prices are different**—sometimes astronomically different—and consumers must not thoughtlessly dismiss those differences.

If you look at the $723 saved on that one comparison and compound the differential over the next fifty years, for a 35-year-old, then we may be talking about in excess of $300,000 in savings. These figures are *real*. They must not be ignored.

Tax-Deductible Plans

Finally, another variable is created when life insurance is purchased in a tax-deductible fashion through a pension or profit-sharing plan, which is often the best way to purchase insurance. Because of tax ramifications, utilizing the same product within a pension will produce an even lower interest-adjusted figure, not reflected in any of the available cost indexes.

Buying Right Can Save a Fortune

The twenty-year interest-adjusted net cost index should not be used as a true cost indication of a policy, but only as a method of comparing one company's policies with another. The interest-adjusted net cost index is definitely superior to traditional methods of establishing the cost of insurance policies. One of its primary deficiencies is that it does not examine the cost of premiums past twenty years. However, this should not be allowed to overshadow its valuable cost-comparison information for shoppers who may have been unaware of the extreme price variations of the life insurance industry.

One index or another does allow the insurance agents the information they need to point out that all policies are not alike, and that all companies do not offer the same rates. A little homework can help save a fortune.

PRACTICAL APPLICATIONS

Part Three reveals the specific savings available when consumers choose to take advantage of the insurance revolution. All of the upcoming facts, comparisons, and charts are based on actual case experiences within my own company when new products such as Extralife-Economatic type plans were put to work.

In all cases, the names of actual clients have been removed: when comparisons are featured, the name of the other insurance company has been deleted. It is not my intention here to point to companies and make judgments on their policies and approaches. I am simply trying to present the dramatic facts involved when comparisons are made between the new products available and those featured by others. It is facts like these that highlight the dramatic impact of the life insurance revolution.

Here are the facts that show why consumers can save more money than ever before on their insurance policies.

We have presented a cross section, from the millionaire doctor to the youthful college student. Comparisons are presented on all major age groups, with a key emphasis on the 35-, 45-, 55- and 63-year-old consumers.

These savings figures are unprecedented, because the state of the insurance industry is unprecedented. Even the most active critics cannot deny the evidence presented in Part Three of this book. The facts are there. It is up to you now to make sure they will eventually apply to you. Then this book will have served its purpose in that you, too, will have learned how to save a fortune on your life insurance.

Summary of Comparisons

In a normal insurance interview, when presentations are made on the following comparisons they also include the actual year-by-year comparison page, proposals on the current policy and the new policy for forty years, and compound interest tables at 4%, 6%, 8%, and 10%. We have not included this backup material since it does require an explanation by a life insurance agent.

The comparisons shown on the following pages are actual examples of clients who used this approach. To reduce the $1 million comparisons to $100,000, simply move the decimal one place to the left.

While these are actual examples, they are only indications of some of the comparisons that can be made with the new products in the marketplace. All of these products with lower premium, when compared with existing policies, may produce the same type of reduction and resulting savings. In many cases comparable savings could be effected with other new available products or with products now in development.

For the purpose of demonstration, and in order to equalize all tax brackets, we have assumed an 8% tax-free net return from a municipal bond fund on all affected savings. There is, of course, no guarantee that an 8% net return will be available in future years.

TABLE 13. SUMMARY OF COMPARISONS

PROPOSAL NO.	SEX	AGE	OCCUPATION	INCOME	DEATH BENEFIT	PREMIUM
1	Male	15	Student	N/A	$ 100,000	$ 1,051
2	Male	15	Student	N/A	250,000	1,390
3	Male	29	Writer	$ 35,000	20,000	219
4	Male	35	Executive	200,000	1,000,000	19,920
5	Male	35	Officer	200,000	1,000,000	20,850
6	Female	40	Secretary	15,000	50,000	794
7	Male	43	Doctor	50,000	268,000	6,740
8	Male	43	President	85,000	500,000	10,290
9	Male	45	Vice-president	300,000	1,000,000	29,210
10	Male	45	President	300,000	1,000,000	31,550
11	Male	45	Dentist	200,000	1,000,000	2,295Term
12	Male	45	Salesman	250,000	1,000,000	31,550
13	Male	48	President	250,000	500,000	9,416
14	Male	49	Keyman	100,000	256,000	7,244
15	Female	54	Psychiatrist	350,000	100,000	3,115
16	Male	55	Psychologist	250,000	1,000,000	45,230
17	Male	55	Professor	250,000	1,000,000	48,260
18	Male	63	President	200,000	1,000,000	68,440

PROPOSAL NO. 1

AGE: 15   OCCUPATION: STUDENT   DEATH BENEFIT: $100,000
SEX: MALE   INCOME: N/A   CURRENT PREM.: $ 1,051

A 15-year-old boy currently has a $100,000 permanent policy. For the same outlay he will have $1,427,115 additional cash available and $1,398,221 additional death benefit. Here is how this incredible increase was accomplished:

Currently he has a $100,000 participating Life Paid-Up at 65 Policy. His yearly premium is $1,051 (B in Table 14) to age 65. The premium remains level because he is using his dividends to purchase additional paid-up insurance. He also has a cash surrender value of $6,785.

The new Extralife-Economatic Type policy has a yearly premium of $571. If he surrendered his current policy for its cash value of $6,785 and added to it the $480 premium difference between the original $1,051 and the new $571 premium, he would have $7,265 (C in Table 14) to deposit in an 8% Municipal Bond Fund. Each year he would deposit the premium difference into the fund. At age 77 he will have deposited $23,933 (F in the table). This was calcuated as follows: because of the current surrender value of the old policy, the total premium outlay for this individual at age 77 is $28,617 (D in the table) versus $52,550 (E) with his current policy. His savings compounded at 8% would grow to $1,538,658 at age 77.

At age 77, the surrender value of the new policy would be $122,313 (H in the table) versus $233,856 (I) with his current policy. This is $111,543 (J) less with the new policy. However, he has a fund of $1,538,658, so he still has $1,427,115 additional cash available (K in the table).

At age 77 if he has not taken the available cash, he would have a death benefit with the new plan of $1,732,721 (L) versus $334,500 (M) with this old policy. This is an increase at death of $1,398,221 (N).

If he lives to age 85, and continues this program, the premium savings with the new policy would be $19,365 (O in the table). This compounded at 8% would grow to $2,841,390 (P). The policy surrender value of the new policy is $125,455 less (Q). However, with the 8% fund taken into account, he would still have $2,715,935 additional cash available (R in the table).

If death should occur at age 85, and he has not taken the cash, the total death benefit with the new policy (policy and savings fund) would be $2,684,465 more (S in the table).

NOTE: A NUMBER OF THE FIGURES ABOVE INCLUDE DIVI-
DENDS THAT ARE NOT GUARANTEED BUT ARE BASED ON THE
CURRENT DIVIDEND SCHEDULE, WHICH MAY BE CHANGED
AT ANY TIME.

Table 14. PREPARED FOR: MALE AGE 15
$100,000 EXTRALIFE-ECONOMATIC TYPE (SUPP-ADDS) VS.
$100,000 CURRENT LPU @ 65 (ADDS)
SUMMARY PAGE

The First Year Annual Premium (1) on the Extra. Econo Policy = $ −6,214(A)
The Current Annual Premium on the LPU @ 65 Policy............= 1,051(B)
　　　First Year Savings with Extralife Policy.............= $ 7,265(C)

	AGE 77 Summary	AGE 85 Summary
1. Extralife Econo. Pol. Total Annual Outlay.....	$ 28,617(D)	$ 33,185
LPU @ 65 Policy Total Annual Outlay	52,550(E)	52,550
Savings With Extralife Econo. Policy	$ 23,933(F)	$ 19,365(O)
Savings compounded at 8%	$1,538,658(G)	$2,841,390(P)

Your current LPU @ 65 Policy has a $6,785
surrender value which was used to reduce the
first year outlay on the Extralife Policy.

2. Extralife Econo. Pol. Total Surrender Value*	$ 122,313(H)	$ 146,113
LPU @ 65 Policy Total Surrender Value*......	233,856(I)	271,568
Additional Extralife Econo. Policy Value*	$ −111,543(J)	$ −125,455(Q)

Plus savings of Premium Outlay and
Surrender Value of Current Policy

Total Additional Cash Available....................	$1,427,115(K)	$2,715,935(R)
3. Total Death Benefit**with Extralife Econo*	$1,732,721(L)	$3,054,165
Total Death Benefit with LPU @ 65 Policy*	334,500(M)	369,700
Additional Death Benefit With Extralife*	$1,398,221(N)	$2,684,465(S)

IN OTHER WORDS:

AGE 77 SUMMARY
FOR THE SAME OUTLAY YOU WILL HAVE $1,427,115 MORE CASH AVAILABLE AND $1,398,221 MORE DEATH BENEFIT;*

OR

YOU CAN SPEND $23,933 LESS AND HAVE $111,543 LESS CASH AVAILABLE AND $140,437 LESS DEATH BENEFIT.*

AGE 85 SUMMARY
FOR THE SAME OUTLAY YOU WILL HAVE $2,715,935 MORE CASH AVAILABLE AND $2,684,465 MORE DEATH BENEFIT;*

OR

YOU CAN SPEND $19,365 LESS AND HAVE $125,455 LESS CASH AVAILABLE AND $156,925 LESS DEATH BENEFIT.*

(1) Extralife First Year Annual Outlay calculated as follows: (Annual Premium) $571 minus (LPU @ 65 Surrender Value) $6,785 equals $−6,214.

* Dividends are not guaranteed but are based on the current dividend schedule, which may be changed at any time.

** Death Benefit includes: A) Death Benefit of Policy, and B) Side fund (Premium difference and current surrender value compounded at 8%).

PROPOSAL NO. 2

AGE: 15	OCCUPATION: STUDENT	DEATH BENEFIT: $100,000
SEX: MALE	INCOME: N/A	CURRENT PREM.: $ 1,051

A 15-year-old boy currently has a $100,000 permanent policy. For the same outlay he will have $356,104 additional cash available and $387,967 additional death benefit. Here is how these savings were accomplished:

Currently he has a $100,000 Life-Paid Up at 65 participating policy with a surrender value of $6,785. His yearly premium is $1,051 and will continue on a level basis until he is age 65. He is using his dividends to purchase additional insurance to increase his death benefit.

The new Extralife-Economatic type policy has a yearly premium of $1,390, which is $339 more yearly than his current policy. However, he has a surrender value of $6,785, which could be invested at 8% and would earn $543; this will pay the $339 premium difference and accumulate $204 more in the side fund with the $6,785 in the first year.

The total outlay to age 77 with the new policy is $80,785 (B in Table 15) versus $52,550 (C in the table) with the old policy. As you can see, the new policy has a cost of $28,235 (D). However, as I indicated there is a surrender value of $6,785, which can earn 8% yearly and will pay the premium difference and still build a savings fund of $241,015 (E in the table).

The total surrender value at age 77 with the new policy will be $348,945 (F in Table 15) versus $233,856 with the old policy (G in the table). This is an increase of $115,089 (H) in total cash value. He will also have the savings fund of $241,015, so he will have increased his total cash available by $356,104 (I) with the new policy.

If death should occur at age 77, and he has not taken the cash, his total death benefit (policy and savings fund) will be $722,467 (J in the table) versus $334,500 (K) with his old policy. This is an increase of $387,967 (L) with the new type policy.

If he continues the program after age 77 and death does not occur, the premium cost with the new policy will be $39,355 (M). However, with the current surrender value invested in an 8% Municipal Bond Fund he would have a savings fund of $430,135 (N) after paying the additional premium from the fund.

The total surrender value with the new type policy would be $165,697 more (O in the table) than the current policy. This plus the savings fund will give him $595,832 (P) additional cash available at age 85.

If death should occur and he has not taken the cash, his total death benefit (policy and savings fund) will be $594,095 more (Q in the table) with the new policy.

NOTE: A NUMBER OF THE FIGURES ABOVE INCLUDE DIVIDENDS THAT ARE NOT GUARANTEED BUT ARE BASED ON THE CURRENT DIVIDEND SCHEDULE, WHICH MAY BE CHANGED AT ANY TIME.

Table 15. PREPARED FOR: MALE AGE 15
$250,000 EXTRALIFE-ECONOMATIC TYPE (SUPP-ADDS) VS.
$100,000 CURRENT LPU @ 65 (ADDS)
SUMMARY PAGE

The FIRST YEAR Annual Premium (1) on the Extra. Econo Policy = $ −5,395
The CURRENT Annual Premium on the LPU @ 65 Policy............=   1,051
      FIRST YEAR SAVINGS WITH EXTRALIFE POLICY.............= $ 6,446(A)

	AGE 77 Summary	AGE 85 Summary
1. Extralife Econo. Pol. Total Annual Outlay.....	$ 80,785(B)	$ 91,905
LPU @ 65 Policy Total Annual Outlay	52,550(C)	52,550
SAVINGS WITH EXTRALIFE ECONO. POLICY	$ −28,235(D)	$ −39,355(M)
SAVINGS compounded at 8%............................	$ 241,015(E)	$ 430,135(N)

Your current LPU @ 65 Policy has a $6,785
surrender value which was used to reduce the
first year outlay on the Extralife Policy.

2. Extralife Econo. Pol. Total Surrender Value*	$ 348,945(F)	$ 437,265
LPU @ 65 Policy Total Surrender Value*......	233,856(G)	271,568
ADDITIONAL EXTRALIFE ECONO. POLICY VALUE*	$ 115,089(H)	$ 165,697(O)

Plus savings of Premium Outlay and
Surrender Value of Current Policy
TOTAL ADDITIONAL CASH AVAILABLE.................... $ 356,104(I) $ 595,832(P)

3. Total Death Benefit**with Extralife Econo*	$ 722,467(J)	$ 963,795
Total Death Benefit with LPU @ 65 Policy*	334,500(K)	369,700
ADDITIONAL DEATH BENEFIT WITH EXTRALIFE*	$ 387,967(L)	$ 594,095(Q)

IN OTHER WORDS

AGE 77 SUMMARY
FOR THE SAME OUTLAY YOU WILL
HAVE $356,104 MORE CASH AVAIL-
ABLE AND $387,967 MORE DEATH
BENEFIT;*

OR

YOU CAN SPEND $28,235 MORE AND
HAVE $115,089 MORE CASH AVAILABLE
AND $146,952 MORE DEATH BENEFIT.*

AGE 85 SUMMARY
FOR THE SAME OUTLAY YOU WILL
HAVE $595,832 MORE CASH AVAIL-
ABLE AND $594,095 MORE DEATH
BENEFIT;*

OR

YOU CAN SPEND $39,355 MORE AND
HAVE $165,697 MORE CASH AVAILABLE
AND $163,960 MORE DEATH BENEFIT.*

(1) Extralife First Year Annual Outlay calculated as follows: (Annual Premium) $1,390
minus (LPU @ 65 Surrender Value) $6,785 equals $−5,395.

 * Dividends are not guaranteed but are based on the current dividend schedule, which
may be changed at any time.

** Death Benefit includes: A) Death Benefit of Policy, and B) Side fund (Premium difference and current surrender value compounded at 8%).

PROPOSAL NO. 3

AGE: 29   OCCUPATION: WRITER   DEATH BENEFIT: $20,000
SEX: MALE   INCOME: $35,000   CURRENT PREM.: $ 219

A 29-year-old man currently owns a $20,000 permanent policy on which he pays $219 annually. For the same $219 yearly outlay he can have, at age 77, $95,704 additional cash available and $100,634 additional death benefit. At age 85, he would have $183,727 additional cash available and $189,841 additional death benefit. Here is how these remarkable savings were accomplished:

His parents purchased a $20,000 cash value permanent policy ten years ago. He now has a surrender value of $1,640. He pays a yearly premium of $219 to age 65, when the policy is paid up. His premium is always the same because it is a non-participating policy.

The premium for the new participating Extralife-Economatic Type policy will be $191 for twenty-one years. At age 51, the premium will be $115, since there is now a $76 dividend. At age 52, the premium will be $2, because the dividend is now $189. Thereafter, he will have no premium outlay since starting in the twenty-fourth year the dividend is large enough to cover the premium and give him cash in his pocket.

If he surrendered his current policy for its cash value of $1,640 and added to it the $28 premium difference between the original $219 and the new $191 premium he would have $1,668 (A in Table 16) to deposit in an 8% Municipal Bond fund. Each year he would deposit the premium difference into the fund. In forty-eight years (age 77) he will have deposited $8,731 (D in the table). This was calculated as follows:

Because of yearly dividends and the current surrender value of the old policy, the total premium outlay for this man at age 77 is actually –$847 (B in Table 16); in other words, rather than taking money out of this man's pocket over a lifetime, he actually got money back ($847). In addition, he would have saved his current policy's premium outlay of $7,884 (C in the table). This total savings compounded at 8% annually would grow to $100,634 (E), which can be added to this man's $20,000 death benefit or taken in cash prior to death.

At age 77, the surrender value of the new policy would be $14,630 (F in Table 16) versus $19,560 (G) with his current policy. The difference is $4,930 (H) less cash value in the new policy contract. But why would this man want to pay $8,731 to have $4,930 more cash value when he could have $100,634 available in his Municipal Bond fund? If you subtract the $4,930 less cash value from the total savings of $100,634 this man would have $95,704 additional cash available (I in the table) with the new program.

At age 77 if this man does not take the available cash ($100,634 bond fund plus $14,630 surrender value of his policy contract, which equals $115,264) he would have a death benefit with the new plan of $120,634 (J in the table) versus $20,000 (K) with the old policy. This is an increase in cash at death of $100,634 (L).

If he lives to age 85, the figures are even more astounding. The premium outlay difference is $11,255 (O). This compounded at 8% would grow to $189,841 (P). The surrender value of his old policy is $6,114 (S) more than the new policy. However, the new program has a fund of $189,841, so you still have $183,727 (T) additional cash available. If he does not take the cash, his death benefit with the new program would also be $189,841 (W) more than his current policy.

(This policy belongs to my editorial adviser Steve Rubin, who until he became involved in this book project did not realize the savings he could achieve on his policy. Since these observations were made, Mr. Rubin has purchased another $80,000 in personal insurance so as to take advantage of the low Extralife-Economatic rates.)

NOTE: A NUMBER OF THE FIGURES ABOVE INCLUDE DIVIDENDS THAT ARE NOT GUARANTEED BUT ARE BASED ON THE CURRENT DIVIDEND SCHEDULE, WHICH MAY BE CHANGED AT ANY TIME.

Table 16. PREPARED FOR: MALE AGE 29
$20,000 EXTRALIFE-ECONOMATIC TYPE (SUPP-REDUCE) VS. $20,000 CURRENT LPU @ 65 (NON-PAR)
SUMMARY PAGE

The FIRST YEAR Annual Premium (1) on the Extra. Econo Policy = $ -1,449
The CURRENT Annual Premium on the LPU @ 65 Policy............. =   219
    FIRST YEAR SAVINGS WITH EXTRALIFE POLICY............. = $ 1,668(A)

	AGE 77 Summary	AGE 85 Summary
1. Extralife Econo. Pol. Total Annual Outlay*	$ -847(B)	$ -3,371(M)
LPU @ 65 Policy Total Annual Outlay...........	7,884(C)	7,884(N)
SAVINGS WITH EXTRALIFE ECONO. POLICY*	$ 8,731(D)	$ 11,255(O)
SAVINGS compounded at 8%............................	$ 100,634(E)	$ 189,841(P)

Your current LPU @ 65 Policy has a $1,640
surrender value which was used to reduce the
first year outlay on the Extralife Policy.

2. Extralife Econo. Pol. Total Surrender Value*	$ 14,630(F)	$ 17,286(Q)
LPU @ 65 Policy Total Surrender Value........	19,560(G)	23,400(R)
ADDITIONAL EXTRALIFE ECONO. POLICY VALUE*	$ -4,930(H)	$ -6,114(S)

Plus savings of Premium Outlay
TOTAL ADDITIONAL CASH AVAILABLE.................... $ 95,704(I) $ 183,727(T)

3. TOTAL DEATH BENEFIT**WITH EXTRALIFE ECONO*	$ 120,634(J)	$ 209,841(U)
TOTAL DEATH BENEFIT WITH LPU @ 65 POLICY	20,000(K)	20,000(V)
ADDITIONAL DEATH BENEFIT WITH EXTRALIFE*	$ 100,634(L)	$ 189,841(W)

IN OTHER WORDS:

AGE 77 SUMMARY	AGE 85 SUMMARY
FOR THE SAME OUTLAY YOU WILL HAVE $95,704 MORE CASH AVAILABLE AND $100,634 MORE DEATH BENEFIT;*	FOR THE SAME OUTLAY YOU WILL HAVE $183,727 MORE CASH AVAILABLE AND $189,841 MORE DEATH BENEFIT;*
OR	OR
YOU CAN SPEND $8,731 LESS AND HAVE $4,930 LESS CASH AVAILABLE AND THE SAME DEATH BENEFIT.*	YOU CAN SPEND $11,255 LESS AND HAVE $6,114 LESS CASH AVAILABLE AND THE SAME DEATH BENEFIT.*

(1) Extralife First Year Annual Outlay calculated as follows: (Annual Premium) $191 minus (LPU @ 65 Surrender Value) $1,640 equals $-1,449.

 * Dividends are not guaranteed but are based on the current dividend schedule, which may be changed at any time.

** Death Benefit includes: A) Death Benefit of Policy, and B) Side fund (Premium difference and current surrender value compounded at 8%).

PROPOSAL NO. 4

| AGE: 35 | OCCUPATION: EXECUTIVE | DEATH BENEFIT: $1,000,000 |
| SEX: MALE | INCOME: $200,000 | CURRENT PREM.: $ 19,920 |

A 35-year-old man has a choice of what type of policy to purchase to fill a need for a $1,000,000 death benefit. He can buy the old low premium and cash value policy and have $44,700 additional cash value, or he can buy the new Extra-life-Economatic policy and invest his savings of $2,573, and have $623,510 additional available in a savings fund. Here is how these policies compare:

The old low premium and cash value policy with a $1,000,000 death benefit has a first year premium of $19,920 (B in Table 17), while the Extralife-Economatic Type has a first year premium of $10,895 (A in the table). If he did purchase the new policy he would save $9,025 (C) in the first year.

The total premiums on the new policy, to age 77, would be $86,943 (D in Table 17) versus $84,370 (E) with the old type policy. This is an extra cost of $2,573 (F) with the new type policy. If the individual invested the premium difference yearly in an 8% Municipal Bond Fund he would have a fund equal to $668,210 (G) even though his total premium outlay is more. This is because the new type policy has a lower premium in the beginning years.

The total surrender value of the new type policy, at age 77, is $709,030 (H) versus $753,730 (I in the table) with the old type policy. As you can see, there is $44,700 (J) less surrender value with the new type policy. However, the premium difference compounded at 8% has grown to $668,210 so he really has $623,510 (K) additional cash available with the new type policy.

If death should occur at age 77 and he has not taken the cash, the total death benefit (policy and fund) with the new policy would be $1,668,210 (L in Table 17) versus $1,000,000 (M) with the old policy. This means that if the death should occur his family would receive $668,210 (N) additional cash at no additional cost.

If he should continue the program after age 77 and death does not occur, at age 85 the additional premium cost with the Extralife-Economatic would be $11,157 (O in the table). However, if the premium difference was invested at 8% he would still have a total fund of $1,224,419 (P) with the Extralife-Economatic policy.

The total surrender value at age 85 with the new policy would be $39,580 (Q in the table) less than the old type policy. However, he has invested the premium difference and has a fund of $1,224,419 with the new policy, so he really has $1,184,839 (R) additional cash available with the new type policy.

If death should occur at age 85 and he has not taken the cash, the total death benefit (policy and fund) with the new policy would be $1,224,419 (S) more than the old type policy.

NOTE: A NUMBER OF THE FIGURES ABOVE INCLUDE DIVIDENDS THAT ARE NOT GUARANTEED BUT ARE BASED ON THE CURRENT DIVIDEND SCHEDULE, WHICH MAY BE CHANGED AT ANY TIME.

Table 17. PREPARED FOR: MALE AGE 35

$1,000,000 EXTRALIFE-ECONOMATIC TYPE (SUPP-REDUCE) VS.
$1,000,000 OLD LOW PREMIUM AND CASH VALUE POLICY (REDUCE)

SUMMARY PAGE

The FIRST YEAR Annual Premium on the Extra. Econo Policy =	$ 10,895(A)	
The FIRST YEAR Annual Premium on the Old Type Policy .... =	19,920(B)	
FIRST YEAR SAVINGS WITH EXTRALIFE POLICY .... =	$ 9,025(C)	

	AGE 77 Summary	AGE 85 Summary
1. Extralife Econo. Pol. Total Annual Outlay*	$ 86,943(D)	$ −20,273
LPU @ 65 Policy Total Annual Outlay*	84,370(E)	−31,430
SAVINGS WITH EXTRALIFE ECONO. POLICY*	$ −2,573(F)	$ −11,157(O)
SAVINGS compounded at 8%	$ 668,210(G)	$1,224,419(P)
2. Extralife Econo. Pol. Total Surrender Value*	$ 709,030(H)	$ 835,110
Old Type Policy Total Surrender Value*	753,730(I)	874,690
ADDITIONAL EXTRALIFE ECONO. POLICY VALUE*	$ −44,700(J)	$ −39,580(Q)
Plus savings of Premium Outlay TOTAL ADDITIONAL CASH AVAILABLE	$ 623,510(K)	$1,184,839(R)
3. Total Death Benefit**with Extralife Econo*	$1,668,210(L)	$2,224,419
Total Death Benefit with Old Type Policy	1,000,000(M)	1,000,000
ADDITIONAL DEATH BENEFIT WITH EXTRALIFE*	$ 668,210(N)	$1,224,419(S)

IN OTHER WORDS:

AGE 77 SUMMARY
FOR THE SAME OUTLAY YOU WILL
HAVE $623,510 MORE CASH AVAIL-
ABLE AND $668,210 MORE DEATH
BENEFIT;*

OR

YOU CAN SPEND $2,573 MORE AND
HAVE $44,700 LESS CASH AVAILABLE
AND THE SAME DEATH BENEFIT.*

AGE 85 SUMMARY
FOR THE SAME OUTLAY YOU WILL
HAVE $1,184,839 MORE CASH AVAIL-
ABLE AND $1,224,419 MORE DEATH
BENEFIT;*

OR

YOU CAN SPEND $11,157 MORE AND
HAVE $39,580 LESS CASH AVAILABLE
AND THE SAME DEATH BENEFIT.*

* Dividends are not guaranteed but are based on the current dividend schedule, which may be changed at any time.

** Death Benefit includes: A) Death Benefit of Policy, and B) Side fund (Premium difference and current surrender value compounded at 8%).

PROPOSAL NO. 5

AGE: 35   OCCUPATION: OFFICER   DEATH BENEFIT: $1,000,000
SEX: MALE   INCOME: $200,000   CURRENT PREM.: $ 20,850

A 35-year-old man has a choice of what type of policy to purchase to fill a need for a $1,000,000 death benefit. He can buy the old high premium and cash value policy and have a $184,980 additional cash value or he can buy the new Extralife-Economatic policy and invest his premium savings of $47,627 and have $983,099 additional available in a side fund. Here is how these policies compare:

The old high premium and cash value policy with a $1,000,000 death benefit has a first year premium of $20,850 (B in Table 18), while the Extralife Economatic Type has a first year premium of $10,895 (A in the table). If he did purchase the new policy he would save $9,955 (C) in the first year.

The total premiums on the new policy, to age 77, would be $86,943 (D in the table) versus $134,570 (E) with the old type policy. This is a savings of $47,627 (F) with the new type policy. If the individual invested the premium difference yearly in an 8% Municipal Bond Fund he would have a fund equal to $1,168,079 (G).

The total surrender value of the new type policy, at age 77, is $709,030 (H) versus $894,010 (I in the table) with the old type policy. As you can see, there is $184,980 (J) less surrender value with the new type policy. However, the premium difference compounded at 8% has grown to $1,168,079, so he really has $983,099 (K) additional cash available with the new type policy.

If death should occur at age 77 and he has not taken the cash, the total death benefit (policy and savings fund) with the new policy would be $2,168,079 (L) versus $1,000,000 (M) with the old policy. This means that his family would receive $1,168,079 (N) additional cash, if the death should occur, at no additional cost.

If he should continue the program after age 77 and death

does not occur, at age 85 the premium savings with the new type policy would be $90,063 (O in Table 18). Again, if the premium difference was invested at 8% he would have a total fund of $2,021,828 (P) with the new type policy.

The total surrender value at age 85 with the new policy would be $275,220 (Q in the table) less than the old type policy. However, he has invested the premium difference and has a fund of $2,021,828 with the new policy, so he really has $1,746,608 (R) additional cash available with the new type policy.

If death should occur at age 85 and he has not taken the cash, the total death benefit (policy and savings fund) with the new policy would be $2,021,828 (S) more than the old type policy.

Why send the insurance company $47,627 more over your lifetime for an old high premium high cash value policy so that you could have $184,980 additional cash value? If you buy an Extralife-Economatic type policy and invest the $47,627 savings, you can have $983,099 additional cash available and $1,168,079 additional death benefit.

NOTE: A NUMBER OF THE ABOVE FIGURES INCLUDE DIVIDENDS THAT ARE NOT GUARANTEED BUT ARE BASED ON THE CURRENT DIVIDEND SCHEDULE, WHICH MAY BE CHANGED AT ANY TIME.

Table 18. PREPARED FOR: MALE AGE 35

$1,000,000 EXTRALIFE-ECONOMATIC TYPE (SUPP-REDUCE) VS.
$1,000,000 OLD HIGH PREMIUM AND CASH VALUE POLICY (REDUCE)

SUMMARY PAGE

The FIRST YEAR Annual Premium on the Extra. Econo Policy =	$	10,895(A)
The FIRST YEAR Annual Premium on the Old Type Policy .... =		20,850(B)
FIRST YEAR SAVINGS WITH EXTRALIFE POLICY .... =	$	9,955(C)

	AGE 77 Summary	AGE 85 Summary
1. Extralife Econo. Pol. Total Annual Outlay*	$ 86,943(D)	$ −20,273
Old Type Policy Total Annual Outlay*	134,570(E)	69,790
SAVINGS WITH EXTRALIFE ECONO. POLICY*	$ 47,627(F)	$ 90,063(O)
SAVINGS compounded at 8%	$1,168,079(G)	$2,021,828(P)
2. Extralife Econo. Pol. Total Surrender Value*	$ 709,030(H)	$ 835,110
Old Type Policy Total Surrender Value*	894,010(I)	1,110,330
ADDITIONAL EXTRALIFE ECONO. POLICY VALUE*	$ −184,980(J)	$ −275,220(Q)
Plus savings of Premium Outlay TOTAL ADDITIONAL CASH AVAILABLE	$ 983,099(K)	$1,746,608(R)
3. Total Death Benefit**with Extralife Econo*	$2,168,079(L)	$3,021,828
Total Death Benefit with Old Type Policy	1,000,000(M)	1,000,000
ADDITIONAL DEATH BENEFIT WITH EXTRALIFE*	$1,168,079(N)	$2,021,828(S)

IN OTHER WORDS:

AGE 77 SUMMARY	AGE 85 SUMMARY
FOR THE SAME OUTLAY YOU WILL HAVE $983,099 MORE CASH AVAILABLE AND $1,168,079 MORE DEATH BENEFIT;*	FOR THE SAME OUTLAY YOU WILL HAVE $1,746,608 MORE CASH AVAILABLE AND $2,021,828 MORE DEATH BENEFIT;*
OR	OR
YOU CAN SPEND $47,627 LESS AND HAVE $184,980 LESS CASH AVAILABLE AND THE SAME DEATH BENEFIT.*	YOU CAN SPEND $90,063 LESS AND HAVE $275,220 LESS CASH AVAILABLE AND THE SAME DEATH BENEFIT.*

* Dividends are not guaranteed but are based on the current dividend schedule, which may be changed at any time.

** Death Benefit includes: A) Death Benefit of Policy, and B) Side fund (Premium difference and current surrender value compounded at 8%).

PROPOSAL NO. 6

AGE: 40   OCCUPATION: SECRETARY   DEATH BENEFIT: $50,000
SEX: FEMALE   INCOME: $15,000   CURRENT PREM.: $ 794

A 40-year-old woman has a choice of what type of policy to purchase to fill a need for $50,000 death benefit. She can buy a non-participating Whole Life Policy or she can buy the New Extralife-Economatic policy and invest her premium savings of $20,080 and have $46,578 additional cash available in a side fund. Here is how these policies compare:

The non-participating Whole Life Policy has a premium of $794 (B in Table 19), while the Extralife-Economatic type has a first-year premium of $677 (A in the table). If she did purchase the new policy she would save $117 (C) in the first year.

The total premiums on the new policy, to age 77, would be $9,298 (D in the table) versus $29,378 (E) with the non-par policy. This is a savings of $20,080 (F) with the new type policy. If the individual invested the premium difference yearly in an 8% Municipal Bond Fund, she would have a fund equal to $57,720 (G).

The total surrender value of the new type policy, at age 77, is $34,658 (H in Table 19) versus $45,800 (I in the table) with the non-par policy. As you can see, there is $11,142 (J) less surrender value with the new type policy. However, the premium difference compounded at 8% has grown to $57,720 so she really has $46,578 (K) additional cash available with the new type policy.

If death should occur at age 77 and she has not taken the cash, the total death benefit (policy and savings fund) with the new policy would be $107,720 (L) versus $50,000 (M) with the non-par policy. This means that her family would receive $57,720 (N) additional cash if the death should occur, at no additional cost.

If she should continue the program after age 77 and death does not occur, at age 85 the premium savings with the new type policy would be $30,829 (O in the table). If the premium difference was invested at 8% she would have a total fund of $122,175 (P) with the new type policy.

The total surrender value at age 85 with the new policy would be $17,227 (Q) less than the non-par policy. However, she has invested the premium difference and has a fund of $122,175 with the new type policy so she really has $104,948 (R) additional cash available with the new type policy.

If death should occur at age 85 and she has not taken the cash, the total death benefit (policy and savings fund) with the new policy would be $122,175 (S) more than the non-par policy.

Why would you send the insurance company $20,080 more over your lifetime for a non-participating whole life policy so that you could have $11,142 additional cash value? If you purchased an Extralife-Economatic Type policy and invested the $20,080 savings, you would have $46,578 additional cash available and $57,720 additional death benefit.

NOTE: A NUMBER OF THE ABOVE FIGURES INCLUDE DIVI-DENDS THAT ARE NOT GUARANTEED BUT ARE BASED ON THE CURRENT DIVIDEND SCHEDULE, WHICH MAY BE CHANGED AT ANY TIME.

Table 19. PREPARED FOR: FEMALE AGE 40
$50,000 EXTRALIFE-ECONOMATIC TYPE (SUPP-REDUCE) VS.
$50,000 WHOLE LIFE (NON-PAR)
SUMMARY PAGE

The FIRST YEAR Annual Premium on the Extra. Econo Policy =	$	677(A)
The FIRST YEAR Annual Premium on the Whole Life Policy....... =		794(B)
FIRST YEAR SAVINGS WITH EXTRALIFE POLICY.............. =	$	117(C)

	AGE 77 Summary		AGE 85 Summary	
1. Extralife Econo. Pol. Total Annual Outlay*	$	9,298(D)	$	4,901
Whole Life Policy Total Annual Outlay..........		29,378(E)		35,730
SAVINGS WITH EXTRALIFE ECONO. POLICY*	$	20,080(F)	$	30,829(O)
SAVINGS compounded at 8%............................	$	57,720(G)	$	122,175(P)
2. Extralife Econo. Pol. Total Surrender Value*	$	34,658(H)	$	38,973
Whole Life Policy Total Surrender Value.......		45,800(I)		56,200
ADDITIONAL EXTRALIFE ECONO. POLICY VALUE*	$	−11,142(J)	$	−17,227(Q)
Plus savings of Premium Outlay				
TOTAL ADDITIONAL CASH AVAILABLE....................	$	46,578(K)	$	104,948(R)
3. Total Death Benefit**with Extralife Econo*	$	107,720(L)	$	172,175
Total Death Benefit with Whole Life Policy		50,000(M)		50,000
ADDITIONAL DEATH BENEFIT WITH EXTRALIFE*	$	57,720(N)	$	122,175(S)

IN OTHER WORDS:

AGE 77 SUMMARY	AGE 85 SUMMARY
FOR THE SAME OUTLAY YOU WILL HAVE $46,578 MORE CASH AVAIL-ABLE AND $57,720 MORE DEATH BENEFIT;*	FOR THE SAME OUTLAY YOU WILL HAVE $104,948 MORE CASH AVAIL-ABLE AND $122,175 MORE DEATH BENEFIT;*
OR	OR
YOU CAN SPEND $20,080 LESS AND HAVE $11,142 LESS CASH AVAILABLE AND THE SAME DEATH BENEFIT.*	YOU CAN SPEND $30,829 LESS AND HAVE $17,227 LESS CASH AVAILABLE AND THE SAME DEATH BENEFIT.*

* Dividends are not guaranteed but are based on the current dividend schedule, which may be changed at any time.

** Death Benefit includes: A) Death Benefit of Policy, and B) Side fund (Premium difference and current surrender value compounded at 8%).

PROPOSAL NO. 7

AGE: 43   OCCUPATION: DOCTOR   DEATH BENEFIT: $268,000
SEX: MALE   INCOME: $50,000   CURRENT PREM.: $ 6,740

A 43-year-old male doctor currently has a $268,000 permanent policy. For the same outlay he can have $352,893 additional cash available and $373,775 additional death benefit. At age 85 he will have $672,027 additional cash available and $704,995 additional death benefit. Here is how these incredible savings were accomplished:

His current $268,000 participating permanent policy has a surrender value of $12,191. His premium for this year, with dividends deducted, was $6,740 (B in Table 20).

The premium for the new Extralife-Economatic Type policy is $4,254 (A in the table). Therefore, his first year saving was $2,486 (C) with the new policy.

The premium outlay for the new policy over the next thirty-four years (to age 77) will be $72,176 (D in the table) versus $110,658 (E) with his current policy. The new policy thus would save him $38,482 (F) and if he invested that difference yearly in an 8% Municipal Bond Fund it would grow to $206,879 (G) by age 77. If he takes the current surrender value of his old policy ($12,191) and invests that in an 8% fund, it will grow to $166,896 (H). He would then have a total fund of $373,775 (I in the table).

The total surrender value of the new policy at age 77 is $182,597 (J) versus $203,479 (K) with his old policy. The difference is $20,882 (L) less cash value in the policy contracts. However, why would this man want to pay $38,482 to have $20,882 more cash value when he can have $373,775 available in his Municipal Bond Fund? If you subtract the $20,882 less cash value from the total savings of $373,775, this man would have $352,893 (M) additional cash available with the new program.

The total death benefit with the new policy if the cash is not taken, at age 77, will be $641,775 (N) versus $268,000 (O in the table) with his current policy. This is an increase of $373,775 (P) cash available for his family at no additional cost over his lifetime.

If he lives to age 85 the savings on the premium outlay will be $47,298 (Q). In an 8% Municipal Bond Fund this savings will grow to $396,082 (R). The surrender value if left the eight additional years will grow to $308,913 (S) giving him a total fund of $704,995 (T).

The surrender value of the new policy is $32,698 (U in the table) less than the current policy. However, with the savings fund taken into account he still has $672,027 (V) additional cash available. If he does not take the cash, his death benefit will be $704,995 (W) more with the new program, an enormous savings.

NOTE: A NUMBER OF THE FIGURES ABOVE INCLUDE DIVIDENDS THAT ARE NOT GUARANTEED BUT ARE BASED ON THE CURRENT DIVIDEND SCHEDULE, WHICH MAY BE CHANGED AT ANY TIME.

Table 20. PREPARED FOR: MALE AGE 43
$268,000 EXTRALIFE-ECONOMATIC TYPE (SUPP-REDUCE) VS. $268,000 CURRENT WHOLE LIFE (REDUCE)
SUMMARY PAGE

The FIRST YEAR Annual Premium on the Extra. Econo Policy   = $ 4,254(A)
The CURRENT Annual Premium on the Whole Life Policy........... =   6,740(B)
FIRST YEAR SAVINGS WITH EXTRALIFE POLICY............. = $ 2,486(C)

	AGE 77 Summary	*AGE 85* Summary
1. Extralife Econo. Pol. Total Annual Outlay*	$ 72,176(D)	$ 53,099
Whole Life Policy Total Annual Outlay*........	110,658(E)	100,397
SAVINGS WITH EXTRALIFE ECONO. POLICY*........	$ 38,482(F)	$ 47,298(Q)
SAVINGS compounded at 8%............................	$ 206,879(G)	$ 396,082(R)
Your current Whole Life Policy has a $12,191 surrender value which could be compounded at 8% and will grow to	$ 166,896(H)	$ 308,913(S)
INCREASING YOUR SAVINGS TO	$ 373,775(I)	$ 704,995(T)
2. Extralife Econo. Pol. Total Surrender Value*	$ 182,597(J)	$ 214,267
Whole Life Policy Total Surrender Value*.....	203,479(K)	247,235
ADDITIONAL EXTRALIFE ECONO. POLICY VALUE*	$ −20,882(L)	$ −32,968(U)
Plus savings of Premium Outlay and Surrender Value of Current Policy TOTAL ADDITIONAL CASH AVAILABLE....................	$ 352,893(M)	$ 672,027(V)
3. Total Death Benefit**with Extralife Econo*	$ 641,775(N)	$ 972,995
Total Death Benefit with Whole Life Policy	268,000(O)	268,000
ADDITIONAL DEATH BENEFIT WITH EXTRALIFE*	$ 373,775(P)	$ 704,995(W)

IN OTHER WORDS:

AGE 77 SUMMARY
FOR THE SAME OUTLAY YOU WILL HAVE $352,983 MORE CASH AVAILABLE AND $373,775 MORE DEATH BENEFIT;*

OR

YOU CAN SPEND $38,482 LESS AND HAVE $146,014 MORE CASH AVAILABLE AND $166,896 MORE DEATH BENEFIT.*

AGE 85 SUMMARY
FOR THE SAME OUTLAY YOU WILL HAVE $672,027 MORE CASH AVAILABLE AND $704,995 MORE DEATH BENEFIT;*

OR

YOU CAN SPEND $47,298 LESS AND HAVE $275,945 MORE CASH AVAILABLE AND $308,913 MORE DEATH BENEFIT.*

* Dividends are not guaranteed but are based on the current dividend schedule, which may be changed at any time.

** Death Benefit includes: A) Death Benefit of Policy, and B) Side fund (Premium difference and current surrender value compounded at 8%).

PROPOSAL NO. 8

AGE: 43   OCCUPATION: PRESIDENT   DEATH BENEFIT: $500,000
SEX: MALE   INCOME: $85,000   CURRENT PREM.: $ 10,290

A 43-year-old man currently has a $500,000 permanent policy. For the same outlay he will have $669,764 additional cash available and $713,099 additional death benefit. Here is how these savings were accomplished:

Currently he has a $500,000 non-participating permanent policy with a surrender value of $4,667. His yearly premium is $10,290 (B in Table 21).

The new Extralife-Economatic Type policy has a yearly premium of $7,915 (A in Table 21), saving him $2,375 (C in the table) in the first year.

The total outlay to age 77 with the new policy is $133,947 (D) versus $349,860 (E) with his current policy. His savings will be $215,913 (F). If he deposited the yearly difference in an 8% Municipal Bond Fund, at age 77 he would have a fund equal to $649,208 (G). If he also deposited his current surrender value of $4,667 in an 8% fund it would grow to $63,891 (H) giving him a total fund of $713,099 (I).

The total surrender value of the new policy, at age 77, will be $340,665 (J in the table) versus $384,000 (K) with his current policy. The new policy has $43,335 (L) less in policy surrender value. However, because he has built a fund of $713,099, he still has $669,764 (M) additional cash available.

If death should occur at age 77, and he has not taken the cash, his total death benefit with the new policy plus the savings fund would be $1,213,099 (N) versus $500,000 (O in the table) with the current policy. This is an increase of $713,099 (P) available cash for his family.

If he continues the program after age 77 and lives to age 85, the premium savings would be $333,995 (Q). This compounded at 8% would produce a fund of $1,370,274 (R on the summary page). His current surrender value compounded at

8% would grow to $118,259 (S) giving him a total combined fund of $1,488,533 (T).

The new policy has $72,248 (U) less surrender value at age 85. However, again he has saved $333,995 on the premium outlay and has a total fund of $1,488,533 so he still has $1,416,285 (V) additional cash available, an incredible saving.

If death should occur, and he has not taken the cash, his total death benefit with the new policy plus the fund would be $1,488,533 (W) more.

Why would this man want to pay $215,913 more to age 77 and have $20,556 less cash available and $63,891 less death benefit when he can pay the same outlay and have $669,764 additional cash available and $713,099 additional death benefit for his family?

NOTE: A NUMBER OF THE FIGURES ABOVE INCLUDE DIVI-
DENDS THAT ARE NOT GUARANTEED BUT ARE BASED ON THE
CURRENT DIVIDEND SCHEDULE, WHICH MAY BE CHANGED
AT ANY TIME.

Table 21. PREPARED FOR: MALE AGE 43
$500,000 EXTRALIFE-ECONOMATIC TYPE (SUPP-REDUCE) VS. $500,000 CURRENT WHOLE LIFE (NON-PAR)
SUMMARY PAGE

The FIRST YEAR Annual Premium on the Extra. Econo Policy =	$	7,915(A)
The CURRENT Annual Premium on the Whole Life Policy........... =		10,290(B)
FIRST YEAR SAVINGS WITH EXTRALIFE POLICY............. =	$	2,375(C)

	AGE 77 Summary	AGE 85 Summary
1. Extralife Econo. Pol. Total Annual Outlay*	$ 133,947(D)	$ 98,185
Whole Life Policy Total Annual Outlay..........	349,860(E)	432,180
SAVINGS WITH EXTRALIFE ECONO. POLICY*	$ 215,913(F)	$ 333,995(Q)
SAVINGS compounded at 8%.............................	$ 649,208(G)	$1,370,274(R)
Your current Whole Life Policy has a $5,547 surrender value which could be compounded at 8% and will grow to..	$ 63,891(H)	$ 118,259(S)
INCREASING YOUR SAVINGS TO	$ 713,099(I)	$1,488,533(T)
2. Extralife Econo. Pol. Total Surrender Value*	$ 340,665(J)	$ 399,752
Whole Life Policy Total Surrender Value.......	384,000(K)	472,000
ADDITIONAL EXTRALIFE ECONO. POLICY VALUE*	$ −43,335(L)	$ −72,248(U)
Plus savings of Premium Outlay and Surrender Value of Current Policy TOTAL ADDITIONAL CASH AVAILABLE....................	$ 669,764(M)	$1,416,285(V)
3. Total Death Benefit**with Extralife Econo*	$1,213,099(N)	$1,988,533
Total Death Benefit with Whole Life Policy	500,000(O)	500,000
ADDITIONAL DEATH BENEFIT WITH EXTRALIFE*	$ 713,099(P)	$1,488,533(W)

IN OTHER WORDS:

AGE 77 SUMMARY	*AGE 85 SUMMARY*
FOR THE SAME OUTLAY YOU WILL HAVE $669,764 MORE CASH AVAILABLE AND $713,099 MORE DEATH BENEFIT;*	FOR THE SAME OUTLAY YOU WILL HAVE $1,416,285 MORE CASH AVAILABLE AND $1,488,533 MORE DEATH BENEFIT;*
OR	OR
YOU CAN SPEND $215,913 LESS AND HAVE $20,556 MORE CASH AVAILABLE AND $63,891 MORE DEATH BENEFIT.*	YOU CAN SPEND $333,995 LESS AND HAVE $46,011 MORE CASH AVAILABLE AND $118,259 MORE DEATH BENEFIT.*

* Dividends are not guaranteed but are based on the current dividend schedule, which may be changed at any time.

** Death Benefit includes: A) Death Benefit of Policy, and B) Side fund (Premium difference and current surrender value compounded at 8%).

PROPOSAL NO. 9

AGE: 45   OCCUPATION: VICE-PRESIDENT DEATH BENEFIT: $1,000,000
SEX: MALE   INCOME: $300,000   CURRENT PREM.: $ 29,210

A 45-year-old man has a choice of what type of policy to purchase to fill a need for a $1,000,000 death benefit. He can buy the old low premium and cash value policy and have $28,860 additional cash value or he can buy the new Extralife-Economatic policy and invest his savings of $20,059 and have $341,643 additional available in a savings fund. Here is how these policies compare:

The old low premium and cash value policy with a $1,000,000 death benefit has a first-year premium of $29,210 (B in Table 22), while the Extralife-Economatic type has a first-year premium of $17,375 (A in the table). If he did purchase the new policy he would save $11,835 (C) in the first year.

The total premiums on the new policy, to age 77, would be $290,071 (D) versus $310,130 (E) with the old type policy. This is a savings of $20,059 (F) with the new type policy. If the individual invested the premium difference yearly in an 8% Municipal Bond Fund, he would have a fund equal to $370,503 (G).

The total surrender value of the new type policy, at age 77, is $672,130 (H) versus $700,990 (I) with the old type policy. As you can see, there is $28,860 (J) less surrender value with the new type policy. However, the premium difference compounded at 8% has grown to $370,503, so he really has $341,643 (K) additional cash available with the new type policy.

If death should occur at age 77 and he has not taken the cash, the total death benefit (policy and savings fund) with the new policy would be $1,370,503 (L) versus $1,000,000 (M) with the old policy. This means that his family would receive $370,503 (N) additional cash, if the death should occur, at no additional cost.

If he should continue the program after age 77 and death does not occur, at age 85 the premium savings with the new type policy would be $35,656 (O in the table). Again, if the premium difference was invested at 8% he would have a total fund of $707,772 (P) with the new type policy.

The total surrender value at age 85 with the new policy would be $25,530 (Q) less than the old type policy. However, he has invested the premium difference and has a fund of $707,772 with the new policy, so he really has $682,242 (R) additional cash available with the new type policy.

If death should occur at age 85 and he has not taken the cash, the total death benefit (policy and savings fund) with the new policy would be $707,772 (S) more than the old type policy.

Why would you send the insurance company $20,059 more over your lifetime for an old low premium low cash value policy so that you could have $28,860 additional cash value? You can buy an Extralife-Economatic Type policy and invest the $20,059 savings and have $341,643 additional cash available and $370,503 additional death benefit.

NOTE: A NUMBER OF THE ABOVE FIGURES INCLUDE DIVI-
DENDS THAT ARE NOT GUARANTEED BUT ARE BASED ON THE
CURRENT DIVIDEND SCHEDULE, WHICH MAY BE CHANGED
AT ANY TIME.

Table 22. PREPARED FOR: MALE AGE 45
$1,000,000 EXTRALIFE-ECONOMATIC TYPE (SUPP-REDUCE) VS. $1,000,000 OLD LOW PREMIUM AND CASH VALUE (REDUCE)
SUMMARY PAGE

The First Year Annual Premium on the Extra. Econo Policy = $ 17,375(A)
The Current Annual Premium on the Old Type Policy .... =   29,210(B)
      First Year Savings with Extralife Policy............. = $ 11,835(C)

	AGE 77 Summary	AGE 85 Summary
1. Extralife Econo. Pol. Total Annual Outlay*	$ 290,071(D)	$ 225,874
Old Type Policy Total Annual Outlay*...........	310,130(E)	261,530
Savings With Extralife Econo. Policy*........	$ 20,059(F)	$ 35,656(O)
Savings compounded at 8%............................	$ 370,503(G)	$ 707,772(P)
2. Extralife Econo. Pol. Total Surrender Value*	$ 672,130(H)	$ 793,690
Old Type Policy Total Surrender Value*	700,990(I)	819,220
Additional Extralife Econo. Policy Value*	$ −28,860(J)	$ −25,530(Q)
Plus savings of Premium Outlay Total Additional Cash Available....................	$ 341,643(K)	$ 682,242(R)
3. Total Death Benefit**with Extralife Econo*	$1,370,503(L)	$1,707,772
Total Death Benefit with Old Type Policy	1,000,000(M)	1,000,000
Additional Death Benefit With Extralife*	$ 370,503(N)	$ 707,772(S)

IN OTHER WORDS:

AGE 77 SUMMARY
FOR THE SAME OUTLAY YOU WILL HAVE $341,643 MORE CASH AVAILABLE AND $370,503 MORE DEATH BENEFIT;*

OR

YOU CAN SPEND $20,059 LESS AND HAVE $28,860 LESS CASH AVAILABLE AND THE SAME DEATH BENEFIT.*

AGE 85 SUMMARY
FOR THE SAME OUTLAY YOU WILL HAVE $682,242 MORE CASH AVAILABLE AND $707,772 MORE DEATH BENEFIT;*

OR

YOU CAN SPEND $35,656 LESS AND HAVE $25,530 LESS CASH AVAILABLE AND THE SAME DEATH BENEFIT.*

* Dividends are not guaranteed but are based on the current dividend schedule, which may be changed at any time.

** Death Benefit includes: A) Death Benefit of Policy, and B) Side fund (Premium difference and current surrender value compounded at 8%).

PROPOSAL NO. 10

AGE: 45	OCCUPATION: PRESIDENT	DEATH BENEFIT: $1,000,000
SEX: MALE	INCOME: $300,000	CURRENT PREM.: $ 31,550

A 45-year-old man has a choice of what type of policy to purchase to fill a need for a $1,000,000 death benefit. He can buy the old high premium and cash value policy and have $182,200 additional cash value or he can buy the new Extra-life-Economatic policy and invest his premium savings of $92,529 and have $602,982 additional available in a side fund. Here is how these policies compare:

The old high premium and cash value policy with a $1,000,000 death benefit has a first-year premium of $31,550 (B in Table 23), while the Extralife-Economatic type has a first-year premium of $17,375 (A in the table). If he did purchase the new policy he would save $14,175 (C in the table) in the first year.

The total premiums on the new policy, to age 77, would be $290,071 (D) versus $382,600 (E) with the old type policy. This is a savings of $92,529 (F) with the new type policy. If the man invested the premium difference yearly in an 8% Municipal Bond Fund, he would have a fund equal to $785,182 (G).

The total surrender value of the new type policy, at age 77, is $672,130 (H) versus $854,330 (I) with the old type policy. As you can see, there is $182,200 (J) less surrender value with the new type policy. However, the premium difference compounded at 8% has grown to $785,182 so he really has $602,982 (K) additional cash available with the new type policy.

If death should occur at age 77 and he has not taken the cash, the total death benefit (policy and savings fund) with the new policy would be $1,785,182 (L) versus $1,000,000 (M) with the old policy. This means that his family would receive $785,182 (N) additional cash if the death should occur at no additional cost.

If he should continue the program after age 77 and death does not occur, at age 85 the premium cost with the new type policy would be $47,634 (O in the table). However, if the premium difference was invested at 8% he would have a total fund of $1,251,331 (P) with the new type policy.

The total surrender value at age 85 with the new policy would be $142,710 (Q) less than the old type policy. However, he has invested the premium difference and has a fund of $1,251,331 with the new policy, so he really has $1,108,621 (R) additional cash available with the new type policy.

If death should occur at age 85 and he has not taken the cash, the total death benefit (policy and savings fund) with the new policy would be $1,251,331 (S) more than the old type policy.

Why would you send the insurance company $92,529 more over your lifetime for an old high premium, high cash value policy so that you could have $182,200 additional cash value, when you could buy an Extralife-Economatic type policy and invest the $92,529 savings, and have $602,982 additional cash available and $785,182 additional death benefit?

NOTE: A NUMBER OF THE ABOVE FIGURES INCLUDE DIVIDENDS THAT ARE NOT GUARANTEED BUT ARE BASED ON THE CURRENT DIVIDEND SCHEDULE, WHICH MAY BE CHANGED AT ANY TIME.

Table 23. PREPARED FOR: MALE AGE 45

$1,000,000 EXTRALIFE-ECONOMATIC TYPE (SUPP-REDUCE) VS.
$1,000,000 OLD HIGH PREMIUM AND CASH VALUE POLICY (REDUCE)

SUMMARY PAGE

The FIRST YEAR Annual Premium on the Extra. Econo Policy =	$	17,375(A)
The FIRST YEAR Annual Premium on the Old Type Policy .... =		31,550(B)
FIRST YEAR SAVINGS WITH EXTRALIFE POLICY .... =	$	14,175(C)

	AGE 77 Summary	AGE 85 Summary
1. Extralife Econo. Pol. Total Annual Outlay*	$ 290,071(D)	$ 225,874
Old Type Policy Total Annual Outlay*	382,600(E)	178,240
SAVINGS WITH EXTRALIFE ECONO. POLICY*	$ 92,529(F)	$ −47,634(O)
SAVINGS compounded at 8%	$ 785,182(G)	$1,251,331(P)
2. Extralife Econo. Pol. Total Surrender Value*	$ 672,130(H)	$ 793,690
Old Type Policy Total Surrender Value*	854,330(I)	936,400
ADDITIONAL EXTRALIFE ECONO. POLICY VALUE*	$ −182,200(J)	$ −142,710(Q)
Plus savings of Premium Outlay TOTAL ADDITIONAL CASH AVAILABLE	$ 602,982(K)	$1,108,621(R)
3. Total Death Benefit**with Extralife Econo*	$1,785,182(L)	$2,251,331
Total Death Benefit with Old Type Policy	1,000,000(M)	1,000,000
ADDITIONAL DEATH BENEFIT WITH EXTRALIFE*	$ 785,182(N)	$1,251,331(S)

IN OTHER WORDS:

AGE 77 SUMMARY

FOR THE SAME OUTLAY YOU WILL HAVE $602,982 MORE CASH AVAILABLE AND $785,182 MORE DEATH BENEFIT;*

OR

YOU CAN SPEND $92,529 LESS AND HAVE $182,200 LESS CASH AVAILABLE AND THE SAME DEATH BENEFIT.*

AGE 85 SUMMARY

FOR THE SAME OUTLAY YOU WILL HAVE $1,108,621 MORE CASH AVAILABLE AND $1,251,331 MORE DEATH BENEFIT;*

OR

YOU CAN SPEND $47,634 LESS AND HAVE $142,710 LESS CASH AVAILABLE AND THE SAME DEATH BENEFIT.*

* Dividends are not guaranteed but are based on the current dividend schedule, which may be changed at any time.

** Death Benefit includes: A) Death Benefit of Policy, and B) Side fund (Premium difference and current surrender value compounded at 8%).

PROPOSAL NO. 11

AGE: 45   OCCUPATION: DENTIST   DEATH BENEFIT: $1,000,000
SEX: MALE   INCOME: $200,000   CURRENT PREM.: $ 2,295
                                                          TERM

Why would a 45-year-old man pay $1,312,634 more for a $1,000,000 in term insurance coverage to age 85 and have absolutely no cash available, when he can buy the same death benefit in an Extralife-Economatic plan, save the $1,312,634, and still have $793,690 available cash value? Here is how this works:

At age 45 a $1,000,000 Yearly Renewable Term Policy would cost $2,295 (A in Table 24) versus $17,375 (B in the table) for a new low-cost Extralife-Economatic Type policy. It appears that term is a better buy, since you save $15,080 on the premium for the term policy in the first year. There is only one problem. Each year the premium for the term policy goes up, while the Extralife-Economatic premium, because of the yearly dividends used to reduce that premium, will eventually go down and the policyholder will, at age 67, have no premium outlay whatsoever.

Life insurance is purchased for life, and normal life expectancy is age 77. The total premiums to age 77 for the term policy are $824,810 (C in the table) versus $290,068 (D) for the permanent policy. This is a savings of $534,742 over the thirty-two years. If the policyholder had bought the term policy and deposited the difference (between the term and the Extralife-Economatic) in an 8% Municipal Bond Fund, his total cash available compounded to age 77 would be $39,140 (E). To get the $39,140 figure, we must realize that, although the side fund was increasing so that at age 67 it reached a total of $418,382, after that year, in order to continue with the term insurance since the term premium was now larger than the permanent premium policy (creating a negative differential), the policyholder would have to start eroding his side fund to pay his term premium and keep his cash flow equal. This erosion would continue each year, increasing dramatically until, at age 77, the side fund would be reduced to the $39,140 figure.

On the other hand, the dividend at age 67 for the permanent policy is $17,848, paying the full premium and giving back the policyholder $473. Ten years later, the Extralife-Economatic dividend is $23,509 and the policyholder gets back $6,134 after the premium of $17,375 has been paid.

Meanwhile, the Extralife-Economatic has been building cash values which at age 77 total $672,130 (F). If we compare this total to the $39,140 in the side fund of the term buyer, we see that the Extralife-Economatic policyholder has $632,989 additional cash available (G in the table).

If the individual lives to age 85, the term premium outlay is now a total of $1,755,620 (H) versus $225,868 (I) with the Extralife-Economatic policy. If the term buyer continues his term insurance to this point, the side fund that he built with his differential will have totally disappeared and he will have had to come up with $1,312,634 (J) additional cash to pay his annual term premiums for the eight-year period (age 77 to 85).

The Extralife-Economatic buyer also has a cash value of $793,690 (K) which would thus give him $2,106,324 (L in the table) additional cash available over the term.

NOTE: A NUMBER OF THE ABOVE FIGURES INCLUDE DIVIDENDS THAT ARE NOT GUARANTEED BUT ARE BASED ON THE CURRENT DIVIDEND SCHEDULE, WHICH MAY BE CHANGED AT ANY TIME.

Table 24. CUMULATIVE COST COMPARISON

BETWEEN

TERM INSURANCE AND PERMANENT INSURANCE

$1,000,000   MALE AGE 45

	TERM INSURANCE		PERMANENT INSURANCE		
YR	CUMULATIVE COST	CUMULATIVE DEPOSITS	8.00 PCT CUMULATIVE DIFFERENCE IN INPUT	CUMULATIVE POLICY VALUE	CUMULATIVE NET COST OF PERMANENT OVER TERM
1	2,295(A)	17,375(B)	16,286	1,830	14,456
2	6,870	34,750	31,413	3,660	27,753
3	11,875	52,125	47,285	18,860	28,425
4	17,350	69,500	63,920	34,770	29,150
5	23,295	86,875	81,378	51,550	29,828
6	29,820	104,250	99,607	69,180	30,427
7	36,935	121,625	118,656	87,730	30,926
8	44,670	139,000	138,560	107,210	31,350
9	53,095	156,375	159,311	127,700	31,611
10	62,270	173,750	180,912	149,210	31,702
11	72,365	191,125	203,247	172,590	30,657
12	83,040	203,500	226,743	197,200	29,543
13	95,675	225,875	250,001	223,120	26,881
14	108,730	243,250	274,667	250,420	24,247
15	123,085	260,625	299,902	279,240	20,662
16	138,700	278,000	325,795	309,680	16,115
17	156,035	295,375	351,902	341,690	10,212
18	174,990	312,750	378,348	375,470	2,878
19	196,015	328,300	402,703	411,150	−8,446
20	219,380	329,204	410,662	446,970	−36,307
21	244,935	329,411	416,139	467,250	−51,110
22	273,210	328,938	418,382	487,350	−68,967
23	304,365	327,771	416,945	507,230	−90,284
24	338,720	325,905	411,181	526,820	−115,638
25	376,455	323,359	400,573	546,050	−145,476
26	426,640	320,151	374,955	564,890	−189,934
27	481,095	316,349	342,033	583,360	−241,326
28	539,950	311,991	301,126	601,520	−300,393
29	603,365	307,164	251,514	619,430	−367,915
30	671,650	301,888	192,190	637,160	−444,969
31	745,265	296,202	121,920	654,740	−532,819
AGE 77					
32	824,810(C)	290,068(D)	39,140(E)	672,130(F)	−632,989(G)
33	911,035	283,506	−57,937	689,220	−747,157
34	1,004,710	276,484	−171,326	705,890	−877,216
35	1,106,525	268,989	−303,086	722,030	−1,025,116
36	1,217,070	261,052	−455,294	737,560	−1,192,854
37	1,336,855	252,714	−630,089	752,450	−1,382,539
38	1,466,270	244,031	−829,643	766,730	−1,596,373
39	1,605,715	235,054	−1,056,310	780,460	−1,836,770
AGE 85					
40	1,755,620(H)	225,868(I)	−1,312,634(J)	793,690(K)	−2,106,324(L)

Table 25. TERM INSURANCE SCHEDULE

$1,000,000 ANNUAL RENEWABLE TERM TO 100
MALE AGE 45   FIRST-YEAR PREMIUM −$2,295

YEAR	AGE	ANNUAL PREMIUM	CUMULATIVE PREMIUMS	DEATH BENEFIT
1	45	2,295	2,295	1,000,000
2	46	4,575	6,870	1,000,000
3	47	5,005	11,875	1,000,000
4	48	5,475	17,350	1,000,000
5	49	5,945	23,295	1,000,000
6	50	6,525	29,820	1,000,000
7	51	7,115	36,935	1,000,000
8	52	7,735	44,670	1,000,000
9	53	8,425	53,095	1,000,000
10	54	9,175	62,270	1,000,000
11	55	10,095	72,365	1,000,000
12	56	10,675	83,040	1,000,000
13	57	12,635	95,675	1,000,000
14	58	13,055	108,730	1,000,000
15	59	14,355	123,085	1,000,000
16	60	15,615	138,700	1,000,000
17	61	17,335	156,035	1,000,000
18	62	18,955	174,990	1,000,000
19	63	21,025	196,015	1,000,000
20	64	23,365	219,380	1,000,000
21	65	25,555	244,935	1,000,000
22	66	28,275	273,210	1,000,000
23	67	31,155	304,365	1,000,000
24	68	34,355	338,720	1,000,000
25	69	37,735	376,455	1,000,000
26	70	50,185	426,640	1,000,000
27	71	54,455	481,095	1,000,000
28	72	58,855	539,950	1,000,000
29	73	63,415	603,365	1,000,000
30	74	68,285	671,650	1,000,000
31	75	73,615	745,265	1,000,000
32	76	79,545	824,810	1,000,000
33	77	86,225	911,035	1,000,000
34	78	93,675	1,004,710	1,000,000
35	79	101,815	1,106,525	1,000,000
36	80	110,545	1,217,070	1,000,000
37	81	119,785	1,336,855	1,000,000
38	82	129,415	1,466,270	1,000,000
39	83	139,445	1,605,715	1,000,000
40	84	149,905	1,755,620	1,000,000

Table 26. LEDGER STATEMENT

$1,000,000 EXTRALIFE PLAN

DIVIDENDS SUPPLEMENTAL/REDUCE
BASIC PREMIUM – $17,375.00

MALE AGE 45

YR	ANNUAL PREMIUMS	INCREASE IN TOTAL CASH VALUE*	NET GAIN	TOTAL PREMIUMS	TOTAL CASH VALUE*	DEATH BENEFIT	PAID-UP INSURANCE
1	17,375	1,830	−15,545	17,375	1,830	1,000,000	6,430
2	17,375	1,830	−15,545	34,750	3,660	1,000,000	12,070
3	17,375	15,200	−2,175	52,125	18,860	1,000,000	53,670
4	17,375	15,910	−1,465	69,500	34,770	1,000,000	94,670
5	17,375	16,780	−595	86,875	51,550	1,000,000	135,440
6	17,375	17,630	255	104,250	69,180	1,000,000	175,950
7	17,375	18,550	1,175	121,625	87,730	1,000,000	216,280
8	17,375	19,480	2,105	139,000	107,210	1,000,000	256,420
9	17,375	20,490	3,115	156,375	127,700	1,000,000	296,510
10	17,375	21,510	4,135	173,750	149,210	1,000,000	336,540
11	17,375	23,380	6,005	191,125	172,590	1,000,000	378,290
12	17,375	24,610	7,235	208,500	197,200	1,000,000	420,250
13	17,375	25,920	8,545	225,875	223,120	1,000,000	462,570
14	17,375	27,300	9,925	243,250	250,420	1,000,000	505,340
15	17,375	28,820	11,445	260,625	279,240	1,000,000	548,790
16	17,375	30,440	13,065	278,000	309,680	1,000,000	593,050
17	17,375	32,010	14,635	295,375	341,690	1,000,000	637,980
18	17,375	33,780	16,405	312,750	375,470	1,000,000	732,630
19	15,550	35,680	20,129	328,300	411,150	1,000,000	779,580
20	904	35,820	34,915	329,204	446,970	1,000,000	824,170
21	206	20,280	20,073	329,411	467,250	1,000,000	838,520
22	−473	20,100	20,573	328,938	487,350	1,000,000	851,910

YR	ANNUAL PREMIUMS	INCREASE IN TOTAL CASH VALUE*	NET GAIN	TOTAL PREMIUMS	TOTAL CASH VALUE*	DEATH BENEFIT	PAID-UP INSURANCE
23	−1,166	19,880	21,046	327,771	507,230	1,000,000	864,440
24	−1,866	19,590	21,456	325,905	526,820	1,000,000	876,150
25	−2,545	19,230	21,775	323,359	546,050	1,000,000	887,040
26	−3,208	18,840	22,048	320,151	564,890	1,000,000	897,160
27	−3,802	18,470	22,272	316,349	583,360	1,000,000	906,550
28	−4,357	18,160	22,517	311,991	601,520	1,000,000	915,300
29	−4,827	17,910	22,737	307,164	619,430	1,000,000	923,450
30	−5,275	17,730	23,005	301,888	637,160	1,000,000	931,100
31	−5,686	17,580	23,266	296,202	654,740	1,000,000	938,330
32	−6,134	17,390	23,524	290,068	672,130	1,000,000	945,180
33	−6,561	17,090	23,651	283,506	689,220	1,000,000	951,620
34	−7,022	16,670	23,692	276,484	705,890	1,000,000	957,670
35	−7,494	16,140	23,634	268,989	722,030	1,000,000	963,320
36	−7,937	15,530	23,467	261,052	737,560	1,000,000	968,530
37	−8,337	14,890	23,227	252,714	752,450	1,000,000	973,330
38	−8,683	14,280	22,963	244,031	766,730	1,000,000	977,730
39	−8,977	13,730	22,707	235,054	780,460	1,000,000	981,790
40	−9,186	13,230	22,416	225,868	793,690	1,000,000	985,490

SUMMARY VALUES AT:	YEAR 20	YEAR 40
TOTAL CASH VALUE	$446,970	$793,690
LESS: TOTAL DEPOSITS	329,204	225,868
NET GAIN (COST)	$117,765	$567,821
TOTAL PAID-UP INSURANCE	$824,170	$985,490

* Dividends are not guaranteed but are based on the current dividend schedule, which may be changed at any time.

PROPOSAL NO. 12

AGE: 45   OCCUPATION: SALESMAN   DEATH BENEFIT: $1,000,000
SEX: MALE   INCOME: $250,000   CURRENT PREM.: $ 31,550

Let's compare Extralife-Economatic with an ordinary permanent insurance policy on the minimum-deposit approach, for a 45-year-old male. Why pay $154,919 more for $1,000,000 in coverage to age 85, when you can invest that $154,919, have $1,788,560 in additional cash available and $1,944,531 additional death benefit? Here's how this plan works:

The premium for the old high premium and cash value policy with a $1,000,000 death benefit is $31,550 (B in Table 27) while the Extralife-Economatic policy has a premium of $17,375 (A in the table). If he purchased the Extralife-Economatic policy he would save $14,175 (C) in the first year.

In minimum deposit, the policyholder borrows from the cash values of the policy after four of the first seven premiums are paid in full and then pays only tax-deductible interest.

The total after-tax outlay (assuming 50% tax bracket) on the new Extralife-Economatic, to age 77, would be $332,482 (D in the table) versus $463,189 (E) with the old type policy. This is a saving of $130,707 (F) with the new type policy. If the individual invested the premium difference yearly in an 8% fund, he would have a savings fund equal to $708,179 (G).

The total surrender value of the new Extralife-Economatic, at age 77, is $389,777 (H), versus $145,221 (I) with the old type policy. As you can see, there is $244,556 (J) more surrender value with the new type policy. Also, the premium difference compounded at 8% has grown to $708,179, so he really has $962,735 (K) additional cash available with the Extralife-Economatic.

If death should occur at age 77 and he has not taken the cash, the total death benefit ($906,570 death benefit plus $708,179 in the side savings fund) in the Extralife-Economatic would be $1,614,749 (L in the table), versus $691,444 (M) with the old policy. This means that his family would receive

$923,305 (N) additional cash if death should occur at no additional cost.

If he should continue the program after age 77 and death does not occur at age 85, the premium savings with the new type policy would be $154,919 (O in the table). Again, if the premium difference was invested at 8% he would have a total fund of $1,348,762 (P) with the new type policy.

The total surrender value at age 85 with the new policy would be $439,798 (Q) more than the old type policy. Also, he has invested the premium difference and has a fund of $1,348,762 with the new policy, so he really has $1,788,560 (R) additional cash available with the new type policy.

If death should occur at age 85 and he has not taken the cash, the total death benefit (policy and fund) with the Extra-life-Economatic would be $1,944,531 (S) more than the old type policy.

NOTE: A NUMBER OF THE ABOVE FIGURES INCLUDE DIVIDENDS THAT ARE NOT GUARANTEED BUT ARE BASED ON THE CURRENT DIVIDEND SCHEDULE, WHICH MAY BE CHANGED AT ANY TIME.

Table 27. PREPARED FOR: MALE AGE 45
$1,000,000 NEW TYPE MINIMUM DEPOSIT (SUPP-REDUCE) VS.
$1,000,000 OLD TYPE MINIMUM DEPOSIT (TDO/REDUCE)
SUMMARY PAGE

The FIRST YEAR Annual Premium on the Extra. Econo Policy = $ 17,375(A)
The FIRST YEAR Annual Premium on the Old Type Policy .... =   31,550(B)
FIRST YEAR SAVINGS WITH EXTRALIFE POLICY............. = $ 14,175(C)

	AGE 77 Summary	AGE 85 Summary
1. Extra. Econo. Pol. Total Annual A.T.***Outlay*	$ 332,482(D)	$ 507,622
Old Type Policy Total Annual A.T. Outlay*	463,189(E)	662,541
SAVINGS WITH EXTRALIFE ECONO. POLICY*	$ 130,707(F)	$ 154,919(O)
SAVINGS compounded at 8%	$ 708,179(G)	$1,348,762(P)
2. Extralife Econo. Pol. Total Surrender Value*	$ 389,777(H)	$ 659,574
Old Type Policy Total Surrender Value*	145,221(I)	219,776
ADDITIONAL EXTRALIFE ECONO. POLICY VALUE ...	$ 244,556(J)	$ 439,798(Q)
Plus savings of Premium Outlay TOTAL ADDITIONAL CASH AVAILABLE....................	$ 952,735(K)	$1,788,560(R)
3. Total Death Benefit**with Extralife Econo*	$1,614,749(L)	$2,457,722
Total Death Benefit with Old Type Policy* ...	691,444(M)	513,191
ADDITIONAL DEATH BENEFIT WITH EXTRALIFE*	$ 923,305(N)	$1,944,531(S)

IN OTHER WORDS:

AGE 77 SUMMARY
FOR THE SAME OUTLAY YOU WILL HAVE $952,735 MORE CASH AVAILABLE AND $923,305 MORE DEATH BENEFIT;*
OR
YOU CAN SPEND $130,707 LESS AND HAVE $244,556 MORE CASH AVAILABLE AND $215,126 MORE DEATH BENEFIT.*

AGE 85 SUMMARY
FOR THE SAME OUTLAY YOU WILL HAVE $1,788,560 MORE CASH AVAILABLE AND $1,944,531 MORE DEATH BENEFIT;*
OR
YOU CAN SPEND $154,919 LESS AND HAVE $439,798 MORE CASH AVAILABLE AND $595,769 MORE DEATH BENEFIT.*

* Dividends are not guaranteed but are based on the current dividend schedule, which may be changed at any time.

** Death Benefit includes: A) Death Benefit of Policy, and B) Side fund (Premium difference and current surrender value compounded at 8%).

*** (A.T.) after tax outlay assumes 50% tax bracket.

PROPOSAL NO. 13

AGE: 48   OCCUPATION: PRESIDENT   DEATH BENEFIT: $500,000
SEX: MALE   INCOME: $250,000   CURRENT PREM.: $ 9,416

During the life insurance revolution, stock companies that normally offer non-participating permanent insurance policies are beginning to offer products that appear to be competitive.

In this case, a 48-year-old man has bought $500,000 of insurance from a stock company. The stock company offers a discount on the first year's premiums. Instead of $10,460, the man pays only $9,416 the first year.

When comparing this premium with the new Extralife-Economatic premium of $10,135, we find that the stock company premium is definitely less expensive—but only in the first year. Starting in year two, the policy goes up to $10,460, so the discount is really only a merchandising gimmick. And in this case, the Extralife-Economatic policy is clearly less expensive.

In addition, the stock company states that the initial premium is guaranteed for only two years. Thereafter, the stock company can actually raise the premium to as high as $13,205 yearly. Thus, the consumer never really knows how much his yearly premium will be. Whereas, the Extralife-Economatic policy premium cannot exceed $10,135.

On the same policy, the stock company offers a level premium option of $11,315 that is guaranteed. If the consumer utilizes that approach, he is simply buying another non-participating policy. The $11,315 premium is obviously larger than the $10,135 Extralife-Economatic premium, but there are other factors involved that also weigh against the stock company's new product.

First, the twenty-year interest-adjusted net cost index on the Extralife-Economatic is $5.73 per thousand, while the stock company interest-adjusted rate varies from $10.07 per thousand for the level premium product to as high as $14.44 per thousand for the varied premium product.

At age 65 the Extralife-Economatic has a surrender value of $192,719, which is larger than the stock company surrender value; the latter can be as low as $96,835 or as high as $153,500.

Over the seventeen-year period to age 65, this man will save $729 the first year, but from then on, if the premiums are not increased, the Extralife-Economatic will offer the same insurance for $325 less annually—a total of $3,861 for that period. If this saving was compounded at 8%, it would grow to $7,946.

Why would you pay $3,861 more to have $46,165 less cash available and $7,946 less death benefit? Since this man will actuarially live longer than 65, these figures become even more dramatic in the later years.

Finally, everything we have compared is based on the stock company premium remaining level and the maximum offered cash values being available. However, the stock company states in its own policy that, should you take advantage of this plan, nothing is guaranteed after two years.

NOTE: A NUMBER OF THE FIGURES ABOVE INCLUDE DIVIDENDS THAT ARE NOT GUARANTEED BUT ARE BASED ON THE CURRENT DIVIDEND SCHEDULE, WHICH MAY BE CHANGED AT ANY TIME.

PROPOSAL NO. 14

AGE: 49	OCCUPATION: KEYMAN	DEATH BENEFIT: $256,000
SEX: MALE	INCOME: $100,000	CURRENT PREM.: $ 7,244

A 49-year-old man currently has a $256,000 permanent policy. For the same outlay he will have $311,105 additional cash available and $309,555 additional death benefit at age 77. Here is how this saving was accomplished:

He currently has a $256,000 non-participating permanent policy with a surrender value of $5,547. His yearly premium is $7,244 (B in Table 28).

The premium for the new Extralife Economatic Type policy is $5,473 (A in the table). The first year savings with the new policy is thus $1,771 (C).

The total premiums, to age 77, for the new policy are $100,913 (D) versus $202,832 (E) with the current policy. This is a saving of $101,919 (F) over this man's lifetime. If he invests this premium difference in an 8% Municipal Bond Fund it will grow to $261,701 (G). If he also invests the current surrender value of $5,547 in an 8% Municipal Bond Fund it will grow to $47,854 (H). Combined, his total savings fund will be $309,555 (I in the table).

The total surrender value, at age 77, of the new policy will be $166,414 (J) versus $164,864 (K) with the current policy. This is an increase of $1,550 (L). Plus combined fund of $309,555, he has $311,105 (M) additional cash available.

If death should occur at age 77, and he has not taken the cash, his total death benefit with the new policy (which includes the savings fund) would be $565,555 (N in the table) versus $256,000 (O) with his current policy. His family will end up with $309,555 (P) additional cash at death.

Should he continue this program and live to age 85, his savings with the new policy would be $168,789 (Q), which when invested at 8% would equal $579,874 (R). His current surrender value, if invested at 8%, would grow to $88,575 (S), giving him a combined total fund of $668,449 (T).

At age 85 the surrender value of the policy is $10,289 (U) less than the current policy. However, he has a fund of $668,449, so he still has $658,160 (V) additional cash available.

If death should occur at age 85, he would have $668,449 (W) additional cash for his family if he had not taken the cash from the policy and fund. By spending the same amount, this man increased his death benefit at age 77 by 121% and increased his available cash by 189%. At age 85, he will increase his death benefit by 261% and his available cash by 313%, another example of an extraordinary lifetime saving.

NOTE: A NUMBER OF THE ABOVE FIGURES INCLUDE DIVIDENDS THAT ARE NOT GUARANTEED BUT ARE BASED ON THE CURRENT DIVIDEND SCHEDULE, WHICH MAY BE CHANGED AT ANY TIME.

Table 28. PREPARED FOR: MALE AGE 49
$256,000 EXTRALIFE-ECONOMATIC TYPE (SUPP-REDUCE) VS. $256,000 CURRENT WHOLE LIFE (NON-PAR)
SUMMARY PAGE

The FIRST YEAR Annual Premium on the Extra. Econo Policy   = $ 5,473(A)
The CURRENT Annual Premium on the Whole Life Policy............=   7,244(B)
       FIRST YEAR SAVINGS WITH EXTRALIFE POLICY..............= $ 1,771(C)

	AGE 77 Summary	AGE 85 Summary
1. Extralife Econo. Pol. Total Annual Outlay*	$ 100,913(D)	$ 91,995
Whole Life Policy Total Annual Outlay..........	202,832(E)	260,784
SAVINGS WITH EXTRALIFE ECONO. POLICY*	$ 101,919(F)	$ 168,789(Q)
SAVINGS compounded at 8%..............................	$ 261,701(G)	$ 579,874(R)
Your current Whole Life Policy has a $5,547 surrender value which could be compounded at 8% and will grow to	$ 47,854(H)	$ 88,575(S)
INCREASING YOUR SAVINGS TO	$ 309,555(I)	$ 668,449(T)
2. Extralife Econo. Pol. Total Surrender Value*	$ 166,414(J)	$ 199,631
Whole Life Policy Total Surrender Value*.....	164,864(K)	209,920
ADDITIONAL EXTRALIFE ECONO. POLICY VALUE*	$ 1,550(L)	$ −10,289(U)
Plus savings of Premium Outlay and Surrender Value of Current Policy TOTAL ADDITIONAL CASH AVAILABLE....................	$ 311,105(M)	$ 658,160(V)
3. Total Death Benefit**with Extralife Econo*	$ 565,555(N)	$ 924,449
Total Death Benefit with Whole Life Policy	256,000(O)	256,000
ADDITIONAL DEATH BENEFIT WITH EXTRALIFE*	$ 309,555(P)	$ 668,449 (W)

IN OTHER WORDS:

AGE 77 SUMMARY
FOR THE SAME OUTLAY YOU WILL HAVE $311,105 MORE CASH AVAILABLE AND $309,555 MORE DEATH BENEFIT;*

OR

YOU CAN SPEND $101,919 LESS AND HAVE $49,404 MORE CASH AVAILABLE AND $47,854 MORE DEATH BENEFIT.*

AGE 85 SUMMARY
FOR THE SAME OUTLAY YOU WILL HAVE $658,160 MORE CASH AVAILABLE AND $668,449 MORE DEATH BENEFIT;*

OR

YOU CAN SPEND $168,789 LESS AND HAVE $78,286 MORE CASH AVAILABLE AND $88,575 MORE DEATH BENEFIT.*

  * Dividends are not guaranteed but are based on the current dividend schedule, which may be changed at any time.

  ** Death Benefit includes: A) Death Benefit of Policy, and B) Side fund (Premium difference and current surrender value compounded at 8%).

PROPOSAL NO. 15

AGE: 54   OCCUPATION: PSYCHIATRIST DEATH BENEFIT: $100,000
SEX: FEMALE   INCOME: $350,000   CURRENT PREM.: $ 3,115

A 54-year-old woman currently owns a $100,000 permanent policy. For the same outlay she can have an additonal $66,849 cash available and $46,151 additional death benefit. Here is how this remarkable saving was accomplished:

She currently has a $100,000 participating permanent policy with a net surrender value of $2,200. Her yearly premium is $3,342. The current dividend is $227, making this year's premium outlay $3,115 (B in Table 29).

The premium for the new Extralife-Economatic Type policy is $2,606 (A in Table 29). Her first-year saving is then $509 (C in the table).

At age 77, the total annual premiums with the new policy will be $59,938 (D) versus $74,272 (E) with her current policy. Therefore, her savings over twenty-three years would be $14,334 (F). If she invested this premium difference yearly into an 8% Municipal Bond Fund it would grow to $37,771 (G). If she also invests the current surrender value of $2,200 in the 8% fund it will grow to $12,917 (H). This will make her total savings fund $50,688 (I).

The surrender value on the new policy is $81,621 (J), versus $65,460 (K) with her current policy. This is an increase of $16,161 (L). This increase plus her total fund will give her $66,849 (M) additional cash available at age 77.

If she doesn't take the cash, her death benefit with the new program would be $178,771 (N) versus $132,620 (O) with her current policy. Therefore, the additional death benefit with the new program would be $46,151 (P).

At age 85 the figures would increase to $20,222 (Q) savings over the previous policy. This invested yearly at 8% would grow to $78,367 (R). The invested current surrender value would increase to $23,909 (S). The total savings would then be $102,275 (T).

The new plan's cash surrender value would be $38,838 (U) more than her current policy, thus increasing her cash available by $141,113 (V). Her death benefit, if she does not take the cash, will be $140,908 more than her current policy (W).

By spending the same amount this woman increased her death benefit at age 77 by 35% and more than doubled her available cash. At age 85, she will increase her death benefit by 114% and her cash available by 160%, an extraordinary saving over her lifetime.

NOTE: A NUMBER OF THE ABOVE FIGURES INCLUDE DIVIDENDS THAT ARE NOT GUARANTEED BUT ARE BASED ON THE CURRENT DIVIDEND SCHEDULE, WHICH MAY BE CHANGED AT ANY TIME.

Table 29. PREPARED FOR: FEMALE AGE 54

$100,000 EXTRALIFE-ECONOMATIC TYPE (SUPP-REDUCE) VS.
$100,000 CURRENT WHOLE LIFE (TDO-REDUCE)

SUMMARY PAGE

The First Year Annual Premium on the Extra. Econo Policy = $ 2,606(A)
The Current Annual Premium on the Whole Life Policy............= 3,115(B)
FIRST YEAR SAVINGS WITH EXTRALIFE POLICY..............= $ 509(C)

	AGE 77 Summary	AGE 85 Summary
1. Extralife Econo. Pol. Total Annual Outlay*	$ 59,938(D)	$ 80,786
Whole Life Policy Total Annual Outlay*........	74,272(E)	101,008
SAVINGS WITH EXTRALIFE ECONO. POLICY*........	$ 14,334(F)	$ 20,222(Q)
SAVINGS compounded at 8%.............................	$ 37,771(G)	$ 78,367(R)
Your current Whole Life Policy has a $2,200 surrender value which could be compounded at 8% and will grow to......................................	$ 12,917(H)	$ 23,908(S)
INCREASING YOUR SAVINGS TO.............................	$ 50,688(I)	$ 102,275(T)
2. Extralife Econo. Pol. Total Surrender Value*	$ 81,621(J)	$ 126,866
Whole Life Policy Total Surrender Value*.....	65,460(K)	88,028
ADDITIONAL EXTRALIFE ECONO. POLICY VALUE ...	$ 16,161(L)	$ 38,838(U)
Plus savings of Premium Outlay and Surrender Value of Current Policy TOTAL ADDITIONAL CASH AVAILABLE....................	$ 66,849(M)	$ 141,113(V)
3. Total Death Benefit**with Extralife Econo*	$ 178,771(N)	$ 264,749
Total Death Benefit with Whole Life Policy*	132,620(O)	123,841
ADDITIONAL DEATH BENEFIT WITH EXTRALIFE*	$ 46,151(P)	$ 140,908(W)

IN OTHER WORDS:

AGE 77 SUMMARY	AGE 85 SUMMARY
FOR THE SAME OUTLAY YOU WILL HAVE $66,849 MORE CASH AVAILABLE AND $46,151 MORE DEATH BENEFIT;*	FOR THE SAME OUTLAY YOU WILL HAVE $141,113 MORE CASH AVAILABLE AND $140,908 MORE DEATH BENEFIT;*
OR	OR
YOU CAN SPEND $14,334 LESS AND HAVE $29,078 MORE CASH AVAILABLE AND $8,380 MORE DEATH BENEFIT.*	YOU CAN SPEND $20,222 LESS AND HAVE $62,746 MORE CASH AVAILABLE AND $62,541 MORE DEATH BENEFIT.*

* Dividends are not guaranteed but are based on the current dividend schedule, which may be changed at any time.

** Death Benefit includes: A) Death Benefit of Policy, and B) Side fund (Premium difference and current surrender value compounded at 8%).

PROPOSAL NO. 16

AGE: 55   OCCUPATION: PSYCHOLOGIST   DEATH BENEFIT: $1,000,000
SEX: MALE   INCOME: $250,000   CURRENT PREM.: $ 45,230

A 55-year-old man has a choice of what type of policy to purchase to fill a need for a $1,000,000 death benefit. He can buy the old low premium and cash value policy and have $7,320 additional cash value, or he can buy the new Extralife-Economatic policy and invest his savings of $34,100 and have $188,187 additional cash available in a savings fund. Here is how these policies compare:

The old low premium and cash value policy with a $1,000,000 death benefit has a first-year premium of $45,230 (B in Table 30), while the Extralife-Economatic type has a first year premium of $28,755 (A in the table). If he did purchase the new policy he would save $16,475 (C) in the first year.

The total premiums on the new policy, to age 77, would be $481,000 (D), versus $515,100 (E) with the old type policy. This is a saving of $34,100 (F) with the new type policy. If the man invested the premium difference yearly in an 8% Municipal Bond Fund he would have a fund equal to $195,507 (G).

The total surrender value of the new type policy, at age 77, is $603,810 (H in the table), versus $611,130 (I) with the old type policy. As you can see, there is $7,320 (J) less surrender value with the new type policy. However, the premium difference compounded at 8% has grown to $195,507, so he really has $188,187 (K) additional cash available with the new type policy.

If death should occur at age 77 and he has not taken the cash, the total death benefit (policy and fund) with the new policy would be $1,195,507 (L in the table), versus $1,000,000 (M) with the old policy. This means that his family would receive $195,507 (N) additional cash, if the death should occur, at no additional cost.

If he should continue the program after age 77 and death

does not occur, at age 85 the premium savings with the new type policy would be $79,807 (O in the table). However, if the premium difference was invested at 8% he would have a total fund of $426,872 (P) with the new type policy.

The total surrender value at age 85 with the new policy would be $11,500 (Q) less than the old type policy. However, he has invested the premium difference and has a fund of $426,872 with the new policy so he really has $415,372 (R) additional cash available with the new type policy.

If death should occur at age 85 and he has not taken the cash, the total death benefit (policy and fund) with the new policy would be $426,872 (S) more than the old type policy.

Why would you send the insurance company $34,100 more over your lifetime for an old low premium cash value policy so that you could have $7,320 additional cash value, when you could buy an Extralife-Economatic Type policy and invest the $34,100 savings and have $188,187 additional cash available and $195,507 additional death benefit?

NOTE: A NUMBER OF THE FIGURES ABOVE INCLUDE DIVI-
DENDS THAT ARE NOT GUARANTEED BUT ARE BASED ON THE
CURRENT DIVIDEND SCHEDULE, WHICH MAY BE CHANGED
AT ANY TIME.

Table 30. PREPARED FOR: MALE AGE 55

**$1,000,000 EXTRALIFE-ECONOMATIC TYPE (SUPP-REDUCE) VS.
$1,000,000 OLD LOW PREMIUM AND CASH VALUE POLICY (REDUCE)**

SUMMARY PAGE

The FIRST YEAR Annual Premium on the Extra. Econo Policy = $ 28,755(A)
The FIRST YEAR Annual Premium on the Old Type Policy ....=   45,230(B)
FIRST YEAR SAVINGS WITH EXTRALIFE POLICY.............= $ 16,475(C)

	AGE 77 Summary	AGE 85 Summary
1. Extralife Econo. Pol. Total Annual Outlay*	$ 481,000(D)	$ 494,653
Old Type Policy Total Annual Outlay*...........	515,100(E)	574,460
SAVINGS WITH EXTRALIFE ECONO. POLICY*........	$ 34,100(F)	$ 79,807(O)
SAVINGS compounded at 8%...........................	$ 195,507(G)	$ 426,872(P)
2. Extralife Econo. Pol. Total Surrender Value*	$ 603,810(H)	$ 750,510
Old Type Policy Total Surrender Value*.......	611,130(I)	762,010
ADDITIONAL EXTRALIFE ECONO. POLICY VALUE*	$ −7,320(J)	$ −11,500(Q)
Plus savings of Premium Outlay TOTAL ADDITIONAL CASH AVAILABLE.....................	$ 188,187(K)	$ 415,372(R)
3. Total Death Benefit**with Extralife Econo*	$1,195,507(L)	$1,426,872
Total Death Benefit with Old Type Policy*...	1,000,000(M)	1,000,000
ADDITIONAL DEATH BENEFIT WITH EXTRALIFE*	$ 195,507(N)	$ 426,872(S)

IN OTHER WORDS:

AGE 77 SUMMARY
FOR THE SAME OUTLAY YOU WILL
HAVE $188,187 MORE CASH AVAIL-
ABLE AND $195,507 MORE DEATH
BENEFIT;*

OR

YOU CAN SPEND $34,100 LESS AND
HAVE $7,320 LESS CASH AVAILABLE
AND THE SAME DEATH BENEFIT.*

AGE 85 SUMMARY
FOR THE SAME OUTLAY YOU WILL
HAVE $415,372 MORE CASH AVAIL-
ABLE AND $426,872 MORE DEATH
BENEFIT;*

OR

YOU CAN SPEND $79,807 LESS AND
HAVE $11,500 LESS CASH AVAILABLE
AND THE SAME DEATH BENEFIT.*

* Dividends are not guaranteed but are based on the current dividend schedule, which may be changed at any time.

** Death Benefit includes: A) Death Benefit of Policy, and B) Side fund (Premium difference and current surrender value compounded at 8%).

PROPOSAL NO. 17

AGE: 55   OCCUPATION: PROFESSOR   DEATH BENEFIT: $1,000,000
SEX: MALE   INCOME: $250,000   CURRENT PREM.: $ 48,260

A 55-year-old man has a choice of what type of policy to purchase to fill a need for a $1,000,000 death benefit. He can buy the old high premium and cash value policy and have $149,090 additional cash value or he can buy the new Extra-life-Economatic policy and invest his premium savings of $161,190 and have $348,853 additional available in a side fund. Here is how these policies compare:

The old high premium and cash value policy with a $1,000,000 death benefit has a first-year premium of $48,260 (B in Table 31), while the Extralife-Economatic Type has a first-year premium of $28,755 (A in the table). If he did purchase the new policy, he would save $19,505 (C) in the first year.

The total premiums on the new policy, to age 77, would be $481,000 (D), versus $642,190 (E) with the old type policy. This is a saving of $161,190 (F) with the new type policy. If the individual invested the premium difference yearly in an 8% Municipal Bond Fund he would have a fund equal to $497,943 (G).

The total surrender value of the new type policy, at age 77, is $603,810 (H), versus $752,900 (I) with the old type policy. As you can see there is $149,090 (J) less surrender value with the new type policy. However, the premium difference compounded at 8% has grown to $497,943, so he really has $348,853 (K) additional cash available with the new type policy.

If death should occur at age 77 and he has not taken the cash, the total death benefit (policy and savings fund) with the new policy would be $1,497,943 (L), versus $1,000,000 (M) with the old policy. This means that his family would receive $497,943 (N) additional cash, if the death should occur, at no additional cost.

If he should continue the program after age 77 and death does not occur at age 85, the premium savings with the new type policy would be $57,767 (O in the table). Again, if the premium difference was invested at 8% he would have a total fund of $805,814 (P) with the new type policy.

The total surrender value at age 85 with the new policy would be $185,890 (Q) less than the old type policy. However, he has invested the premium difference and has a fund of $805,814 with the new policy, so he really has $619,924 (R) additional cash available with the new type policy.

If death should occur at age 85 and he has not taken the cash, the total death benefit (policy and savings fund) with the new policy would be $805,814 (S) more than the old type policy.

Why send the insurance company $161,190 more over your lifetime for an old high premium high cash value policy so that you could have $149,090 additional cash value? You can instead buy an Extralife-Economatic Type policy and invest the $161,190 savings and have $348,853 additional cash available and $497,943 additional death benefit.

NOTE: A NUMBER OF THE ABOVE FIGURES INCLUDE DIVIDENDS THAT ARE NOT GUARANTEED BUT ARE BASED ON THE CURRENT DIVIDEND SCHEDULE, WHICH MAY BE CHANGED AT ANY TIME.

Table 31. PREPARED FOR: MALE AGE 55

$1,000,000 EXTRALIFE-ECONOMATIC TYPE (SUPP-REDUCE) VS. $1,000,000 OLD HIGH PREMIUM AND CASH VALUE POLICY (REDUCE)

SUMMARY PAGE

The First Year Annual Premium on the Extra. Econo Policy =	$	28,755(A)
The First Year Annual Premium on the Old Type Policy ....=		48,260(B)
First Year Savings with Extralife Policy.............=	$	19,505(C)

	AGE 77 Summary	AGE 85 Summary
1. Extralife Econo. Pol. Total Annual Outlay*	$ 481,000(D)	$ 494,653
Old Type Policy Total Annual Outlay*...........	642,190(E)	552,420
Savings With Extralife Econo. Policy*........	$ 161,190(F)	$ 57,767(O)
Savings compounded at 8%............................	$ 497,943(G)	$ 805,814(P)
2. Extralife Econo. Pol. Total Surrender Value*	$ 603,810(H)	$ 750,510
Old Type Policy Total Surrender Value*	752,900(I)	936,400
Additional Extralife Econo. Policy Value*	$ −149,090(J)	$ −185,890(Q)
Plus savings of Premium Outlay Total Additional Cash Available....................	$ 348,853(K)	$ 619,924(R)
3. Total Death Benefit**with Extralife Econo*	$1,497,943(L)	$1,805,814
Total Death Benefit with Old Type Policy* ...	1,000,000(M)	1,000,000
Additional Death Benefit With Extralife*	$ 497,943(N)	$ 805,814(S)

IN OTHER WORDS:

AGE 77 SUMMARY	AGE 85 SUMMARY
FOR THE SAME OUTLAY YOU WILL HAVE $348,853 MORE CASH AVAILABLE AND $497,943 MORE DEATH BENEFIT;*	FOR THE SAME OUTLAY YOU WILL HAVE $619,924 MORE CASH AVAILABLE AND $805,814 MORE DEATH BENEFIT;*
OR	OR
YOU CAN SPEND $161,190 LESS AND HAVE $149,090 LESS CASH AVAILABLE AND THE SAME DEATH BENEFIT.*	YOU CAN SPEND $57,767 LESS AND HAVE $185,890 LESS CASH AVAILABLE AND THE SAME DEATH BENEFIT.*

* Dividends are not guaranteed but are based on the current dividend schedule, which may be changed at any time.

** Death Benefit includes: A) Death Benefit of Policy, and B) Side fund (Premium difference and current surrender value compounded at 8%).

PROPOSAL NO. 18

AGE: 63   OCCUPATION: PRESIDENT   DEATH BENEFIT: $1,000,000
SEX: MALE   INCOME: $200,000   CURRENT PREM.: $ 68,440

A 63-year-old man has a choice of what type of policy to purchase to fill a need for a $1,000,000 death benefit. He can buy the old high premium and cash value policy and have $19,350 additional cash value, or he can buy the new Extra-life-Economatic policy and invest his savings of $33,821, and have $88,306 additional available cash in a savings fund. Here is how these policies compare:

The old high premium and cash value policy with a $1,000,000 death benefit has a first-year premium of $68,440 (B in Table 32), while the Extralife-Economatic Type policy has a first-year premium of $46,205 (A in the table). If he did purchase the new policy, he would save $22,235 (C) in the first year.

The total premiums on the new type policy, to age 77, would be $617,109 (D), versus $650,930 (E) with the old type policy. This is a savings of $33,821 (F) with the new type policy. If the individual invested the premium difference yearly in a 8% Municipal Bond Fund he would have a fund equal to $107,656 (G).

The total surrender value of the new type policy, at age 77, is $496,860 (H), versus $516,210 (I) with the old type policy. As you can see, there is $19,350 (J) less surrender value with the new type policy. However, the premium difference compounded at 8% has grown to $107,656, so he really has $88,306 (K) additional cash available with the new type policy.

If death should occur at age 77 and he has not taken the cash, the total death benefit (policy and fund) with the new type policy would be $1,107,656 (L), versus $1,000,000 (M) with the old policy. This means that his family would receive $107,656 (N) additional cash if death should occur, at no additional cost.

If he should continue the program after age 77 and death

does not occur, at age 85 the premium savings with the new type policy would be $150,295 (O in the table). Again, if the premium difference was invested at 8% he would have a total fund of $361,428 (P) with the new type policy.

The total surrender value at age 85 with the new type policy would be $118,140 (Q) less than the old type policy. However, he has invested the premium difference and has a fund of $361,428 with the new type policy so he really has $243,288 (R) additional cash available with the new type policy.

If death should occur at age 85 and he has not taken the cash, the total death benefit (policy and fund) with the new type policy would be $361,428 (S) more than the old type policy.

Why would you send the insurance company $33,821 more over your lifetime for an old high premium cash value policy so that you could have $19,350 additional cash value, when you can buy an Extralife Economatic Type policy and invest the $33,821 savings and have $88,306 additional cash available and $107,656 additional death benefit?

NOTE: A NUMBER OF THE ABOVE FIGURES INCLUDE DIVIDENDS THAT ARE NOT GUARANTEED BUT ARE BASED ON THE CURRENT DIVIDEND SCHEDULE, WHICH MAY BE CHANGED AT ANY TIME.

Table 32. PREPARED FOR: MALE AGE 63

$1,000,000 EXTRALIFE-ECONOMATIC TYPE (SUPP-REDUCE) VS.
$1,000,000 OLD HIGH PREMIUM AND CASH VALUE POLICY (REDUCE)

SUMMARY PAGE

The FIRST YEAR Annual Premium on the Extra. Econo Policy = $ 46,205(A)
The FIRST YEAR Annual Premium on the Old Type Policy ....= 68,440(B)
      FIRST YEAR SAVINGS WITH EXTRALIFE POLICY..............= $ 22,235(C)

	AGE 77 Summary	AGE 85 Summary
1. Extralife Econo. Pol. Total Annual Outlay*	$ 617,109(D)	$ 746,445
Old Type Policy Total Annual Outlay*...........	650,930(E)	896,740
SAVINGS WITH EXTRALIFE ECONO. POLICY*........	$ 33,821(F)	$ 150,295(O)
SAVINGS compounded at 8%............................	$ 107,656(G)	$ 361,428(P)
2. Extralife Econo. Pol. Total Surrender Value*	$ 496,860(H)	$ 689,570
Old Type Policy Total Surrender Value*.......	516,210(I)	807,710
ADDITIONAL EXTRALIFE ECONO. POLICY VALUE*	$ −19,350(J)	$ −118,140(Q)
Plus savings of Premium Outlay TOTAL ADDITIONAL CASH AVAILABLE....................	$ 88,306(K)	$ 243,288(R)
3. Total Death Benefit**with Extralife Econo*	$1,107,656(L)	$1,361,428
Total Death Benefit with Old Type Policy* ...	1,000,000(M)	1,000,000
ADDITIONAL DEATH BENEFIT WITH EXTRALIFE*	$ 107,656(N)	$ 361,428(S)

IN OTHER WORDS:

AGE 77 SUMMARY	AGE 85 SUMMARY
FOR THE SAME OUTLAY YOU WILL HAVE $88,306 MORE CASH AVAILABLE AND $107,656 MORE DEATH BENEFIT;*	FOR THE SAME OUTLAY YOU WILL HAVE $243,288 MORE CASH AVAILABLE AND $361,428 MORE DEATH BENEFIT;*
OR	OR
YOU CAN SPEND $33,821 LESS AND HAVE $19,350 LESS CASH AVAILABLE AND THE SAME DEATH BENEFIT.*	YOU CAN SPEND $150,295 LESS AND HAVE $118,140 LESS CASH AVAILABLE AND THE SAME DEATH BENEFIT.*

 * Dividends are not guaranteed but are based on the current dividend schedule, which may be changed at any time.

** Death Benefit includes: A) Death Benefit of Policy, and B) Side fund (Premium difference and current surrender value compounded at 8%).

INDEX

Advertising of insurance, 25, 101–4
Agent, 40–44, 78, 84–85, 123–24, 177; commissions, 24, 25–26, 33, 95–100; communication with, 67–71, 73–76, 77–81, 100, 207–10; loyalty to, 36, 79–80; vs. agent, 77–81, 83–88, 209; vs. investment broker, 89–93

Brokering of insurance, 84–5
Business, life insurance in, 161–69; for key man, 161–62, 163, 281–83; for partnerships, 166; protecting investments with, 164
Buy/sell agreements, 166–67
Buying while insurable, 153, 186–87, 215

Case histories (policies compared), 226–99
Cash value, advantages of, 56, 91–92, 202; as asset, 37; borrowing against, 37, 119, 202, 204, 214; extent of, 47, 111, 118, 269–70
Children, insurance for, 183–87, 189–96, 215; figuring amount of, 155–60; proposals for, 190–97, 229–31, 233–35; when to insure, 69, 177, 182

Commissions. See Agent, commissions.
Compound interest, impact of, 57–60, 61–62 (tables), 226–99
Convertible vs. non–convertible term insurance, 116
Cost comparison: factors involved in, 43–44, 52–56, 86–87, 98, 100, 217–23; policies juxtaposed, 109, 111, 129–45 (tables), 226–99; in replacement, 79
Cost index. See Interest-adjusted net-cost index.

Death benefit, defined, 202
Dividends: effect of, on premium, 49, 52–53, 111, 237; guarantee of, 47, 108; on par and non-par policies, 49, 107–9, 110–13; uses of, 86, 110, 203
Double or triple indemnity, 214

Endowment policy, 120
Estate taxes. See Taxes, estate.
Extralife-Economatic Policies, 26, 4͜–50, 119, 190–97, 203; arguments against, refuted, 46–47; term insurance in, 46; vs. new non-par policy, 279–80; vs. old policy types, 221–22; 229–99

301